FONTAINEBLEAU CLIMBS

A generalised grading comparison

Fontainebleau	British technical grades	US Boulder (Hueco Tanks, Bishop etc.)
3a, 3b, 3c	4a – 4c	V0
4a, 4b, 4c	4c – 5b	V0–V2
5a, 5b	5b – 6b	V0–V2
6a, 6a+	6a – 6b	V0–V3
6b	6a – 6b	V1-V3
6b+	6a – 6b	V2–V3
6c	6a+ – 6b	V3–V4
6c+	6b – 6b-	V4–V5
7a	6b – 6c-	V5–V6
7a+	6b – 6c	V6–V7
7b	6b – 6c	V7–V8
7b+	6c	V8–V9
7c	6c – 7a	V9–V10
7c+	6c – 7a	V10–V11
8a	7a – 7b	V10–V11
8a+	7a – 7b	V11–V12
8b	7b – 7c	V12–V13
8b+	7c	V14

This is a very rough guide as local conditions and traditions greatly influence grading

This is a translation of the main French selected guide to the best boulder groups in the celebrated Fontainebleau climbing area, 50kms south of Paris. It is printed in conjunction with French publisher Arthaud/Flammarion and published simultaneously in Great Britain and the United States.

Those unfamiliar with the Fontainebleau Forest will find it bewilderingly complex. Climbers are advised to purchase the 1.25,000 Forêt de Fontainebleau map (IGN 2417OT) and for the north-eastern areas – Beauvais and La Padôle, and the Buthiers Malesherbes area to the south-west – the adjoining sheet (IGN 2316ET). These maps used in conjunction with the main location maps in the guide (listed below) should solve all approach problems.

In addition to these general maps each main group of boulders has a detailed layout map with an inset approach map. In some cases these two maps are orientated in the same direction (not always with north towards the top of the page) and in other cases they are orientated differently (these maps have north arrow added for clarity).

© Editions Arthaud, Paris, 1999

Published under license simultaneously in Great Britain and the United States in 2001 by Bâton Wicks Publications, London and The Mountaineers, Seattle.

ISBN 1-898573-49-2 (UK) ISBN 0-89886-842-5 (US)

© 2001 in English translation by Bâton Wicks, London

Catalogue records for this book exist in the British Library and the Library of Congress.

Trade enquiries – Great Britain, Europe and Commonwealth (except Canada):
Bâton Wicks c/o Cordee, 3a De Montfort Street, Leicester LE1 7HD
Trade enquiries – United States and Canada etc.
The Mountaineers Books, 1001 S.W. Klickitat Way, Suite 201, Seattle, WA 98134, U.S.A.

Printed by I.M.E., France.

Jo & Françoise Montchaussé and Jacky Godoffe

Fontainebleau Climbs

The finest bouldering and circuits

Translated by Sue Harper

Bâton Wicks • London
The Mountaineers • Seattle

THE NATIONAL FOREST OF FONTAINEBLEAU
(La Forêt Domaniale de Fontainebleau)

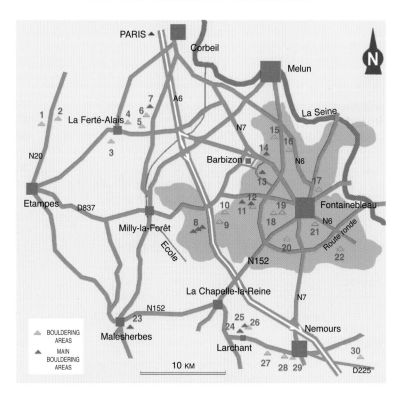

CONTENTS

A Beginner's Guide

So you have not yet set foot on Fontainebleau sandstone, nor felt the roughness of the rock under your fingertips, even though these beautifully shaped boulders are constantly urging you to climb them? It is a unique place, a wilderness of silver birch, pine trees, beech, oak intermingled with sandstone boulders scattered over an area of some one thousand two hundred square kilometres. Would the boulders be so alluring without this symbiosis of rock and trees, the interplay between body and spirit?

The rock does not give up its secrets easily and your first climbing attempts will probably be punctuated by a few unplanned returns to ground level. Experience is everything here and some moves need to be practised, sometimes for months, before they can be strung together to complete a problem. So if at first there seem to be more difficulties than solutions, have a little patience. It is worth it for the pleasure of climbing rung by rung up the ladder of what must be some of the most difficult climbing grades in the world.

There will be times when you will not understand or have the answers within you to some of the problems. But wherever you climb you will always find someone who will inspire you, infuse you with an inner sense of balance, or help you to work out a problem.

You will eventually be won over as much by the variety and complexity of moves as by the beauty of your surroundings. Patience and energy combined with a good choice of bouldering area and some free time are all the ingredients needed in order to improve or, to simply enjoy yourself. We hope the following information will get you off to a good start.

FINDING BOOTS TO FIT YOUR FEET

A single visit to a climbing shop, far from being reassuring, is enough to daunt any beginner. Rock boots with a low ankle, high ankle,

slippers, ballet-type slippers, with laces, velcro, style, fit, price, make. So many things to consider when choosing a rock boot.

• **High or low boot?** For bouldering a low boot is better as it allows for greater ankle flexibility.

• **Ballet-type slipper or stiff boot?** On sandstone (particularly for the harder problems) you need to be able to feel the rock through your boot, the closer to the rock your foot is the better: ballet-type slippers are better for this; and even if they are painful to wear at first, it is advisable to buy them close-fitting.

• **Velcro, lacing?** You will probably want to undo your boots several times a session, so think about it.

• **For a good fit,** it is better to choose one of the more classic styles than one of the new asymmetric technical boots, which are better for crag climbing.

• **As for the make,** there are so many different ones, each with their own specifications, style and price, that you will be spoilt for choice.

• **Prices** range from about £25 for the cheapest to £70 for the most expensive ($35–$100). The most important factor to consider when buying a rock boot for bouldering is the stickiness of the sole. Each type of rubber has its own particular characteristics and it is important to ascertain the quality of the sole on each boot before deciding which one to buy. The rubber on the sole will last from about three months to several years, depending on how often the boots are used and it is also possible to get them resoled if the rest of the boot is still in good condition.

THE GRADING SYSTEM

The French grading system, which is used for bouldering as well as other climbing related activities, was inherited from Willo Welzenbach. In the early years of the 20th century he devised a scale, beginning at 1 being the lowest level and going up as high as 6, being the limit of

GRADE OF CIRCUIT

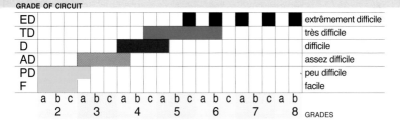

ED																			extrêmement difficile
TD																			très difficile
D																			difficile
AD																			assez difficile
PD																			peu difficile
F																			facile

a b c a b c a b c a b c a b c a b c a b c a b
2   3   4   5   6   7   8   GRADES

human possibility at the time, with sub-divisions of 'plus' or 'minus' to give more precision to the grades. This scale is still used today, for bouldering, crag climbing and mountaineering. But these activities, though similar in nature differ from each other in many ways and the grade of a particular problem or route allows for this. In other words, bouldering is comparable to a sprint, crag climbing to middle-distance running and alpinism to a marathon. It is therefore pointless to compare grades.

The grade of a particular boulder problem depends on various objective criteria: how far apart the holds are, the size and shape of the holds, how steep the rock is, how long it took to do the problem originally, how many times it has been repeated, how it is affected by weather conditions. But this assessment also incorporates an element of subjectivity: the personality of the person who is grading it, his experience, whether he has just made a first ascent or repeated the problem, the way in which he did it which may not necessarily be the only way of doing it and which could therefore affect the perception of the difficulty. A grade is suggested by the first ascensionist and then confirmed by those repeating the problem. Therefore it could be several months or even longer after the first ascent before the grade of a particular problem is confirmed as this confirmation depends on the problem being repeated and the grade will not change unless a new way of climbing it is miraculously found. Which sometimes happens.

The difficulty of the grade is expressed as a figure which is subdivided by the addition of a letter: "a" being the lowest, "b" the

intermediate and "c" the highest. After 6a and above, there is another subdivision of "plus" refining the grade still further.

The colour coded marking of the different circuits corresponds to that shown on the table above.

Finally, as if all this was not difficult enough to understand, the Fontainebleau grading system has not been universally adopted. But it is used in most European countries and in South Africa.

The graph below is an attempt to compare this grading system with that used in the United States, in particular at Hueco Tanks (Texas) and Bishop (California). It should be used with care, particularly in the lower grades, because the climbing styles are very different and each grading system has its own logic.

Bleau

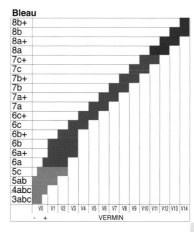

Lastly, if you find a particular 6a+ easier than a 5b problem, remember that the true grade and how difficult a problem feels can be very different. Combined in all this is the type of problem (slab, overhang, wall), one's own particular intrinsic qualities (technical or physical), height (small or tall) and the way it was climbed (there are sometimes several different ways of doing a problem and new ones are regularly found).

You think it's complex? That's a euphemism. But that is part of its charm. Keep smiling, it's only a game, a source of endless debate ...

TO FALL OR NOT TO FALL?

Whether he likes it or not, at some point in his career a climber is going to fall off. It is a reality which goes hand in hand with the activity and there is no point in ignoring it just as there is no point in exaggerating the risk involved. Every fall risks injury, but these risks can be largely minimised by considering the following:

• A fall is never nothing; to master the art is not to trivialise it.

• The climber must always have a mental picture of the location of obstacles (rocks, tree roots ...) within his landing zone, and anticipate the trajectory of his fall. Beware of standing on a rock to reach the first holds, this can be potentially very dangerous.

USE A SPOTTER!

The idea of unacceptable risk has become less and less acceptable as climbing has developed, which has led climbers to have 'a spotter' to catch them if they fall, as often as possible. To make a fall safe, the spotter must be able to fulfil four roles which are not mutually exclusive:

• Reduce the force of impact by absorbing some of the energy generated by the fall;
• Stabilize the climber so that he can absorb the force of the fall himself with his legs;
• Correct his trajectory so he can avoid dangerous obstacles;
• Give confidence by making a safe fall possible, which often results in the climber not falling off at all ...

The spotter is an essential actor in the whole scene, he must be as concentrated and aware as the climber who has placed his trust in him.

A FEW COMMON SITUATIONS:

On a wall, slab or any other piece of rock which is not steeply overhanging, the falling climber is most effectively supported near his centre of gravity and on parts of his body which are easy to grab hold of, in other words his

buttocks. And for this reason at least it is always preferable to ask the person beforehand if they wish to be spotted ...

The speed of the falling climber determines the degree of cushioning provided by the spotter, who must be as close to the climber as possible, without actually touching him ...

The spotter must also pay attention to the position of his thumbs, as a climber's buttocks are harder and less yielding than a volley ball!

Brushing is essential before and after climbing.
Overleaf: support by the spotter may help in getting the feel of a move.

On the other hand, on an overhang, spotting at buttock level is dangerous because in this situation the climber's buttocks are below the centre of gravity (which is now at waist level)

and grabbing him there will cause him to overbalance and fall head first ...

For this reason, the spotter must support the body above the centre of gravity, at shoulder level, in order to keep the falling climber upright so he lands on his feet in a natural position.

Above a certain height, spotting loses its relevance, not only for the climber who cannot be held correctly if he falls, but also for the spotter who risks overbalancing and being injured himself ...

It is generally preferable to be as close to the climber as possible in order to be able to alter the potentially dangerous trajectory of a fall before the energy generated by that fall makes any assistance more apparent than real ...

In a particularly dangerous or complicated situation there could be several spotters (even including one to spot the spotter).

— ✳ —

Kaleidoscope

Some of the first bleausards at Apremont in 1897.

1889 THE FIRST BLEAUSARDS

It would be impossible to try to trace the name of the first person to set foot on Fontainebleau rock. However it is possible to put a date on the time when climbers first showed an interest in the boulders. This engraving dates from the end of the 19th century, suggesting that 1889 would be a plausible date.

Who would have thought at that time, that bouldering would one day become so popular that it would be accepted as an activity in its own right, just as alpinism is?

1913 CLIMBING BOOTS ARE RELEGATED TO THE CUPBOARD

Phew! If Jacques de Lépiney had not quickly relegated nailed climbing boots to the back of the cupboard our playground would not look the same as it does today.

1935 FINALLY A ROCK BOOT

Pierre Allain was not only a great alpinist, he was also one of the most accomplished boulderers of the 20th century. It was he who dreamt up the idea of the rock boot; at the beginning of the 1940s [in collaboration with Edouard Bourdonneau] he made a boot for his bleausard friends.

[Note: Allain and Bourdonneau eventually had a business disagreement and separated – the classic boot, initially the "PA" thus became the "EB". "PA" was transferred to a boot of different design. The "EB" was the world's most popular rock boot until c.1982 when it was superseded by boots with improved frictional properties ("sticky boots").]

206	l'angle du cuvier (sorti e A)		II
"	La bizut (sortie B)		VIa
207	la Dalle aux 2 arêtes voie normale		IV
207A	"	traversée supérieure	V
207B	"	traversée inférieure	V
208	"	directe de gauche	V
209	"	directe de droite	V sup.
210	"	arête Sud	IV sup.
211	sortie A "	traversée Sud	VIa
"	sortie B "	la marie rose (sort.dir.)	VIb
212	sortie A "	face Sud	V inf.
"	sortie B "	la cocktail	VIc
212B	"	la bidule	V sup.
213	"	la 3e arête	VIa
213B	"	la 4e arête	VIf
214	"	face nord	V
215	"	angle nord	IV sup.
215B	"	la jocker	VIf
216	le coin du Suzanne		V sup.

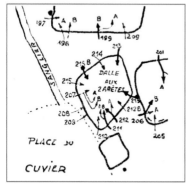

1945 FIRST BOULDERING TOPO

In this year, when the rest of the world was sadly more occupied with less peaceful affairs, Maurice Martin became the first person to record routes on the Bas Cuvier boulders. This first climbing topo is in some ways the grandfather to this book and we pay tribute to him for this.

1947 THE LITTLE ARROWS

Why paint arrows on the rock? The idea of a circuit was devised by Fred Bernick as a sort of horizontal alpinism, a substitute for a mountaineering route. Training for great alpine exploits necessitated good physical preparation and the chaos of the Cuvier Rempart boulders was the setting for the first circuit. It followed the obvious lines of the area with the last route climbing up to the modest summit of the Rempart. Fred Bernick indisputably broke new ground on that day in 1947 and furthered the development of the type of climbing which is peculiar to Bleau today. [Note: This is unique to the area and the markings are discreet. Nevertheless it is not to be emulated for obvious environmental reasons.]

TIMELESS BLEAUSARD ESSENTIALS

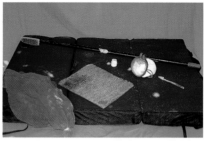

Brushes, carpet, resin and chalk, crash mat, slippers and the rest ... Things which are still considered today as necessary accoutrements to an activity which is perpetually evolving in the minds of the protagonists. These essential objects are no longer just used by climbers in the Fontainebleau forest but are now used by them in climbing areas all over the world.

1982 STICKY RUBBER

Yvon Chouinard revolutionised climbing when he injected resin into the soles of rock boots. As happens with Formula One tyres, the resin soles become more adherent as they are heated by friction. However it took another five years for this innovation to catch on, as stiffer rock boots were more popular at the time.

1997 http : //www.bleausards.fr

With the approach of the third millennium and thanks to modern communications, bouldering has entered the virtual world. Long gone is the time when the early climbers would only have chance to discuss their future plans when they met at weekends. Today they only have to tap away on their keyboard to quench their thirst for gossip. If you join them on the Web. YOU will see that they have lost none of their passion.

to come across a climber with one of these pads, the main virtue of which is to cushion ones falls in the short term and protect ones back in the long term.

2010 PERHAPS TOMORROW

Working along the same lines as the idea of the air bag used in cars nowadays, a French company has perfected a safety belt designed to protect climbers. A fall of more than two metres triggers the inflation of cushions designed to protect the back.

1998 A SOFTER LANDING

The crash pad is about to steal a lead over the famous straw mattress which bleausards used to use. Our American friends thought of the idea at the end of the eighties, before it caught on here, and nowadays it is no longer unusual

2010, visionaries or jokers?

How to use this guide

BOULDERING AREAS, CIRCUITS AND ROUTES

For each area there is an introduction together with an exhaustive list of circuits; also mentioned are routes which are not marked and are listed as "off-circuit"; where they are quite a long way from the circuit, they are indicated as being "off-site". Thus, for the area called 95.2 where there are four circuits, several unmarked routes and several off-site routes, this information is represented by the following symbols:

CIRCUITS		
Yellow PD+	❑	*the square indicates the existence of a circuit which is not described*
Blue D	●	*the coloured circle indicates that the circuits are described (maps*
Red TD-	◉	*and graded lists)*
WHITE ED-	◔	
Off-circuit	✗	*the cross indicates the description of unmarked route*
Off-site	★	*the star indicates the description of off-site routes around area 95.2*

LOCATIONS AND GRADES

• Because of the concentration of boulders and circuits, the climbing areas at Fontainebleau are very varied and different in nature. For example, it is much easier to find your way around the Rochers des Potets than the Gorges d'Apremont. So we have decided not to arrange the information in a uniform way for each area:
• In an area where the quantity of routes is fairly small all problems/circuits are listed in a single table;
• Otherwise, circuits will be described in the following way:

THE NUMBERING PRINCIPLE

• The boulders in each area or zone are numbered from 1 to n;
• On each boulder the routes are marked with either:
• Their number on the circuit;
• Or, for classic off-circuit routes, a lower case letter is used;
• And for very hard off-site routes an upper case letter is used.

MAP

In order to make the maps easy to read, on each side you will find:
• Either, layer tinting to show relief in areas of steeper ground, such as Apremont;
• Or colouring to show areas with shade from the sun, such as at La Roche aux Sabots.

In general maps are orientated as far as possible with north to the top.

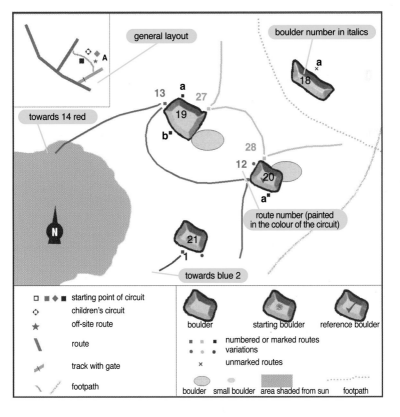

The map shows:

- Numbers 27 and 28 of a yellow circuit,
- Numbers 12 and 13 of a red circuit,
- Number 1 of a blue circuit and its starting block,
- 3 very difficult routes, marked but not numbered, problems (a) and (b) on boulder 19 and (a) on boulder 20,
- 1 unmarked, very hard route, problem (a) on boulder 18,
- 1 reference boulder which stands out because of its situation, height or notoriety, which is useful for orientation,
- On the layout map, a very hard off-site route is marked with a capital A.

GIRDLE TRAVERSES AND GRADES

- Generally, girdle traverses on individual boulders are reversible or can even be done there and back; there is an infinite variety of possibilities and only the usual direction is indicated. For example, traverse G>D (or R>L) indicates a traverse from right to left.
- The symbol / indicates any marked differences in grade depending on how the problem is done.

HOW TO FIND
SPECIFIC INFORMATION

At the end of the book there is a general list which groups together all the routes of the major areas; it is organised in such a way that if you know either the name, number on a particular coloured circuit or the location (number of the boulder on the map) you will be able to find a complete description of the route.

— ✳ —

15

QUESTIONS / ANSWERS

What is the grade of a route in a known location?

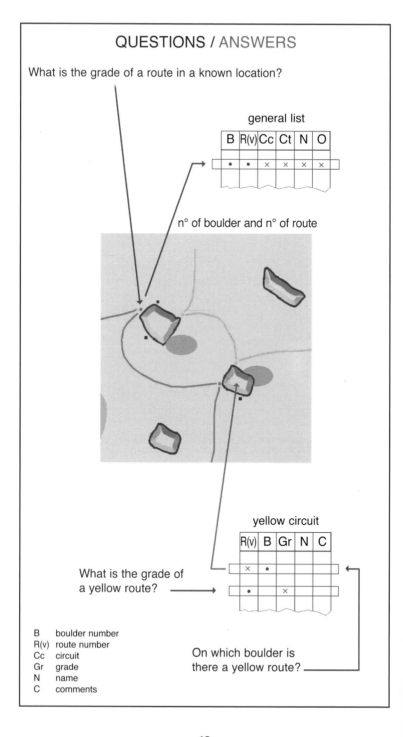

general list

B	R(v)	Cc	Ct	N	O
•	•	×	×	×	×

n° of boulder and n° of route

yellow circuit

R(v)	B	Gr	N	C
×	•			
•	×			

What is the grade of a yellow route? →

On which boulder is there a yellow route?

What is the grade of a yellow route? →

B   boulder number
R(v) route number
Cc   circuit
Gr   grade
N   name
C   comments

THE PICTOGRAMS

The multiplicity of bouldering areas on offer give the climber a wide variety of choice. In order to help you to choose where to climb, we have used what we feel are the six essential criteria for a choice of climbing area: the pictograms referred to will help you to find the place most suited to your needs of the moment, the weather, aspect, how busy it gets and how you are feeling today. They are as follows:

Signposts unlovely but useful.

• How busy it gets (from quiet to very busy, at the weekend for example);

• How much sun it gets, from shady to full sun;

• Whether the rock dries quickly after rain (whether or not it catches the wind);

• How committing the problems are (from not very to total exposure);

• How practical it is to take the family there;

• Finally, how far, in metres, the circuit is from the nearest car-park.

Loïc climbs with cat-like stealth on La dalle de fer.

LE CUVIER

The keys to the kingdom
Michel Libert, singled out
by Robert Paragot at the
end of the fifties as being
the true spiritual son of the
"Cuviéristes", was
entrusted with the secret of
the master's bivouac site
and, symbolically and very
solemnly, with the keys to
Bas Cuvier with instructions
to make good use of them.
Which is what he did as he
put up many new routes
including the famous
L'abattoir, Fontainebleau's
first 7a.

Michel Libert, originator of the
seventh grade.

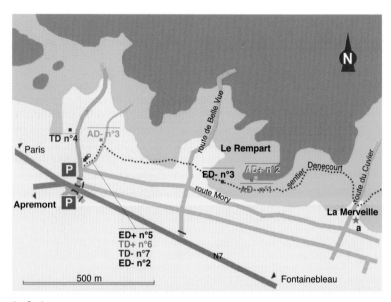

Le Cuvier.

Bas Cuvier

CIRCUITS

Orange AD- n°3 ●
Blue TD- n°7 ❑
Blue D- n°1 ●
Red TD+ n°6 ●
Black ED- n°2 ❑
White ED+ n°5 ○

Off-circuit ✗

Fontainebleau's temple of climbing ... it has been the favourite haunt of generation after generation of climbers and its popularity does not seem to be waning. Originally it's popularity was born out of a lack of transport before and just after the war, as it was one of the nearest places to the station at Bois-le-Roi. Then latterly because there are a large number of boulders at this particular spot and there is very good parking close by (less than ten metres from the nearest boulders). And finally because the beautiful shapes of the sandstone boulders are an invitation to climb in themselves. Le Bas Cuvier has been honoured many times by illustrious climbers who have laid the foundations of the sixth and then the seventh grade. The reputation of many of the problems has become international, further increasing the area's popularity. Today, this area still easily merits its nickname "laboratory of technique" because every season new ideas still seem to turn up.

Each circuit is a kind of quintessence of the art of bouldering and some of the problems outside the circuits are amongst the most difficult in the world. The bouldering in this area is particularly known for its round and flat holds. They are the locals staple diet; but can be a little indigestible for the non-initiated, especially for those who start their bleausard trip here.

The sardine can test

This curious test was reserved by Cuvier climbers as an initiation for newcomers wishing to join the "Cuvier academic club" in the forties. The climber who wished to become a member of this very exclusive fraternity found himself pointed up the slab which is today marked as 40 blue. Balanced on each tiny rugosity was a sardine can opener and it was essential to climb the route without knocking any of them off and of course, to do it first time. Try it for yourself and see!

Bas Cuvier

orange circuit

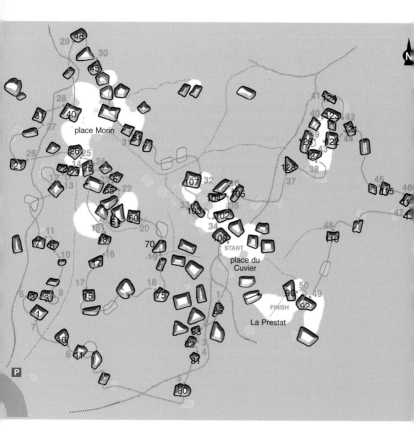

Dany Crenn doing a
dynamic move on
L'Abbé Résina.

This is not really an easy circuit, because as a result of its great popularity many of the problems have become highly polished. On all the boulders in this area you require a degree of prehensile ability and this circuit is not recommended for complete beginners, who are likely to leave somewhat frustrated. The price of success as it were.

ORANGE CIRCUIT

route	boulder	grade	name	route	boulder	grade	name
0	100	2a	La fissure de la place du Cuvier	26	21	2a	Le "trois"
1	86	2b	Le petit rétab	27	31	3a	Le petit surplomb
2	83	2c	La fissure de l'auto	28	40	3a	La rigole ouest de la solitude
3	82	3a	L'envers des trois	29	48	2b	La delta
4	81	3a	Le second rétab	30	45	2c	La fissure des enfants
5	80	2c	Le onzième trou	31	51	2a	La grenouille
6	10	2b	La sans les mains	32	107	3b	La dalle aux trous
7	1	3b	La voie de l'arbre	33	103	3a	La traversée de la dalle des flics
8	2	2b	La dalle du tondu	34	102	4a	La jarretelle
9	3	3b	L'envers du J	35	104	2b	Le zéro sup
10	6	3b	L'oreille cassée	36	105	2c	Le boulot
11	7	2b	La dalle de l'élan	37	128	2b	La dalle aux demis
12	22	2b	La petite côtelette	38	127	3a	Les tripes
13	23	2a	La fissure sud du coq	39	126	3c	La dalle du 106
14	23	2a	La traversée de la crête du coq	40	123	1c	Le coin du 5
15	18	2c	La proue	41	124	2b	Les lunettes
16	17	3a	La tenaille	42	123	2c	Les pinces
17	15	2c	La deux temps	43	122	3c	La traversée du doigt
18	75	2a	La voie bidon	44	121	2b	Les lichens
19	70	2b	La dalle du pape	45	115	2b	La verte
20	60	2a	La fissure est de la gamelle	46	114	3b	La déviation
21	61	2c	La traversée du bock	47	112	3c	Le petit mur
22	65	2c	La petit angle	48	110	2c	L'envers de pascal
23	67	2c	Le muret	49	92	2c	L'envers du réveil matin
24	25	4a	Le tire bras	50	90	3c	La Prestat
25	26	3a	Le mur aux fênes				

Bas Cuvier

blue circuit

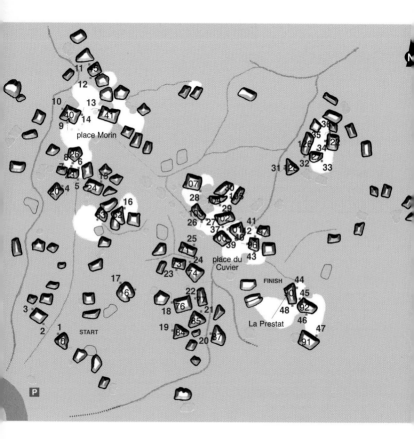

O f all the areas in the forest this particular circuit is one where all the routes have a well balanced level of difficulty. Fine lines, a great variety of styles and good value. A must, without a shadow of a doubt. The circuit is an excellent test of one's fitness, as so many of the problems combine both strength and technical ability and as such is a rite of passage for those wishing to become a true "bleausard".

On the Cuvier boulders, La Gaulle.

BLUE CIRCUIT

route	boulder	grade	name	route	boulder	grade	name
1	10	5a	La sans les mains	24	74	5a	La nouvelle
2	1	4c		25	71	5a	Le dernier des six
3	1	5a	Le surplomb nord ouest	26	103	4b	L'angle olive
3b	63	4c	La demi dalle	27	103	4c	La dalle olive
4	20	5c	Fissure Authenac	28	107	5a	La baquet
5	23	4a	Pilier	29	104	4c	La dalle d'ardoise
6	23	4c	Le coq	30	105	4c	Le 7 sup
7	23	4c	Le coq droite	31	128	3b	La dalle au demi
8	26	4a	La poule	32	126	4b	La dalle au pernod
9	40	4c	Le tuyau Morin	33	127	5b	La dévissante
10	40	4c	La solitaire	34	127	5c	Les tripes
11	45	4c	Les grattons Morin	35	122	5a	Le surplomb du doigt
12	45	4c	La dalle du réveil matin	36	122	4c	Le dièdre du doigt
13	40	5a	Le surplomb du réveil matin	37	102	5c	L'angle Authenac
14	41	4c	Fissure Morin	38	101	5c	Le jus d'orange
15	24	4a	L'inexistante	39	101	5a	La Porthos
16	62	5a	Faux ligament	40	96	5b	
17	16	4c	Le K	41	97	5b	L'Innominata
1b	16	5b	Le faux K	42	96	5b	La face nord
18	76	5b	Le fantôme	43	96	4c	Le bidule
19	87	4c	La dalle de la rouge	44	90	5a	La nationale
20	87	5b	La Borniol	45	92	4c	La fissure de la lionne
21	85	4c	Le vide ordure	46	92	5a	Les grattons du réveil-matin
22	77	5b	La fissure	47	91	5b	Le baquet normal
23	73	5b	Le coup	48	90	4c	La Paillon directe

Rock, sky and trees, a magical combination.

Bas Cuvier

red circuit

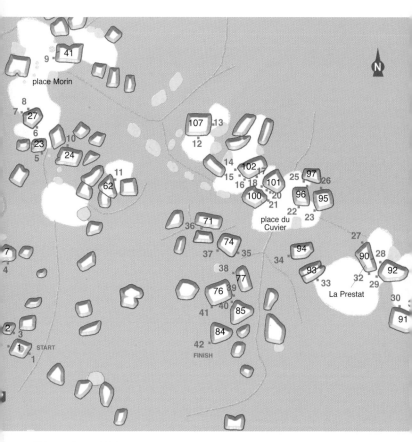

place Morin

place du Cuvier

La Prestat

START

FINISH

D one in the blink of an eye but an outstanding record which still stands today; this whole circuit was done in less than twenty minutes as a result of a bitter duel between two protagonists: Jérôme Jean Charles and Thierry Bienvenu. The latter holds the record after a year of attempts; in his opinion the most difficult thing was working out the quickest way to link the boulders in order to gain precious seconds. The same climber also holds the staggering record of doing the whole circuit thirteen and a half times in six hours.

RED CIRCUIT

route	boulder	grade	name
1	1	5c	L'envers du un
2	1	5c	La goulotte sans la goulotte
3	2	5c	Le trou du tondu
4	7	6a	Le trou du Simon
5	23	5c	La genouillère
6	27	5c	La gugusse
7	27	5c	Les frites
8	27	5b	La vire Authenac
9	41	6c+	La daubé
10	24	5b	La bijou
11	62	5c	Le ligament gauche
12	107	5b	La dalle au trou
13	107	5c	La voie de la vire
14	102	6b	Les bretelles
15	102	5b	L'Authenac
16	102	5b	La V1
17	102	5c	La traversée Authenac
18	101	5c	La parallèle
19	101	5c	La Leininger
20	101	6a	La Suzanne
21	100	6a	La nescafé
22	96	6a	La Marie Rose The first 6a at Fontainebleau
23	95	5b	La bizuth
24	96	5c	La troisième arête
25	97	5c	L'angle rond
26	95	5c	L'huitre
27	90	5b	Le quartier d'orange
28	92	5c	La Nasser
29	92	5b	Le réveil matin
30	91	6a	La Couppel
31	91	6a	Les grattons du baquet
32	90	5c	La dalle du baquet
33	93	5c	La dalle au chocolat
34	94	5b	La côtelette
35	74	5b	Les esgourdes
36	71	6a	Le soufflet
37	74	5c	Le coup de rouge
38	77	5c	La bicolore
39	76	5c	La clavicule
40	85	5b	L'orientale
41	76	5c	L'ectoplasme
42	84	6a	La fauchée

Bas Cuvier

white circuit and off-circuit routes

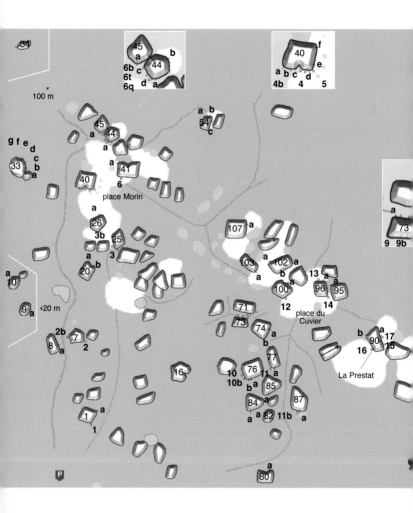

100 m

place Morin

place du Cuvier

La Prestat

20 m

LE CUVIER

WHITE CIRCUIT

route	boulder	grade	name
1	1	6c	La Lili
2	7	6a	L'emporte pièce
2b	7	7c	L'aérodynamite
3	25	6a	Le dernier jeu
3b	25	6b	La Ravensbruck
4	40	6c	La charcuterie
4b	40	7b	L'angle incarné
5	40	7a	La boucherie
6	41	6c	La défroquée
6b	44	7a	L'abattoir
6t	44	7b+	Le carnage
6q	44	7c	L'abbé Résina
7	71	6b	la résistante
8	71	6c	La forge
9	73	6b	La folle
9b	73	6b	L'enclume
9t	73	7a	La rhume folle
10	76	7a	La vie d'ange
10b	76	6b	La dix tractions
11	77	6c+	La clé
11b	87	6c	La tour de Pise
12	100	6c	La chicorée
13	96	7a	La joker
14	96	6c	Le 4ème angle
15	90	6b	La stalingrad
16	90	6c	La chalumeuse
17	90	7b+	La super Prestat

The local experts like to say that the white circuit has always been a true representation of some of the hardest problems for nearly thirty years.

Because there are so many boulders in this area it is still possible to find new problems to add to an already very long list of extremely hard ones. Slabs, overhangs, walls and traverses, bosses, minute incuts, crimps and greasy sloping holds, all help to perpetuate the magic of a place which has still not gone out of fashion after half a century.

All the problems are exceptionally challenging in their way, requiring patience and perseverance.

The routes on the finest boulders have only been done in the last five years and are not marked but are grouped together in the form of an imaginary circuit. A dream or a nightmare trip for anyone thinking of trying it sometime.

Brushing cleans the holds for others.

Bas Cuvier

off-circuit variations |||

OFF-CIRCUIT VARIATIONS

boulder	route	grade	name
1	a	7b	Croix de fer
8	a	7a	Platinium
9	a	7a	La tonsure
10	a	7b	Fluide magéntique
16	a	7c	Plats toniques
20	a	7a+	Le mur du feu Stand on a stone to start
20	b	6c+	
26	a	7c	Photo sensible D>G (R>L) traverse
33	a1	8b	Encore Obsession + Biceps dur
33	a2	7c+	Obsession G>D (L>R) traverse
33	b	7b	Pince mi
33	c	7b+	Vers Nulle part
33	d	7b+	Vers Claire7c Sitting start
33	e	7b	Biceps mou
33	f	7c+	Biceps dur D>G (R>L) traverse
33	g	7a	Holey Moley
34	a	7c	La Gaulle Sitting start
40	a	7c	Infidèle
40	b	7c	Hypothèse
40	c	7c+	Antithèse
40	d	7a	Araignée
40	f	8b	Mouvement perpétuel D>G (R>L) girdle traverse
40	e	7a	Le picon bière
41	a	7a	Cortomaltèse
44	a	6c+	Coton tige
44	b	7c/7c+	Balance Grade depends on technique used
44	c	7a	Hélicoptère
44	d	7c+	Apothéose
45	a	7a	
54	a	6c	Béatrice
54	b	6b	Sanguine
54	c	7c+	Raideur digeste
71	a	7a	La bouiffe
73	a	7a+	Fruits de la passion
74	a	8a	Digitale
76	a	7b	Kilo de beurre G>D (L>R) traverse
76	b	7c	Murmure
77	a	7a	la clé de droite
77	b	7a+	Casse tête
80	a	7b	Technogratt'
82	a	7a	L'aconqueàdoigt
84	a	7b	Dalle siamoise Righthand variation
85	a	7b+	Banlieue nord G>D (L>R) traverse
87	a	7b	Tour de pise directe
90	a	7c	L'ange gardien
90	b	6c	L'angle
95	a	7c+	L'idiot
96	a	7b	Cornemuse
96	b	7c	Le joueur
100	a	6b+	La Marco
101	a	8a	Golden feet
101	b	7c+	Lune de fiel
102	a	7a	La Cinzano
103	a	7b	Alter mégot
107	a	8a+	Coup de feel No longer possible, crucial hold broken

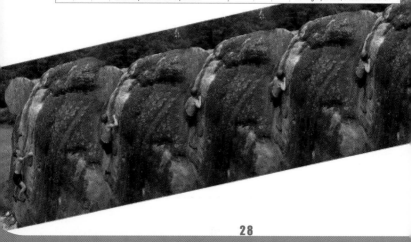

BICEPS MOU

A potted history
In the winter of 1980 Jo Montchaussé made the first ascent of "Le Biceps Mou" and in so doing added another dimension to the bouldering here, roof climbing. The problem was originally graded 6b, but as a result of a hold breaking, it is today given 7b. Twenty years later there are an impressive number of routes on this

overhang and the quality of each of them is as good as the very first: outstanding. This is one of the places to hang out.

The routes
· **Boulder problems**
b: Pince mi, 7b
c: Vers nulle part, 7b+
d: Vers Claire, 7b+ (sitting start)

e: Biceps mou, 7b
g: Holey moley, 7a (7a+ finishing to the right)

· **Traverse problems**
a1: Encore, 8b (linking Obsession and Biceps dur)
a2: Obsession, 7c+
f: Biceps dur, 7c+

LA MARIE ROSE

Location:
number 22 red on Bas Cuvier.

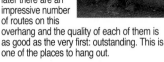

Grade: 6a.
Style: in two words, delicacy and precision.
Climber:
Raphaël Godoffe.

1946. René Ferlet pinched the first ascent of La Marie Rose from under the nose of his friend Pierre Allain and named it after his girlfriend. Little did she know that she would for ever more be associated with the first sixth grade boulder problem ever to be done.
The rounded holds, requiring a delicacy of touch, have not suffered from the passage of time and half a century after its first ascent this superb route remains one of the finest of its grade in the forest.

Technique
Use a tiny crimp to reach the two crux sidepulls.
Place the right foot as far to the left as possible on the flat sloping hold; left foot on a good sidepull; push down on the right hand and left foot.
As you push down on your left foot, move your left hand up to a rounded hold.
Move the right foot up onto a tiny crimp at the same time moving the right hand from the sidepull up to the finishing pocket via an intermediate flat hold.
The finish is more straightforward.

Cuvier Rempart

CIRCUITS

Red AD-	❏
Yellow D	❏
Black ED-	❏
Selected problems	✗

Cuvier Rempart has always fascinated climbers. The Denecourt footpath runs through the jumble of boulders here and it is probably this which originally led to the exploration of this area.

It is here that the first bouldering circuits were done in 1947. The sequence of ascents, descents and jumps gave the climbers of the time as much exercise as if they were doing a small mountain route. In more recent times, this area has contributed to the rise in standards with many new committing, intricate and extremely hard problems being done on boulders outside the circuit. On the route Mory, the road which runs between Bas Cuvier and La Merveille, you will find some of the hardest problems at Fontainebleau.

The high standard climber will be able to try some of the hardest 7c to 8b+ problems in the forest. Very much the preserve of the hard climber.

An original copy

We owe many of the new innovations of the climbing world to the Americans. Indeed the first climber to artificially reproduce a problem was Tony Yaniro, who invented a device for learning to climb off-widths. However tribute must also be paid to Régis Guillaume, professor of philosophy and sometime climber, who recreated, at home, a problem which would become one of the most difficult in the forest. In striving for perfection he was driven to build an artificial structure specifically adapted to this problem. And this was before it had even had a first ascent (when it became Fatman). He recreated an exact copy of the problem, hold by hold, measuring distances to the nearest millimetre, and after a year of painstaking work he had a boulder which effectively laid down the marker of a higher grade of difficulty. Who can boast of having one of the jewels of bleausard art in his cellar? What this anecdote illustrates is the immense passion which the rocks of Fontainebleau have aroused in climbers for over a century.

Marc Le Ménestrel on the pure, clean line of La Merveille.

Cuvier Rempart
selected problems |||

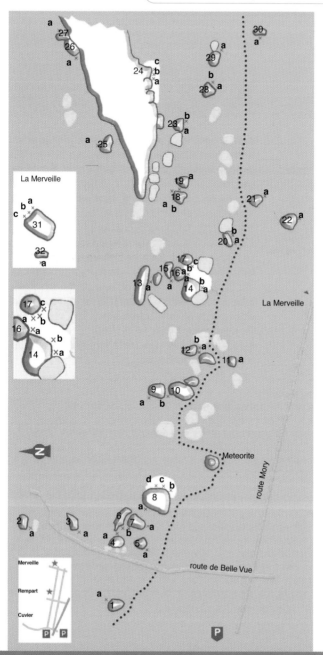

LE CUVIER

SELECTED PROBLEMS

boulder	route	grade	name
1	a	8a+	Souvenir d'été G>D (L>R) traverse
2	a	7c+	Les pieds nickés G>D (L>R) traverse
3	a	7b	On a volé le fresbee G>D (L>R) traverse
4	a	7a	Festin de pierre
6	a	6a	Several variations
7	a	7b	Angel face Committing
7	b	7c	D>G (R>L) traverse
8	a	7b/8a	Les petits anges G>D (L>R) traverse
8	b	6c	Carré d'as Finishing point of black circuit n°2 Trivellini
8	c	6c+	Duroxmanie
8	d	7c	Michel Ange
9	a	7c	Massacre G>D (L>R) traverse, there and back 8b
9	b	7b	Gabonis
11	a	7c+	T. Rex
12	a	8a	C'était demain
12	b	6c+	Troisième ciel
13	a	6c+	Johannis D>G (R>L) traverse
14	a	7c	Big boss
14	b	7c+	Fourmis rouges
15	a	8a+	Dessous chics G>D (L>R) traverse
16	a	7c	Tristesse
17	a	7c+	Big golden
17	b	8a	Atrésie
17	c	7a+	Blitz
18	a	5c	L'angle Allain
18	b	6c	Laser
19	a	6c+	
20	a	8b	Fatman
20	b	8b	Gourmandise
21	a	7c+	Cyclopède D>G (R>L) traverse
22	a	6c	
23	a	6a	
23	b	7c	Noir désir
24	a	8b	Miroir des vanités G>D (L>R) traverse
24	b	7c+	Haute tension
24	c	8a	Hyper tension
25	a	7a+	Salathé wall
26	a	7a+	Philantropie
27	a	7b	L'émeraude
28	a	7a+	Où are you
28	b	7c	Baisers volés
29	a	8b	Khéops
30	a	7c+	Verdict Sitting start
31	a	8a	Merveille
31	b	7a+	Sourire de David
31	c	7c	Dalle de fer
32	a	7c	Swell D>G (R>L) traverse

Laurent Avare masters the fierce bulge of Big golden, an 8a.

Off-circuit
The last twenty years have seen a lot of new route activity. Because they are so scattered and the problems on them are so difficult, many of these boulders have not been marked. Knowledge of them gets around by word of mouth, through the columns of climbing magazines and new topo guides. A sort of complement to circuit climbing, this kind of bouldering goes straight to the basics and has become a totally separate entity compared to other forms of climbing. It is this kind of specificity which you find "off-circuit": going off to climb a particular problem on a particular boulder in the middle of nowhere then going off somewhere else to try another one. Move after move, climbing for its own sake, forgetting any idea of linking problems or of resting. A sign of the times, a sign of a living passion.

Apremont is one of the biggest areas in the Biere forest, forerunner to the forest of today. It stretches from the edge of Barbizon village, internationally famous for its soon to be seven hundred years old oak tree, Jupiter. Which is why, disregarding any interest in climbing, this is a particularly popular area.

You can take your time discovering the many marked circuits in the Gorges, perhaps lose yourself in the wilderness and even dare to uncover new problems on the Envers d'Apremont or the Bizons boulders.

After you have been to the inn at Ganne and the museum at Barbizon do not forget to wander down the "artists' road" which was their inspiration.

Jean-Hervé Baudot on Onde de Choc.

Apremont.

500 m

Barbizon
Bas Bréau
crossroads

N7

Félix-Herbert
crossroads
route de Barbizon à Fontainebleau

Clair Bois
crossroads

TD n°1

PD n°3

Envers d'Apremont

AD n°4

100 m

PD+ n°1

125 m

Apremont
Bizons

Désert
d'Apremont

AD n°3

Gorges
d'Apremont

TD n°1

Gorges
d'Apremont
crossroads

PD+ n°2

125 m

100 m

P

Gorges d'Apremont

CIRCUITS

Circuit	
White for children (n°14)	❏
Yellow PD+ (n°9)	○
Orange AD (n°3)	❏
Green AD	❏
Orange AD+ (n°1)	●
Ultramarine blue D (n°5)	●
Baltic blue D+ (n°13)	●
Crushed strawberry D+ (n°4)	●
Salmon TD- (n°6)	●
Red TD+ (n°10)	●
Red ED- (n°12)	●
Sky blue ED- (n°11)	○
Black and white ED+ (n°7)	○

It is said that it would be impossible for anyone to describe where the circuits finish, so hopelessly intricate is the jumble of boulders that they negotiate, enough to discourage the most ambitious of climbers. Which goes someway to illustrating the complexity of this huge area. Micro mountains in fact. Because it gets so much sunshine and has an abundance of routes of all grades this has always been one of the most popular areas in the forest.

It is sometimes difficult to know where you are; we guarantee that with our help you will be able to find your way around more easily.

Despite the concentration of routes and circuits it does happen that one sometimes stumbles upon an untouched boulder or an unsolved problem. All the various elements of bouldering are brought together here, with, as added spice, a hint of commitment which isn't without its attraction for certain lovers of the vertical.

This particular sandstone labyrinth is one of the areas in the forest which dries most quickly after rain. The circuit grades (particularly ED) are traditional and may seem hard. A quick look back through history tells us that, long before climbers arrived on the scene, the impressionists of the Barbizon school of painting had been charmed by the Gorges d'Apremont. Their now famous canvases are a tribute to the timeless beauty of the place.

THE ZONES

In order to make it easier to understand the maps and tables, the area has been divided into four zones, from zone A in the west to zone D in the east. The boulders are numbered zone by zone.

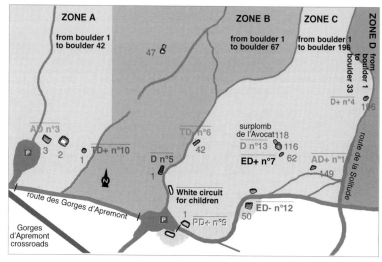

Les Gorges d'Apremont.

Resin v Chalk

If you had to sum up Bleau in one word, it would definitely be resin. How did the idea of making a little cloth bag full of crushed resin originate? It is something of a mystery. However we do know that at first the resin was simply placed in an open bag on the ground. Then someone had the clever idea of tying the bag up with a lace and using this ball to puff resin onto the soles of their boots or a hold.

Chalk is widely used by gymnasts because it absorbs sweat and not surprisingly it was a gymnast – John Gill – who started using it on climbs in the United States in the fifties. But it was not until the end of the seventies that it began to be used at Fontainebleau. At first the use of chalk was very controversial, but today it is commonplace.

Is it any more damaging than resin? Visually certainly, but there is also an ethical debate. The use of resin is actively frowned upon abroad, particularly in the United States and arouses hostile comments, because it "glazes" the surface of holds and reduces the much sought after friction …

The argument rages back and forth.

It is a necessary debate and more and more climbers who use chalk clean the holds afterwards with a tooth brush. The acceptance of responsibility is more effective than an outright ban.

orges d'Apremont
red and white circuit

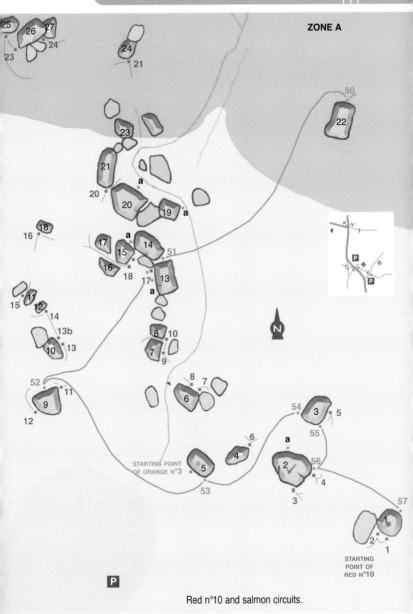

ZONE A

STARTING POINT OF ORANGE N°3

STARTING POINT OF RED N°10

Red n°10 and salmon circuits.

The end of the "yellow circuit" in the Gorges d'Apremont

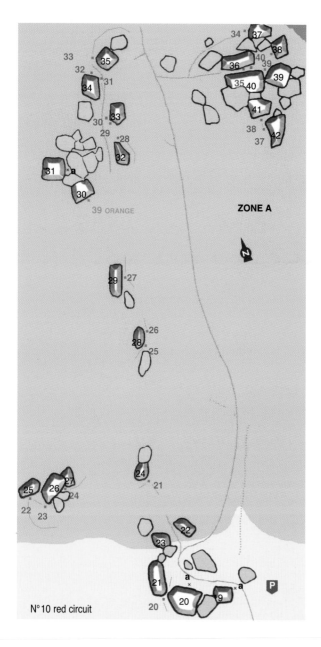

ZONE A

39 ORANGE

N° 10 red circuit

RED AND WHITE CIRCUIT, ZONE A

route	boulder	grade
1	1	5c
2	1	6a
3	2	6a
4	2	5c
5	3	5c
6	4	5b
7	6	5b
8	6	5c
9	7	5c
10	8	5c
11	9	5c
12	9	5b
13	10	5c
13 b	10	5c
14	12	5b
15	11	5b
16	18	5b
17	13	5b
18	15	5c
19	15	5b
20	21	5b
21	24	5b
22	25	5c
23	26	5b
24	27	5c
25	28	5c
26	28	5b
27	29	5b
28	32	5c
29	33	5c
30	33	5c
31	34	5a
32	34	5c
33	35	5a
34	37	5a
35	40	5b
36	40	5c
37	42	4c
38	41	5b
39	40	5a
40	38	5c

Gorges d'Apremont

ultramarine blue circuit

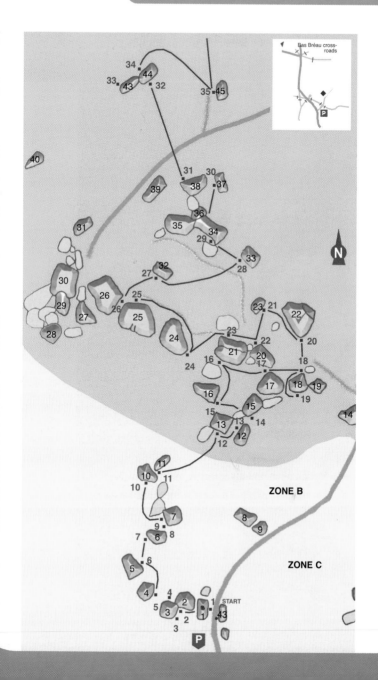

APREMONT

route	boulder	grade
1	1	4a
1b	43	5b
2	2	3b
3	3	4b
4	3	3b
5	4	3c
6	5	4b
7	6	4a
8	7	3c
9	9	3c
10	10	3c
11	11	3c
12	13	4b
13	12	4c
14	15	4b
15	16	3c
16	21	4c
17	17	3c
18	18	3c
19	18	4a
20	22	4a
21	23	4c
22	20	4b
23	21	3c
24	24	3c
25	25	4b
26	26	4c
27	32	3c
28	33	4a
29	34	3c
30	37	3c
31	38	4a
32	44	4b
33	43	4b
34	44	4b
35	45	4c
36	46	4c
37	47	3c
37b	47	4b
38	50	4c
39	51	3c
40	52	3b
41	53	4b
42	54	4a
43	55	4b
44	55	4a

ULTRAMARINE BLUE CIRCUIT, ZONE B

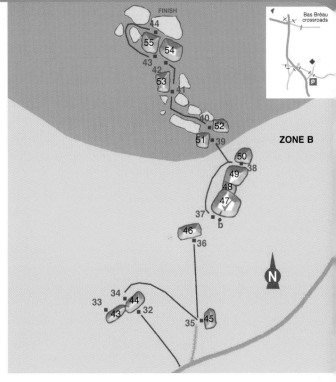

Fun climbing at Apremont.

41

Gorges d'Apremont
sky blue circuit

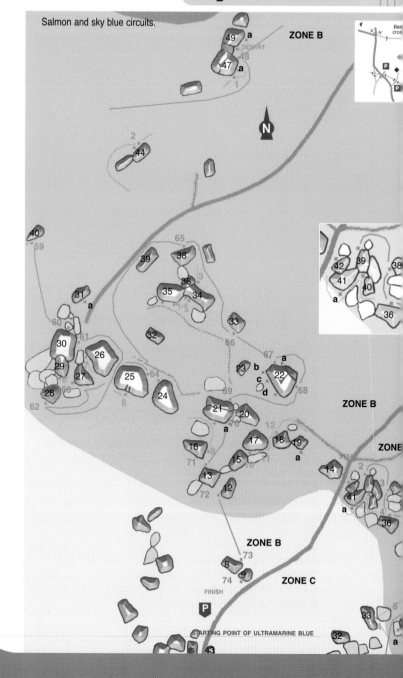

Salmon and sky blue circuits.

...oise Montchaussé at the end of the "salmon circuit".

SKY BLUE CIRCUIT, ZONE B AND C

route	boulder	grade	zone	name
0	49	5c	B	Le croque mitaine
1	47	5c	B	
2	44	5c	B	L'esprit du continent
2b	44	6c	B	Le poulpiquet
3	36	5a	B	L'anti gros
4	34	4b	B	L'effet yau de poele
5	34	4a	B	La bagatelle
4b	35	5c	B	
4t	35	5c	B	
6	29	7a	B	Le toit tranquille
7	26	6a	B	Le gibbon
8	25	6a	B	L'empire des sens
9	16	5b	B	La pavane
10	17	4c	B	Le sabre
11	17	4c	B	Le goupillon
12	18	6c	C	Le mur des lamentations
13	40	5a	C	Le rince dalle
14	33	5c	C	L'ostétoscope
15	108	5c	C	Les fesses à Simon
16	112	5b	C	La michodière
17	59	4c	C	L'across en l'air
18	62	5a	C	L'astrolabe
19	66	5a	C	La vessie
20	65	4c	C	La lanterne
21	65	5b	C	Le pont mirabeau
22	70	5b	C	La super simca
23	74	6a	C	Ignès
24	83	5c	C	La salamandre
25	83	5c	C	La vie lente
26	86	5c	C	La muse hermétique
27	92	5c	C	L'angle obtus
28	90	5b	C	Icare
28b	90	5c	C	
29	166	5b	C	Le merle noir
29b	160	5b	C	L'adieu aux armes
30	161	5b	C	La gnose
31	153	5a	C	La clepsydre
31b	118	5b	C	Le surplomb de l'avocat
32	118	5c	C	La mélodie juste
32b	118	6c	C	Le soupir
33	119	5b	C	Le piano vache
34	122	5c	C	Le surplomb à coulisses
35	121	6a	C	La sortie des artistes

The word which springs to mind when describing this circuit is 'precision". This imaginative route was dreamt up by Robert Mizrahi and is a real encyclopaedia of crack climbing. There are about forty rather unusual routes which are rarely climbed, less because of their intrinsic difficulty than because of the particular techniques required for success: a mixture of crack climbing techniques and commitment, even exposure. The most original route must be across a roof offering a series of precarious moves and will remain an unforgettable experience for anyone who attempts it.

Grey chalk

Chalk arrived in France and at Fontainebleau at the end of the seventies, much to the disgust of many bleausards who considered it damaging, unsightly and useless. Towards the middle of the eighties however, it became widely used by climbers and to silence the critics, someone had the idea of colouring the chalk to blend in with the colour of the rock, making it barely noticeable. Looked at more closely this is not so much a miraculous solution to the problem as a means of placating the rebellious spirit of the bleausards.

Gorges d'Apremont

salmon circuit

Reaching for the sky on the famous Balafre.

SALMON CIRCUIT, ZONES A, B, C

route	boulder	grade	route	boulder	grade	route	boulder	grade	route	boulder	grade
ZONE C			20	81	6a	37	65	5a	56	2	5a
1	42	5c	21	88	5a	38	64	4c	57	1	4c
2	39	4a	22	93	5b	39	64	4a	**ZONE B**		
3	37	4a	23	94	5a	40	63	4a	58	41	4a
4	36	4a	24	118	6a	41	62	4b	59	40	4c
5	34	3c	La balafre			42	61	4a	60	30	4b
6	29	4c	25	132	6a	43	60	5c	61	30	5b
7	27	5a	26	112	5b	44	59	5a	62	28	4b
8	55	5a	27	108	5a	45	57	4a	63	27	4b
9	53	5c	28	110	4c	46	58	3c	64	25	4c
10	54	4c	28 b	104	5c	47	56	5c	65	38	5b
11	56	5b	29	152	5c	48	47	5c	66	33	5c
12	58	4a	30	153	5b	49	42	4c	67	22	5a
13	61	4c	31	165	5a	**ZONE A**			68	22	4c
14	63	4c	32	176	4a	50	22	4a	69	21	4c
15	64	5a	33	173	5c	51	13	4c	70	21	4c
16	67	4a	34	179	4a	52	9	4a	71	13	5a
17	70	5b	**ZONE B**			53	5	4a	72	12	5a
18	71	4c	35	67	4a	54	3	4a	73	8	4b
19	79	5a	36	66	4a	55	3	5b	74	9	4c

The colour is a statement in itself. Why not blue or red? This particular chapter in climbing history was written by Jacques Reppellin and Pierre Port, two ageless and charming alpinists whom it is always a pleasure to meet. This long circuit has seventy four problems, but despite its length has been done in less than forty five minutes. The scale of some of the problems is striking; and if the circuit is sometimes difficult to follow in the labyrinth of the Apremont boulders, well then that is all part of its charm.

Salmon and sky blue circuits.

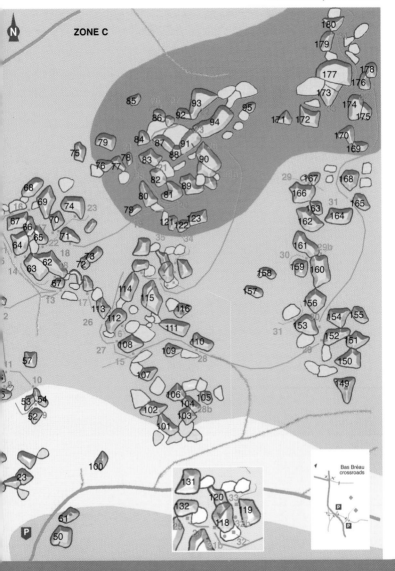

Gorges d'Apremont
yellow circuit

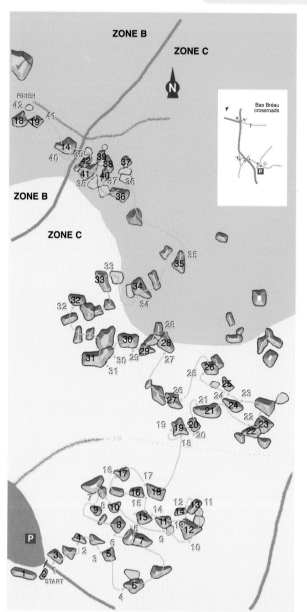

Bas Bréau
crossroads

YELLOW CIRCUIT, ZONE C

route	boulder	grade
1	3	2b
2	4	2b
3	5	2a
4	6	2a
5	7	2b
6	8	2a
7	9	2b
8	10	3a
9	11	3c
10	12	2b
11	13	2b
12	14	2b
13	12	2b
14	15	2c
15	16	3b
16	17	2a
17	18	2c
18	19	2a
19	19	3a
20	20	3c
21	21	3a
22	22	3a
23	24	2b
24	25	2c
25	26	2a
26	27	2c
27	28	2c
28	28	2b
29	30	2a
30	31	3a
31	31	2a
32	32	2c
33	33	2c
34	34	2c
35	35	2c
36	36	2c
37	40	2c
38	41	2c
39	42	2a
40	14	3a
41	19	2c
42	18	2c

Gorges d'Apremont
orange circuit

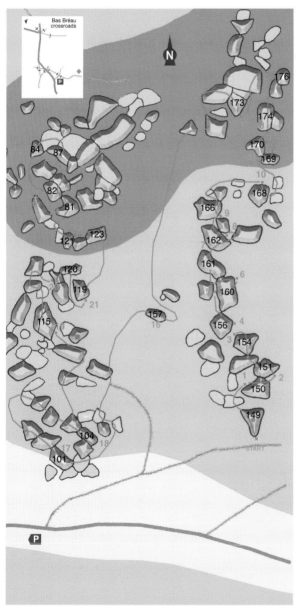

Ochre tones at Apremont.

ORANGE CIRCUIT, ZONE C

route	boulder	grade
0	149	3b
1	150	4a
2	151	3c
3	154	3b
4	156	3b
5	160	3b
6	160	3b
7	161	4b
8	162	3a
9	166	3b
10	168	4c
11	169	3a
12	170	3c
13	174	3a
14	176	3b
15	173	4a
16	157	1b
17	101	3c
18	104	4b
19	115	2b
20	120	4b
21	119	3c
22	123	3a
23	121	2b
24	81	3b
25	82	3c
26	87	4c
27	84	3c
28	82	3b

Gorges d'Apremont
baltic blue circuit

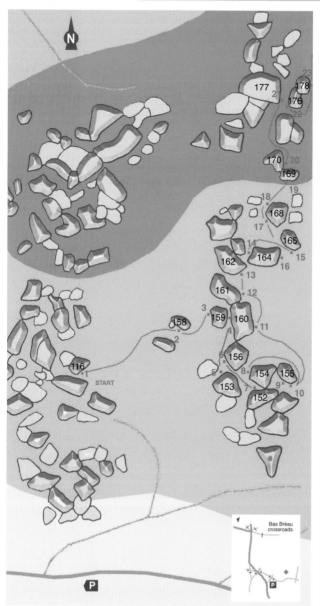

BALTIC BLUE CIRCUIT, ZONE 0

route	boulder	grade
1	116	4c
2	158	4b
3	159	4a
4	160	4a
5	153	4c
6	156	4b
7	152	4a
8	154	4b
9	155	4b
10	155	6a
11	160	5a
12	161	4a
13	162	4b
14	164	3c
15	165	4c
16	164	4b
17	168	4c
18	168	4b
19	169	4a
20	170	4c
21	177	5a
22	176	4b
23	178	4b
24	181	5a
24b	182	4c
25	183	3c
26	184	4b
27	185	4b
28	186	4b
29	187	5b
30	189	3c
31	188	4c
32	189	4b
33	190	4c
34	190	4b
35	190	4a
36	191	4a
37	192	4c
38	194	3c
38b	193	4c
39	195	4c

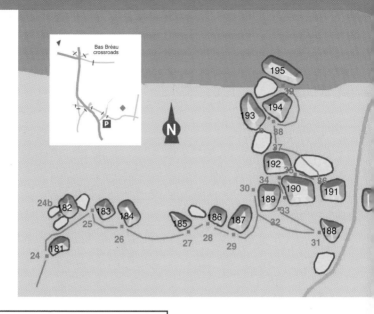

Once upon a time ...
there were climbing circuits

Is it possible to simulate the ascent of a mountain route without actually gaining height? In 1947, Fred Bernick created the first ever circuit at Cuvier Rempart, linking together a series of boulder problems, which actually required the same intensity of effort as a mountain route.

However it was not until the sixties that these circuits became widely used and their intrinsic merit recognised and as a result they became identified with climbing at Fontainebleau.

Both an historical reference and an alluring invitation to climb, the circuits are still the very essence of bleausard climbing. How would you find your way around the tens of thousands of routes in this rocky chaos without these invisible threads? It is their ease of use which has made them so popular.

There are nearly two hundred circuits, which at present is considered to be enough. They are maintained and occasionally remarked as a result of consultation between the Office national des forêts, the Comité de défense des sites et rochers d'escalade (CO-SI-ROC) and volunteers who are happy to give up their time to further the upkeep of their common inheritance.

On L'égoïste.

Gorges d'Apremont
red circuit

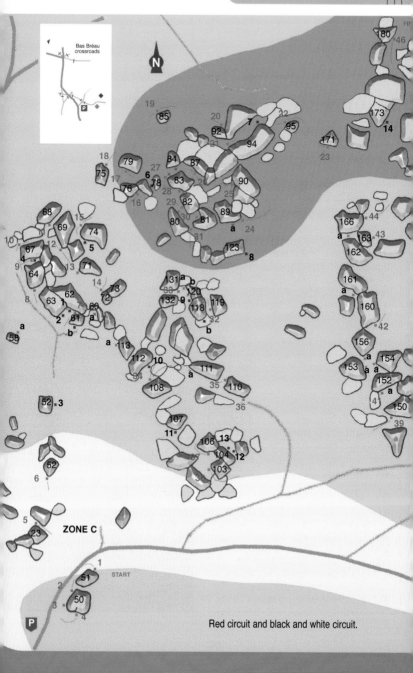

Bas Bréau crossroads

ZONE C

START

Red circuit and black and white circuit.

Morning light at Apremont.

RED CIRCUIT, ZONE C

route	boulder	grade	name	route	boulder	grade	name
1	51	5c	Départ	24	89	6b	Les verrues
2	50	5b	La sans l'arête	25	90	5a	Le réta gras
3	50	5a	Les trois petits tours	26	87	5b	La claque
4	50	6a	Le piano à queue	27	83	5a	Le pilier
5	23	5a	La traversée de la fosse aux ours	28	83	6a	La conque
6	52	5c	Le trompe l'œil	28b	82	6a	Les fausses inversées
7	62	6a	Les crampes à Memère	29	82	5c	L'ancien
7b	62	6a		29b	80	6a	Les chiures
7t	63	5c		30	81	5b	La valse
8	64	5b	Le triste portique	31	80	5c	La que faire
9	67	5b	Le toboggan	32	119	6b	La psycho
10	67	5b	Le vieil os	33	131	5c	Le doigté
11	68	6a	Les yeux	34	108	5c	La science friction
12	69	5c	Le château de sable	35	110	5c	La pilier japonais
13	71	5c	La durandal	36	110	6a	La Ko-Kutsu
14	72	5c	La rampe	37	106	5c	Le médius
15	74	5c	Le marchepied	38	103	5c	La râpe grasse
16	76	5b	La longue marche	39	150	6a	L'anglomanique
17	79	5c	Le bouleau	40	150	5c	Le grand pilier
18	75	5b	Le bonheur des dames	41	152	6a	L'arrache bourse
19	85	5b	La freudienne	42	160	5c	L'alternative
20	92	5a	Le coin pipi	43	163	5a	La dalle à dame
21	94	5a	L'angulaire	44	166	5a	Le cube
22	95	5b	Le baiser vertical	45	175	5b	La croix
23	171	5b	Le dièdre gris	46	180	5b	La John Gill

Gorges d'Apremont
black and white circuit |||

BLACK AND WHITE CIRCUIT

route	boulder	grade	name	route	boulder	grade	name
1	62	7a	L'hyper plomb	9	118	7a+	Le treizième travail Direct variation 7c+
2	63	7a	La dalle du dromadaire	9b	118	7a+	Fleur de rhum
2b	61	7a	Médaille en chocolat	10	112	6c+	La lune
3	52	6b	La croix et la bannière	11	107	6c	Le fruit défendu
4	64	6a	La dalle du toboggan	12	105	6c	L'arc d'Héraclès
5	74	6c	L'ébréchée	13	104	6c	La tarentule
6	78	6c	La térébrante	14	173	6c	Les lames
7	94	6c	L'œuf				
8	123	6c	La conque				

Gorges d'Apremont
crushed strawberry circuit

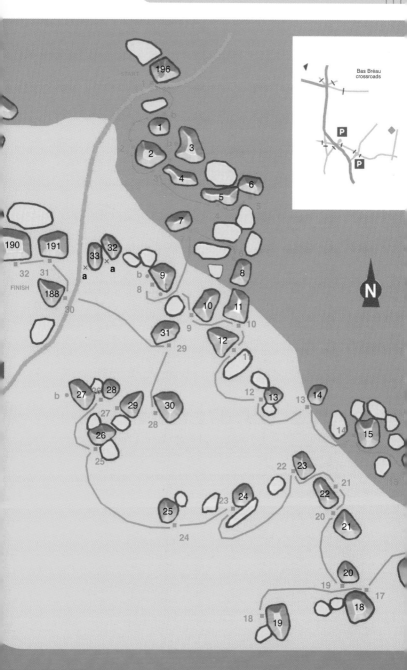

CRUSHED STRAWBERRY CIRCUIT, ZONE D

route	boulder	grade	route	boulder	grade
1	196	3b	17	18	4c
1b	1	4a	18	19	4b
2	2	3c	19	20	4a
3	4	4a	20	21	5b
3b	3	4a	21	22	4b
4	5	4a	22	23	4a
5	6	4c	23	24	4b
6	8	4b	24	25	3c
7	7	4a	25	26	5b
8	9	5a	26	28	4c
8b	9	4c	26b	27	6a
8t	9	4c	27	29	4b
9	10	4a	28	30	4b
10	11	5c	29	31	4c
11	12	5b	30	188	4b
12	13	4a	31	191	5a
13	14	4a		L'ante phallus	
14	15	4b	32	190	5b
15	16	4a		Le phallus	
16	17	4b			

Here again, the originality of the colour is striking. And this circuit must have made an impact when it was first done in 1957 because it was the hardest of the time. Doing it today you get an idea of how good the climbers of that era were given that they did not have the high-performance equipment that we have now. This circuit was also ground-breaking in that it was the first time bouldering was done for its own sake and not simply used as training for the mountains.

Gorges d'Apremont
off-circuit

OFF-CIRCUIT, ZONES A, B, C, D

zone	boulder	route	grade	name	zone	boulder	route	grade	name
A	2	a	7a		C	58	a	6b	D>G (R>L) traverse
A	13	a	7a	Super Stalingrad	C	60	a	6a	Overhang
A	13	b	7a	Tendance de droite	C	83	a	7a+	Dalle d'Alain
A	14	a	7c+	Merry Christmas	C	84	a	7a+	Futur antérieur
A	19	a	7a	Hiéroglyphe	C	89	a	7b	Coup de cœur
A	20	a	7c+	Jolie Môme	C	111	a	7b+	Tarpé diem / Reachy
A	31	a	7a		C	113	a	7c	Travers D / G>D (L>R) traverse
B	19	a	7a	Clin d'œil					
B	21	a	7c+	Koala / Exposed	C	120	a	7a+	Arrête
B	22	a	6c		C	120	b	7c+	Remaniement / Eliminate
B	22	b	6c						
B	22	c	6c	D>G (R>L) traverse 7a	C	152	a	7b	
B	22	d	6b		C	153	a	6c	
B	31	a	7b	Faux contact	C	154	a	7a	
B	47	a	7b	Une idée en l'air	C	156	a	7b	Onde de choc
B	49	a	7b+	Le marginal	C	161	a	8b	L'alchimiste / The crucial hold has broken
C	34	a	6b	Traverse					
C	41	a	6c+	Egoïste / Sitting start 7a+	C	162	a	7b+	
					D	32	a	6c	Quiproquo
					D	33	a		Project

Désert d'Apremont

CIRCUITS

Yellow PD (n°2) ❑
Yellow PD+ (n°1) ⬤
Orange AD (n°3) ❑
Orange AD (n°4) ❑
Orange AD (n°5) ❑
Blue D+ (n°6) ❑

The French word "désert" means wilderness which conjures up images of boundless space, this is a wonderful place for discovering what climbing is all about on one of the six circuits, which are all beginner's circuits. Take the spirit of discovery and add a small amount of isolation: although you are only about ten minutes from the road, there is no noise, or very little, and it is easy to imagine yourself far off in the wilderness.

Margins and limits

How difficult a route feels depends on the relationship between the amount of energy you have expended and the amount of energy you anticipate expending. You can sometimes feel as though you have a big "margin" on a difficult problem, and feel at your "limit" on a less difficult problem. The concept that you are getting the better of both the route and yourself can determine how difficult it feels. To improve you can attempt to push yourself against continually harder problems. You need to become mentally detached from yourself and focus totally on the rock and the problem you choose to do. Conversely you can try to always find an easier way of doing problems, whatever their difficulty. In this case you need to become mentally detached from the rock and more focused on yourself as you choose a route. The ability to combine these two processes can help you to make better use of your energy and to gradually climb up the grades.

It can help you to look at the rock in a different way, help you to know yourself better and lastly to enjoy yourself more.

Marc Le Menestrel

Delicate holds require positive footwork.

Désert d'Apremont
yellow circuit

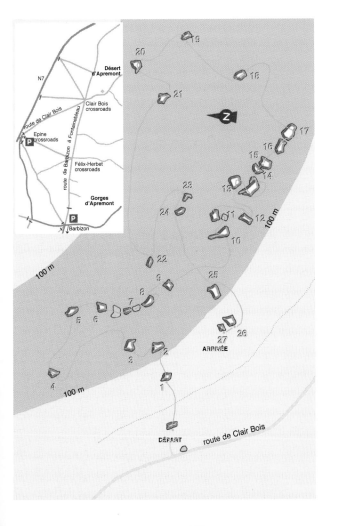

route	grade
YELLOW CIRCUIT	
1	2b
2	2b
3	3a
4	2b
5	2c
6	3a
7	2c
8	3a
9	2b
10	2c
11	2c
12	3b
13	2b
14	2c
15	2a
16	3a
17	3b
18	2b
19	3b
20	2b
21	3c
22	3a
23	3a
24	2c
25	1b
26	3a
27	4a

Envers d'Apremont

CIRCUITS

Yellow PD ❑
Orange AD ❑
Red TD
being re-marked at present ❑

North of the Gorges and their jumble of blocks, the Envers d'Apremont seems particularly peaceful. It has an old circuit running through it, affectionately nicknamed "Farine" (meaning "flour") after the person who first did it thirty years ago and who used to cart around bags of … .flour. More recently, one of the boulders on the circuit (the old number 40), following the fashion for sitting starts, now boasts one of the most difficult problems in the forest: *Pierre philosophale*. You will find it cool in summer and quiet when all the other areas are crowded.

The curve of the tree echoes that of the rock Mathieu Dutray on L'apparemment (8a).

Breaking through five seven

In order to be able to climb everything several symbolic barriers need to be crossed. Notably those of the sixth and seventh grade. As you pause for a moment on the threshold of these two levels, we would like to give you a few pointers. The main one being that the barriers are more psychological than physical or technical.

A few tricks of the trade

First choose a problem most suited to the style of climbing which you prefer. Do not try an overhang first if you are more at home on slabs. As Yannick Noah said about tennis, work on your strong points first.

Watch those who are more experienced and preferably of the same build as yourself; do not hesitate to ask for an explanation of the subtlety of a certain move which seems different. Wait for the right time to try the problem. Friction is better in winter or when the temperature is between 5 and 10 degrees. Any higher, and friction is less good. Have the right rock boots and for more comfort in winter, leave them next to your car heater so they are more pleasant to put on. It will also improve feel and friction. Having a spotter support you while trying moves is an excellent way of learning how to do a problem. The spotter can lightly support your body weight while you do the moves, gradually giving you less and less support until finally you do the problem unaided. It is important that the area of support is at the level of the tops of your thighs to keep your centre of gravity in the right place and to allow you to feel the rock.

Some problems to help you progress to grade 6

- La piscine (black n°4) at the Gros Sablons: a longer route
- John Gill (red n°46) at the Gorges d'Apremont: a 5b roof
- Red n°1 at the Roche aux Sabots: 5c
- La Marie Rose (red n°22) at Bas Cuvier: 6a, very technical (the first ever of its grade)
- La Balafre (salmon n°24) at the Gorges d'Apremont: a big 5c ... 6a.
- Mine de rien (red n°23) at the Roche aux Sabots: a big 5c or a little 6a
- Red bis n°11 in the Vallée de la Mée: a pleasant 6a on lovely rock.
- The Bois Rond red circuit is an excellent place for a first 6a.
- The Roche aux Sabots red circuit is a superb place for learning the technical subtleties of grade 6.

Some problems to help you progress to grade 7

- La dernière croisade (white n°13) at La Padôle: a big 6c/6c+
- White n°50 (finishing point) at Isatis: a psychological 6c (without the arête)
- The Droyer pillar on the Eléphant: a 6c+ tricky and technical
- Le Surplomb de la coquille at Isatis-Hautes Plaines: overhanging with commitment approaching grade 7.
- White n°6 at Isatis by the direct start: 6c/6c+, delicate and technical
- Medaille en chocolat (black and white bis n°2) at the Gorges d'Apremont: a fairly easy 7a using dynos but reachy
- Hélicoptère at Bas Cuvier: an easier 7a for those who are tall, than l'Abattoir
- Holey Moley at Bas Cuvier: a fairly easy 7a especially in winter. and easy to "spot".
- Attention chef d'oeuvre at Buthiers: a fingery 7a wall, absolutely unique
- Chasseur de prises (white n°1) at Rocher Canon: a 6c+ trending towards 7a
- A l'impossible at the Roche aux Sabots: a slabby 7a, fingery and delicate
- Pierre précieuse at area 95.2: 6c+ for "figure of 4" experts (where the right leg is coiled round the left arm)
- Descent aux enfers (black n°5) at Franchard Cuisinière: a physical 7a+ with foot hooking.

Apremont Bizons

CIRCUITS

Orange AD+ ●
Red TD ●

Don't bother looking for buffalo, they have never been domestically reared here. There is not far to walk, the routes start less than fifty metres from the car-park. Although you are near the Gorges here, the scenery is very different: shady and with a certain harshness about it. Lovely in summer.

Apremont Bizons

orange circuit

red circuit

ORANGE CIRCUIT

route	boulder	grade		route	boulder	grade		route	boulder	grade	
1	1	3c		16	13	3a		32	35	4b	4c variation
2	2	3c		17	14	3c		33	41	4a	
3	3	3a	3b variation	18	18	3c		34	45	4a	
4	4	4a	3c variation	19	21	4a		35	44	3b	
5	4	2c		20	22	4a		36	43	3a	
6	5	3b		21	20	3a		37	47	3b	4a variation
7	6	3c		22	19	3b		38	52	3c	4a variation
7b	6	3a		22b	19	3c		39	52	2c	
7t	6	4b		23	17	2c		40	51	3b	4b variation
8	7	2b		24	16	4b+		41	51	2c	
9	7	3		24b	16	2c		42	49	4a	3c variation
10	8	4c		25	16	3a		43	48	2b	
10b	8	3c		26	15	3a		44	49	3b	
11	8	3c		26b	15	3c		45	53	3c	
12	9	3b		27	37	3c		46	54	4a	
13	9	3a		28	38	4c		47	55	3b	
14	10	2c		29	39	3a		48	40	3a	
14b	10	3c		30	39	3c					
15	12	4c		31	36	3c					

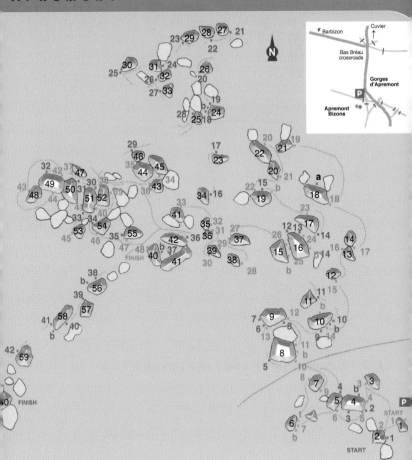

RED CIRCUIT

route	boulder	grade		route	boulder	grade		route	boulder	grade	
1	2	4b	3b variation	15	19	5c		31	50	4b	
2	4	5a	Dynos	16	34	5c		32	49	4b	
2b	4	5b+		17	23	4a		33	51	4b	
3	3	4b		18	24	5a		34	54	3c	
4	5	4c		18b	24	5c		35	55	5b	
5	8	4c	6a variation	19	24	4b		36	42	4b	
6	9	5a		20	26	4a		37	41	3c	
7	9	4c		21	27	4b	5a variation	37b	40	4c	
8	9	4a		22	28	4b		38	56	5b	
9	10	5a		23	29	4a		38b	56	5b	
9b	10	5a		24	31	4a		39	57	4a	4c variation
10	10	4c		25	30	4c		40	58	5b	
11	11	5b		26	32	4c		41	58	5a	
12	16	4c		27	33	5b		41b	58	5a	
13	16	5a	6a variation, G>D (L>R) traverse	28	25	4c		42	59	5b	
				29	46	4c		43	60	5a	
14	17	4c		30	51	6a		a	18	7a	

FRANCHARD

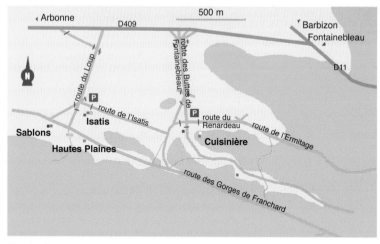

Franchard.

THE SUPER JOKER

Location: Franchard Isatis,one metre right of white number 9.
Grade: 7b+ originally, 7c today.
Style: Two movements and two words: pelvic mobility and co-ordination.
Climber: Didier Girardin.

It was Alain Michaud who cast this special stone into the bleausard garden at the end of the seventies. Initially a 7b+, it was upgraded and is a test of nerve for the taller climber who will find it harder to link together the foot-hand moves than those of smaller stature.

Technique

Right hand on a sidepull on which it is necessary for me to put all five digits; left hand on the edge, right foot smearing; I then lower my pelvis as much as possible, so my body is curved.

The toe of the left foot can then be placed above the left hand at the same time putting as much pressure as possible on your right hand's pinch grip. Gradually move all your weight on to your left foot at the same time continuing to maintain the pinch grip with your right hand.

Stand up to reach the finishing pocket, but do so slowly in order to avoid slipping off. The finish out to the left is but a formality using the rounded holds, but it is best to clean them all the same.

Franchard Isatis

CIRCUITS

Circuit	
Orange AD	☐
Blue D-	●
Red TD-	●
White ED	○

This is one of the best loved sites in the forest. No doubt as a result of the large number of boulders and the elegance of the problems of every grade. This subtle alchemy has made Isatis one of the undisputed classic areas of the forest. Admittedly there is no point in going there hoping for absolute peace and quiet; the area is often crowded at the weekend. But there is nothing to stop you from leaving the hordes behind and it gets quieter towards the end of the circuits. The proximity to the Rochers des Sablons and the new routes which have been put up outside the circuits have done much to disperse the crowds. Lastly, watch out for your fingers and hone the edges of your boots, crimping is the name of the game here and the edges are renowned for their sharpness.

Franchard Isatis
blue circuit

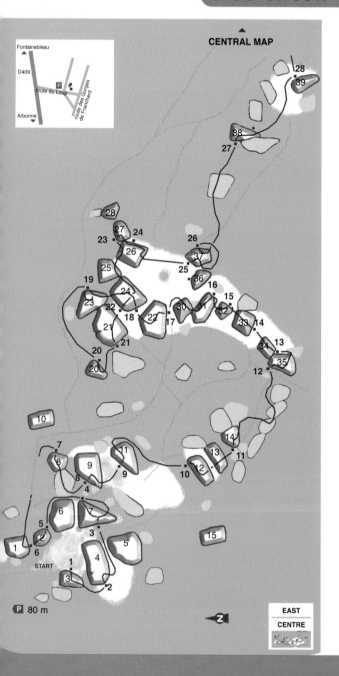

CENTRAL MAP

Fontainebleau
D409
route du Loup
route des Gorges de Franchard
Arbonne

START

P 80 m

N

EAST
CENTRE

Ferns carpet the
forest floor

BLUE CIRCUIT

route	boulder	grade
1	3	3b
2	4	3a
3	7	3c
4	7	3c
5	2	4b
6	1	3c
7	8	3c
8	9	5a
9	11	5a
10	12	4a
11	14	3b
12	35	4b
13	34	5c
14	33	4a
15	32	3a
16	31	3b
17	22	3a
18	24	3b
19	23	3b
20	20	3a
21	21	4a
22	24	4b
23	27	3c
24	26	4a
25	37	3c
26	37	3c
27	38	2c
28	39	4b
28b	39	5a
29	40	3a
30	44	3b
31	46	3b
32	51	3b
32b	51	3c
33	49	3c
34	43	4c
35	41	4c
36	52	4c
37	55	4b
38	54	3c
39	53	3c
40	56	3c
41	58	4a
42	59	4b
43	70	3b
44	70	4a
45	72	3b
45b	72	3a
46	72	4a
47	73	3c
48	74	3b
49	75	4a

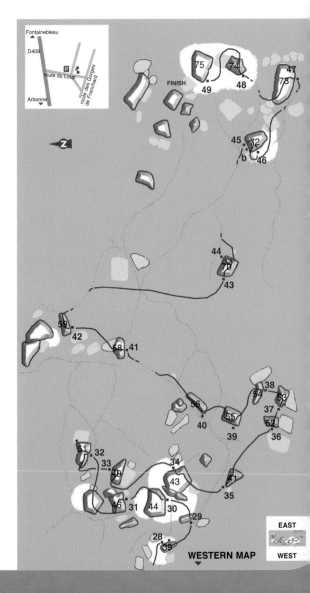

WESTERN MAP

EAST

WEST

Franchard Isatis

red circuit

CENTRAL MAP

Fontainebleau

D409

route du Loup

route des Gorges de Franchard

Arbonne

START

P 80 m

EAST
CENTRE

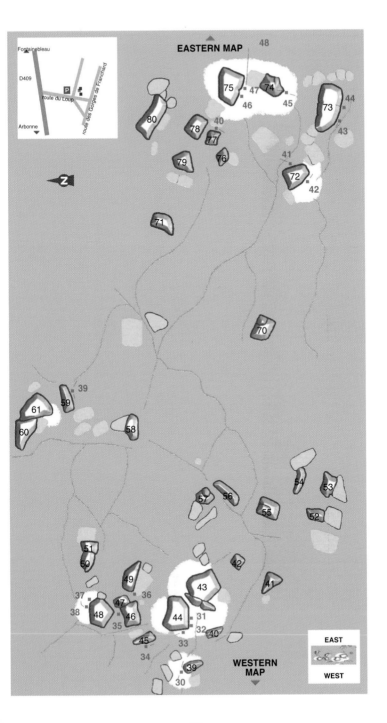

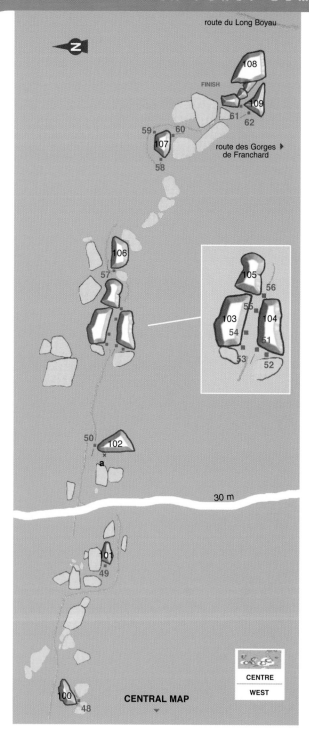

route du Long Boyau

108

FINISH

109

61

62

59 60

107

route des Gorges
de Franchard ▶

58

106

57

105

56

56

103 104

54

51

53 52

50

102

×
a

30 m

101

49

100

48

CENTRAL MAP

CENTRE

WEST

On the technical
arête of Le Cervin
(The Matterhorn).

route	boulder	grade	route	boulder	grade	route	boulder	grade	route	boulder	grade	route	boulder	grade
1	1	4c	14	9	5b	27	24	4c	41	72	4c	53	103	4c
2	1	5b	15	9	5a	28	24	5c	42	72	5b	54	103	5a
3	3	5b	16	9	5a	29	24	5c	43	73	4c	55	104	4c
4	4	4c	17	11	5a	30	39	5b	44	73	4b	56	105	4c
5	4	5a	18	11	4b	31	44	5b	45	74	4c	57	106	4a
6	4	4b	19	13	4c	32	44	5a	46	75	5b	58	107	4c
7	4	4c	20	13	4b	33	44	5b	47	75	5b	59	107	5b
8	7	5b	21	14	4c	34	45	5c	La bissouflante			60	107	5b
9	6	5	22	35	5a	35	46	4c	48	100	4a	61	109	4c
10	6	5b	23	33	4c	36	49	6a	49	101	5a	62	108	5b
11	7	4b	24	33	5b	37	48	4b	50	102	5a			
12	9	5a	25	31	4b	38	48	5b	51	104	5a			
13	9	5a	26	22	4c	40	77	5b	52	104	4c			

RED CIRCUIT

Franchard Isatis

white circuit

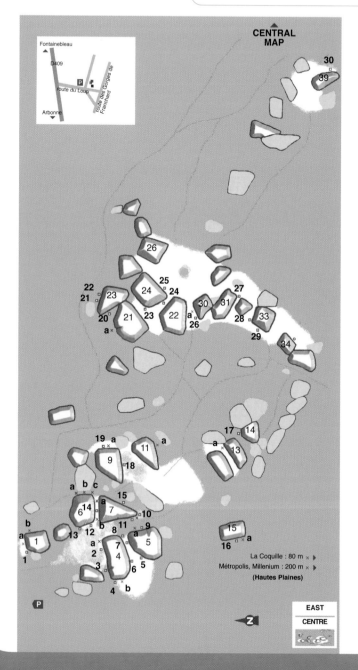

CENTRAL MAP

Fontainebleau

D409

route du Loup

route des Gorges de Franchard

Arbonne

La Coquille : 80 m × ▶
Métropolis, Millenium : 200 m × ▶
(Hautes Plaines)

EAST
CENTRE

WHITE CIRCUIT

route	boulder	grade	name
1	1	6b	L'amoche doigt
2	4	5b	
3	4	5a	
4	4	6c	Composition des forces
5	5	5b	
6	4	5b	
7	5	5b	
8	4	6a	
9	5	5c	Le coup de pompe
10	7	6a	Le statique
11	7	6b	
12	6	5b	
13	6	5b	
14	6	5c	
15	7	5b	
16	15	6a+	Beurre marga
17	14	5b	
18	9	6b	La zip zut
19	9	6b	L'envie des bêtes
20	23	6b	La planquée
21	23	6a	
22	23	5c	
23	24	5c	
24	24	6a	
25	24	5c	
26	30	5a	
27	31	6a	
28	33	6a	
29	33	5b	
30	39	5b	
31	43	6b	
32	43	6a	
33	44	5a	
34	44	5c	
35	44	6a	
36	44	6b	
37	46	6a	
38	48	6a	
39	48	6a	
40	51	6b	
41	51	6a	
42	50	5b	
43	79	6a	
44	72	5b	
45	74	5b	
46	74	6c	Le Cervin
47	74	5b	La patinoire
48	75	6c	
49	75	6a	
50	80	6b	

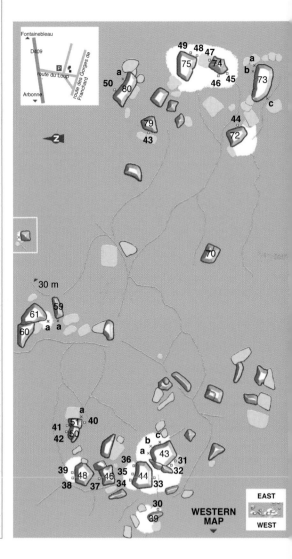

Franchard Isatis
off-circuit

Pierre Gonzalès starting the
crux of L'arrache cœur.

OFF-CIRCUIT PROBLEMS

boulder	route	grade	name
1	a	7b+	Surprise
1	b	7a	
4	a	7b+	L'intégrale Traverse
4	b	7a+	Couenne de merde
5	a	7c	Super joker
6	a	7c	Gnossienne
6	b	7b+	Le mur des lamentations 7c Direct
6	c	7c	Gymnopédie
7	a	7a	
7	b	7a	
7	c	7a	
9	a	6c+	
11	a	6c	
13	a	7c+	Le vin aigre Reachy
15	a	6c	Les troubadours
21	a	6b+	
30	a	7a+	
43	a	6c	
43	b	7c	Alta
43	c	8b	Enigma
51	a	7a	
59	a	7a+	El poussif
61	a	7a	El poussah
73	a	6b	
73	b	?	Project
73	c	7b	La Memel
80	a	7c	L'arrache cœur
102	a	8a	Iceberg

OFF-SITE PROBLEMS

boulder	grade	name
a	6c+	Surplomb de la coquille
b	7c	Métropolis
c	7c+	Millenium
see Franchard Hautes Plaines map		

Hautes Plaines

CIRCUITS

Yellow PD-	❏
Yellow PD+	⚪
Orange AD+	❏

This peaceful sylvan setting is the perfect place to learn the basic techniques of climbing, from the very first steps (PD-) to a more advanced level (AD+).

For those who wish to train for mountain routes or big cliffs, two boulders (located near the end of the yellow circuit PD+) have fixed belay points and you can set up an abseil (take rope, harness and descender). All that is missing is the mountains themselves.

Mother Nature orders chaos.

Hautes Plaines
yellow circuit

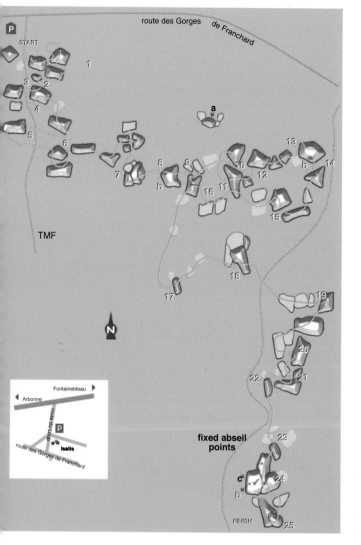

route des Gorges de Franchard

START

TMF

a

route des Gorges de Franchard
Fontainebleau
Arbonne
isatis

fixed abseil points

FINISH

YELLOW CIRCUIT	
route	grade
1	2c
1b	3c
2	3a
3	3a
4	2c
5	2c
5b	1c
6	2b
7	2a
7b	3c
8	2a
8b	3a
9	2c
10	2c
11	2a
12	2a
12b	2c
13	2c
14	2b
14b	3c
15	3a
16	2c
17	2c
18	2c
19	2b
20	2a
21	2b
22	2c
23	2b
24	3b
25	3c

Franchard Sablons

CIRCUITS

Blue D ●
Red TD ●

This area, which is a few hundred metres from Isatis, has in the past been eclipsed by its more famous neighbour, but is now enjoying something of a second childhood, with the refurbishment of the circuits and the creation of new traverses and problems. The average standard of difficulty is well below that at Isatis and you are assured of peace and quiet, making it an attractive choice.

Chestnut trees in bloom.

Franchard Sablons

blue circuit

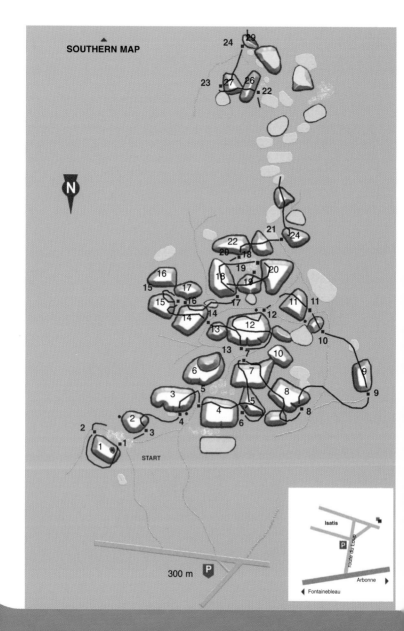

SOUTHERN MAP

N

300 m

Isatis

route du Loup

Arbonne

Fontainebleau

START

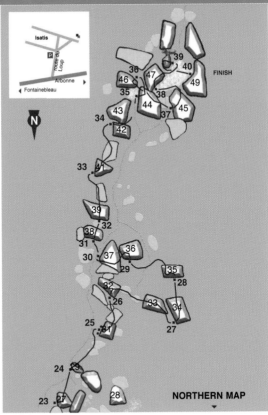

NORTHERN MAP

BLUE CIRCUIT

route	boulder	grade	name	route	boulder	grade	name
1	1	3b	L'accueil tranquille	20	22	4b	Le bon point à Danièle
2	1	4a		21	24	3a	La médaillon
3	2	4c	La verdâtre	22	26	5a	La grat'à Marc
3b	2	3c		23	27	4b	
4	3	4b	L'oiseau bleu	24	29	4c	
4b	b	3	4a	25	31	4a	La Gillette
5	4	4b	Le 4x4	25b	31	3a	La débonnaire
6	5	4a	La voie du gynécologue	25t	31	3c	La Gillette bleue
7	7	4b	L'ascenseur	26	32	4a	L'anonymat
8	8	4b	Le gros bidon	27	34	4a	L'arraché
9	9	4b	Le bloc du forestier	28	35	3c	
10	11	4c	L'équilibriste	29	36	4b	
11	21	3c	L'amanite vaginée	30	37	4c	
11b	21	4c		31	38	4b	La réserve du Président
12	12	4b	La montagne russe	32	39	3c	Le rouleau californien
12b	12	4c	La Migouze	33	41	4a	La soucoupe volante
13	12	5a	Une voie d'O.S.	34	42	4a	L'arête vive
14	13	4b	Les fourmis vertes	35	44	4a	
15	15	4a	L'enchaînement	36	46	4b	
16	14	4a		37	45	3a	La Fonta stick
17	18	4c	L'élégante	38	47	3c	
18	20	4a		39	48	4a	
19	19	3b/5c	Le trou morpho	40	49	4b	La multiprise

Franchard Sablons
red circuit

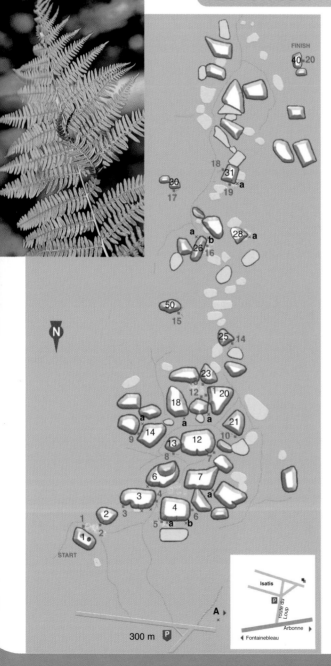

FINISH

40 · 20

18
31
× a
19

80
17

a
b
28 × a
26
16

50
15

25 · 14

23
12
20
18
a a
21
14
9
10
13 12
8 7
6
7
3 4 a
2 a
1 5 a b
2
1

START

N

300 m

Isatis

route du Loup

A ×

◀ Fontainebleau

Arbonne ▶

Ice stops play;
a feast for the eye

RED CIRCUIT

route	boulder	grade	name
1	1	5c	L'accroche doigt
2	2	5b	La réticence
3	3	5b	Le passe plat
4	3	5b	La promptitude
5	4	5c	La dérobade
6	4	5c	Morsure aux doigts
7	12	5c	Les racines
8	13	5b	Saccage au burin
9	14	5b	Le chien assis
10	21	5b	L'arête du poisson
11	20	5b	La traversée
12	19	5a	Le nez
13	23	4c	L'accalmie
14	25	4b	Mise en train
15	50	5a	Coup de canon Sustained 6a
16	26	6a	La dalle à Clément
17	30	4b	Orgasme
18	31	4a	La dalle bleue
19	31	5c	Prise de tête
20	40	6a	Dalle funéraire

Franchard Sablons
off-circuit

OFF-CIRCUIT PROBLEMS

boulder	route	grade	name	boulder	route	grade	name
3	a	6c	Dos d'âne	18	a	7a	Duralex
3	b	6c	Le fer à repasser	19	a	7b+	Modulor
4	a	7b+	Traînée de poudre G>D (L>R) traverse, finish up scoop	26	a	7b	Jokavi Dyno
4	b	7c+	Fragment d'hébétude D>G (R>L) traverse, finish on red	26	b	7a	La vérité
				28	a	6b	Sale affaire
6	a	6c+	Gros tambour G>D (L>R) traverse	31	a	7a+	Talons aiguilles
7	a	7a+	Canyon G>D (L>R) traverse				
14	a	7a	Peine forte G>D (L>R) traverse, sustained 7b+		A	7a	Voltane 8a traverse

Franchard Cuisinière

CIRCUITS

Mountain Orange	●
Orange AD+	❑
Red TD-	●
White ED	○

The Franchard Cuisinière area lies on both sides of the route Amélie, in the shade of great pine trees. It boasts the longest circuit in the whole forest, the historic orange route which is several kilometres long. Its marked circuits are always popular as are the many interesting off-circuit problems.

Its jumble of blocks is a real treasure trove for new route fanatics. Add to that the fact that you can climb there all year round and you will understand the appeal of 'La Cuisinière'.

The shape of the boulder forces an athletic mantel-shelf.

Franchard Cuisinière
mountain circuit

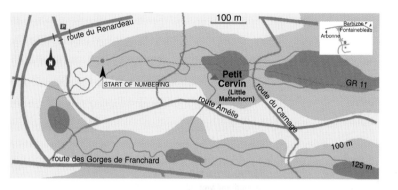

route du Renardeau

100 m

Barbizon
Fontainebleau
Arbonne

START OF NUMBERING

Petit Cervin
(Little Matterhorn)

route Amélie

route du Carnage

GR 11

route des Gorges de Franchard

100 m

125 m

I t was a group from the Club Alpin Français who conceived the idea of this circuit in 1960. The red circuit, 'cerise for beginners', as it was then was a real test of physical fitness: 6km of easy boulders, which are challenging to link together and it is not known whether there is a speed record, but there probably is. Today the circuit is painted orange and is a veritable voyage of climbing discovery, a very physical excursion amongst the magnificent trees and rocky crests of Franchard.

Sky and forest, a magical combination for the climber (Larchant).

Franchard Cuisinière
red circuit

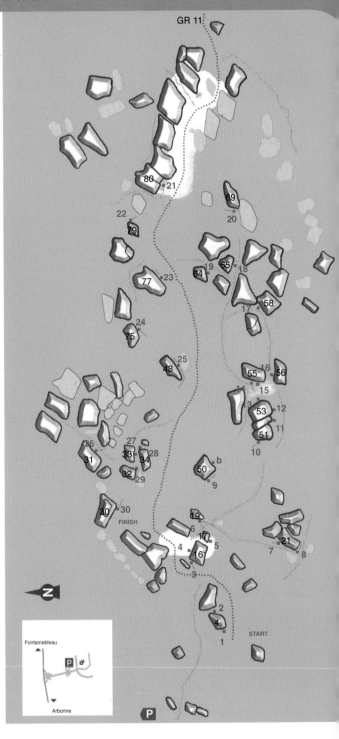

The woodland setting of La teigne.

RED CIRCUIT

route	boulder	grade
1	4	4b
2	4	4c
3	16	4c
4	16	4c
5	17	6a
6	19	4b
7	21	4c
8	21	5a
9	50	5a
9b	50	4c
10	51	4b
11	52	4c/5c
12	53	5a
13	53	4a
14	55	6a
15	55	4b/6b
16	56	4c
17	58	5a
18	65	4c
19	64	4b
20	69	5a
21	80	4c
22	79	4c
23	77	4b
24	75	5b
25	43	4c
26	31	5a/5c
27	34	4a
28	33	4c
29	32	4b
30	30	4c

Franchard Cuisinière
white circuit

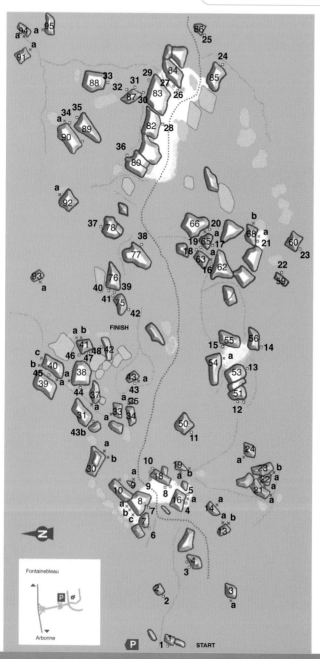

E asy for a white circuit! That is what people often say about this circuit when it is compared with others, like the one at Bas Cuvier for example. First done by Patrick Cordier in the seventies it has a distinctive style of its own which stems from the variety of problems and the commitment demanded of the climber. It is generally agreed that this circuit is indisputably one of the finest in the forest.

Into the unknown, on Impasse du hasard.

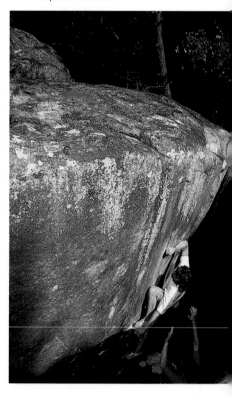

WHITE CIRCUIT

route	boulder	grade	route	boulder	grade
1	1	5c	24	85	5c
2	2	4b	25	86	5c
3	4	4c	26	84	5a
3b	4	5a	26b	84	5b
4	16	5b	27	83	6a
Le hareng saur			28	82	5b
5	16	5c	29	83	5c
6	7	6a	30	87	5C
7	8	4b	31	87	5c
8	18	5b	32	87	4c
8b	18	6a	33	88	4b
9	18	5b	34	90	5c
10	18	6b	34b	90	4b
10b	18	6c	35	89	5c
11	50	5c	36	80	6b
12	51	4c	37	78	5b
12b	51	4b	38	77	6b
13	53	5a	39	76	5b
14	56	4c	40	76	5c
15	55	5c	41	75	5c
16	62	5b	42	75	5c
17	65	5c	43	43	6b
18	63	4b	43b	31	6b
19	65	5c	44	38	5c
20	66	5c	45	39	4c
21	68	5b	46	41	5c
22	59	5a	47	41	6a
23	60	5a	48	42	6b

Franchard Cuisinière
off-circuit

OFF-CIRCUIT PROBLEMS

boulder	route	grade	name
3	a	7c+	Coté cœur
8	a	7a	
8	b	6c	
8	c	6a	
9	a	7b	Alaxis
10	a	8a	The beast Traverse
13	a	6b	
13	b	6c	
14	a	7c	La jouissance du massétar
16	a	7c+	Les yeux pour pleurer
19	a	6c	
19	b	6a+	
21	a	7b	Entorse Reachy
21	b		Project
22	a	7a+	Impasse du hasard
23	a	7b+	Les petits poissons
23	b	6a	
24	a	6c	
30	a	8a	Karma
30	b	7a	Bizarre bizarre Eliminate
33	a	6b+	
35	a	6c	

boulder	route	grade	name
37	a	7a	Traverse
38	a	8a+	Liaisons futiles Traverse
40	a	7c	Eclipse Traverse
40	b	7a+	Pensées cachées
40	c	7c	Atomic power
41	a	6b	
41	b	6c	
43	a	7a	
54	a	7a+	Terre promise Sitting start (7c)
63	a	6c	
66	a	7b+	Corps accord
68	a	7b	Haute tension
68	b	7b	La déferlante Exposed
90	a	7a+	Le magnifique
91	a	7b+	Echine Sitting start (7c+)
92	a	7c	Maudit manège Exposed
93	a	7a+	Soirée brésilienne
94	a	8a	En route pour la joie Traverse
95	a	8a+	Du pareil au même Traverse

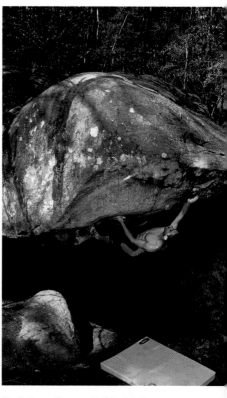

Brice Lefèvre on L'insoutenable légèreté de l'être.

KARMA

Location: Franchard Cuisinière, to the right of the end of the red circuit.
Grade: 8a.
Style: in two words, power and leg strength (adducteurs).
Climber: Laurent Avare.

This problem, one of several unfinished big projects in the forest, was stolen from under the bleusards' noses at the end of the nineties by Frederic Nicole, the exceptional Swiss bouldering specialist. Today it is an international benchmark by which the most difficult problems in the world are measured.

Technique

With both hands on the large starting hold, the outside edge of the right foot on the left side of the crack, make two balancy moves which allow you to dyno for a two finger pocket with your right hand; it is important to mark it beforehand because it is invisible from below. (Note that I have my left hand on the hold the furthest to the left, because I am six feet three inches tall, but most people use the sidepull crimp which is furthest to the right of the jug.)
The fingers are outstretched as you reach this hold but are then crimped as you place your left heel under the left hand which is on the starting hold.
All your weight is now on your leg, turning the hips in order to release the left hand and, after several tries depending on the friction and the strength of your quadriceps, reach for the flat finishing hold.

The story of La comète de Hale Bopp as told by Mathieu Dutray.

Autour de Cuisinière

high standard routes

The following selection of problems, far from being an exhaustive list of possibilities in this part of the forest, represents some of the most outstanding. Nearly all of them are unorthodox in some way or other, such as the famous dyno on *Hale Bopp*, the only route [?] at Fontainebleau whose grade changes with the height of the person climbing it; the superb line of *Duel* which is without question the yardstick by which extreme slab climbing is measured at Fontainebleau; the big 6c arête, or perhaps *La Chose*, with its exclusive flat holds, are also landmarks of their kind. This is where you discover that there is another side to Franchard Cuisinière.

Around Cuisinière.

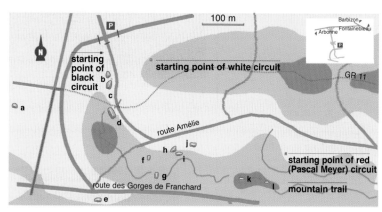

HIGH STANDARD ROUTES

route	grade	name		route	grade	name
a	8b+	L'insoutenable légéreté de l'être		f	6c	De fil en aiguille
b	7a	Excalibur		g	7b	Trois hommes et un coup fin Exposed
c	7a+	Descente aux enfers		h	7a	La teigne
d1	6c	Le Merluchet The big wall (lefthand)		i	7c+	La chose
d2	6a	Moondance The big wall (centre)		j	8a	Duel
d3	6b	Blocage mental The big wall (righthand)		k	7 à 8	Hale Bopp Dynos, grade depends on height
e	7a	Mosquito Coast		l	7c	Toutes peines confondues Rope needed

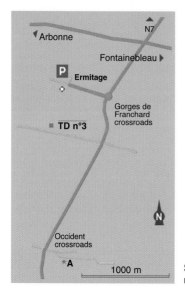

Small boulder for grown ups, but big for little ones.

Jo Montchaussé on the Petit homme traverse.

Ermitage - Route ronde

CIRCUITS

White circuit for children ❑

Red Raymond ❑

Off-circuit
Petit homme (7b+)

The special characteristic of this area is that it has both a particularly good children's circuit, one of the finest traverses in the forest, as well as a red circuit. These have all been recently repainted and run through a very peaceful area. Because the density of the trees filters the sun's rays, it is possible to climb here even when it is very hot; but conversely the rock takes a long time to dry after rain.

In the heart of the forest,
the vertiginous
Trois graines d'éternité.

Rocher Canon.

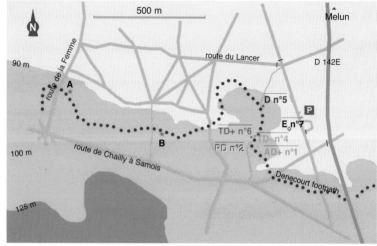

Rocher Canon

CIRCUITS

White children's circuit	❑
Yellow PD	❑
Orange AD+	❑
Dark blue D	❑
Sky blue TD-	●
Red ED-	❑

Selected problems:
Red and dark blue off-circuit routes

The boulders at Rocher Canon (Cannon Rock) are famously rounded, but nevertheless it is a very popular weekend venue. The boulders have their own particular qualities and some of the problems are very technical. The recent fashion for traverses has incited several bravura performances much appreciated by connoisseurs. You will find this a very sociable place to hang out, as long as it is not peace and quiet that you are seeking and in autumn the wonderful colour of the bracken makes this a beautiful place to climb.

Greg Clouzeau on Lévitation.

Rocher Canon
sky blue circuit

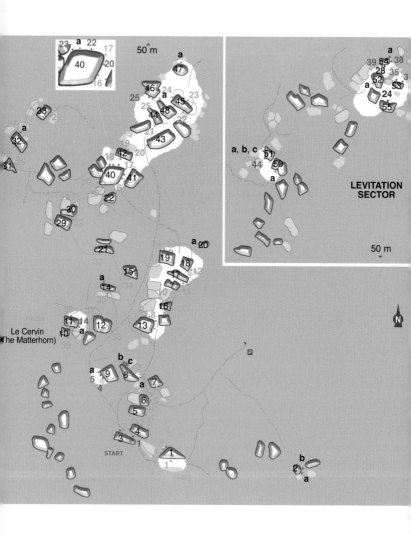

50 m

LEVITATION
SECTOR

50 m

Le Cervin
(The Matterhorn)

START

Desperately seeking holds on a 7a.

SKY BLUE CIRCUIT

route	boulder	grade	name	route	boulder	grade	name
1	1	5a+	Le Cap GAP	20	43	5b	La contrealto
2	4	4c	Le bombé du pied levé	21	44	5c	La Bendix
3	4	5a	Le pied levé	22	45	4a	L'eunuque
4	5	5c	L'appuyette	23	45	4b	Les plats
5	6	4c	Le bloc	24	45	4c	La fourch'mammouth
6	7	5b	L'attrappe-mouche	25	46	5b	Le surplomb du Bengale
7	8	4c	Le dévers	26	33	5a	Le but
8	13	5c	Le sphinx de droite	27	32	4b	L'oubliée
8b	13	4c	Le golgotha	28	32	5a	La spéciale
9	13	5b	Le golgotha de gauche	29	31	4b	La Bizuth
10	16	4c	L'intermédiaire	30	40	4c	Le couloir
11	17	5a	L'ex-souche	31	30	5a	Le prétoire
11b	17	5b	La traversée de l'ex-souche	32	29	5a	La fédérale
12	18	5b	Le beaufort	32b	30	4b	La voie de l'obèse
13	19	4c	La queue du dromadaire	33	21	4c	La norma
13b	19	5a	Le dromadaire	34	15	5a+	L'imprévue
14	19	4c	Le pilier du dromadaire	35	14	4c	La cachée
15	22	4b+	La dalle de marbre	36	12	5a	La French Cancan
16	41	5b+	L'Emmenthal	37	12	5a	Le serpent
16b	40	6a	Le cruciverbiste	38	11	5c	L'impossible
17	40	5c	Le cheval d'arçon	39	10	5b	
18	42	4b	La soprano	40	11	5a+	Le Cervin
19	42	4c	La goulotte				

Rocher Canon
selected routes

SELECTED ROUTES

boulder	route		grade	name
1	a	✗	8b	La valse aux adieux G>D (L>R) traverse
1	b	✗	7a	Fantasia chez les ploucs
2	a	✗	7a+	Caterpillar
2	b	✗	6c+	Chasseur de prises
3	1	●	6a	Force G
3	a	✗	7b/7c+	Le chaînon manquant 7c+ without the arête
8	a	✗	7a+/7c	36.15 power 7c direct Without the holds on the left
8	b	✗	7a+	La mare Attendre une longue période sans pluie
8	c	✗	7b+	La mare directe Attendre Dries slowly after rain
9	4	●	5b	L'ancien
9	5	●	6b	Dure limite
9	a	✗	7a	Traverse from l'ancien to Dure Limite
11	14	●	6c	
11	a	✗	7b	Marquis de Sade Direct
14	a	✗	6c+	Gainage et dévers G>D (L>R) traverse
20	a	✗	7a+	Orange 17 sitting start
32	a	✗	7b+	G>D (L>R) traverse
40	20	●	5c	
40	22	●	6a	Styrax
40	23	●	5c	
40	a	✗	6c	
48	a	✗	7c+	Manus déi G>D (L>R) traverse
46	25	●	6a	Nuage blanc
47	a	✗	7c+	L'œil de Civah Sitting start. Exposed.
50	a	✗	6c+	Sledge hammer D>G (R>L) traverse
51	44	●	5c	
51	a	✗	7b	Vagabond des limbes G>D (L>R) traverse
51	c	✗	7a	Lévitation G>D (L>R) traverse
51	b	✗	8a	Légende Girdle traverse to start of Lévitation
52	a	✗	8a	Crescendo D>G (R>L) traverse
53	34	●	6a	D>G (R>L) traverse
53	35	●	5c	
54	28	●	4c	
54	38	●	5c	
54	39	●	5c	
54	a	✗	7c	Cocaline D>G (R>L) traverse
55	24	●	3c	

everal of the problems here are at the centre of a controversy which has shaken the local climbing community: should the hardest problems be marked?

According to an opinion poll of about a hundred bleausards undertaken by CO.SI.ROC, it seems that the majority of the climbers consulted are not in favour of it. Which is why these boulders do not form part of a circuit and instead are in the form of a topo list enabling you to identify and locate them. The list is supplemented by several of the most interesting problems on the red (ED-) and dark blue (D) circuits.

Crimping is back in fashion on Le Denmat, it'll take some doing.

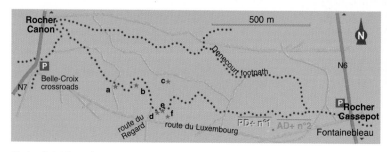

Rocher Saint-Germain.

Rocher Saint-Germain

CIRCUITS

White children's circuit ❑
Yellow PD+ ❑
Orange AD+ ❑

Off-circuit ✗

Rocher Saint-Germain is a huge area broken into two zones, the first, more easterly zone has several beginner's circuits; the second is only of interest to higher standard climbers and is reached via the carrefour de Belle-Croix (Belle-Croix crossroads). Here the boulders are very scattered and sometimes difficult to locate. But this incitement to explore only adds to the charm of the place. You do not come here for the circuits but to savour the quality of the traverses, some of which count amongst the best in the forest. So don't worry if you have a little bit more of an adventure than you bargained for. The tranquillity of the place and the superb problems will more than make up for it. Expect to meet walkers, horse riders and Sunday strollers: although perfect for a little discreet climbing, this is nevertheless a popular area.

Rocher Cassepot
Cassepot, like Rocher de Bouligny, is worth a detour if only for the problem on the Synapses boulder. There is only one line, a 7c+, but it's pretty eyecatching all the same. Round about, there are several worthwhile new problems to add to your collection, although none of them are less than 7b. But even if you don't climb, it's worth going to take in the atmosphere of the place. There are no painted markers here either.

Bleau, a love affair.

Rocher Saint-Germain
off-circuit

OFF-CIRCUIT

boulder	grade	name
a	7c+	Les yeux plus gros que le ventre D>G (R>L) traverse
b1	7c+	Mégalithe (the bloc)
b2	8a	The bloc Mégalithe sitting start
c	7c+	La cité perdue D>G (R>L) traverse
d	7c+	Double croche G>D (L>R) traverse
e	7b+/8b	Danse de printemps D>G (R>L) traverse
f	7c+	Psychose G>D (L>R) traverse

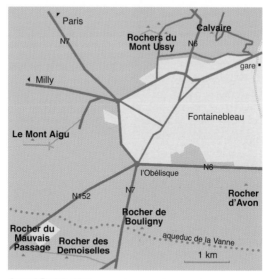

Around Fontainebleau.

These areas are all within a five kilometre radius of the centre of Fontainebleau. Some of them, such as Le Mont Ussy, Le Mont Aigu, La Dame Jeanne d'Avon are amongst the original areas to be developed in Fontainebleau and provide routes for climbers of all standards. Others like the Rocher Bouligny, the Gorges du Houx, the Rochers des Demoiselles or the Rocher Cassepot have recently become fashionable again with new, often very high standard routes being done there. Depending on your climbing grade and your ambitions, each of these areas is worth a visit.

Rocher des Demoiselles

History does not tell us who the young ladies were, but the prominent sculptured rocks at the end of the only exisiting circuit (orange) do have vaguely feminine shapes. Several new routes have been done between the Mauvais Passage path and the orange circuit. Some of the problems are committing, even exposed and will need to be worked on, perhaps necessitating several visits. Few of the routes are below grade seven and none are marked. Here you will also be able to throw yourself at the most amazing finger-locking crack at Fontainebleau.

Rocher de Bouligny

Another new area. There are very few boulders here, but all are of a high quality, with some providing a taste of exposure. The fashion for sitting starts has led to the discovery of several interesting problems and one in particular: a superb 7c+ on an overhanging boulder called Les Beaux quartiers. The few climbers who visit this quiet corner of the forest only come to try this problem, which is why we are mentioning it here. Follow the traces of resin and chalk, don't bother looking for painted arrows.

La Dame Jeanne d'Avon

Like the area named after its big sister the Dame Jeanne de Larchant, this area also has a boulder which dominates gracefully with its noble presence. However this particular area has never enjoyed quite the same reputation because the choice of routes is more restricted.

Several new routes were done in the eighties; you will see signs of them on the scary arêtes, the impossibly smooth slabs and the superb crack lines. We will leave you to find them.

Bring a brush with you to ensure you maximise your enjoyment of this peaceful spot.

Le Mont Ussy

Situated not far from the famous and strikingly ochre coloured "Rocher Hercule", the circuits in this area are mainly for beginners (two PD yellows and an AD+ orange) but there are several traverses of all grades on the boulders. The technical difficulty of the traverses is somewhat unbalanced, but this does allow you to enrich your repertoire of moves by working out new problems. It is a shame that the finest and highest boulder has been blackened by the smoke of campfires, because some of the problems on it are superb.

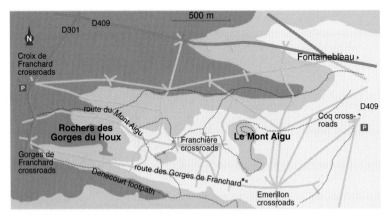

Mont Aigu, the Gorges du Houx and the Franchière crossroads.

Le Mont Aigu

CIRCUITS

White children's circuit	❑
Yellow PD	❑
Orange AD	●
Blue D+/TD-	❑

The car-park is quite close to Fontainebleau town and the Bellifontains come here to use the fitness trail, to mountain bike or simply to walk. You have to walk a little way to find the start of the four circuits, three of which are for beginners and are in a haven of peace and coolness.

The sandstone of this little visited area is particularly rough and the circuits are ideal for beginners and improvers.

Le Mont Aigu

orange circuit

ORANGE CIRCUIT

route	grade
1	2c
2	3b
3	3a
4	3b
5	3a
6	2b
7	3c
8	3b
9	2c
10	3b
11	3c
12	3a
13	4a
14	3b
15	3c
16	4a
17	3b
18	3b
19	3b
20	3c
21	3c
22	3b
23	3a
24	3c
25	3c
26	3b
27	2c
28	3b
29	3c
30	3b
31	3b
32	3c
33	4b
34	4a
35	4b
36	3b
37	3c
38	3b
39	3c
40	3b
41	3a
42	3c
43	4a
44	4a
45	3c
46	4b
47	3c
48	4a
Numerous AD+ variations	

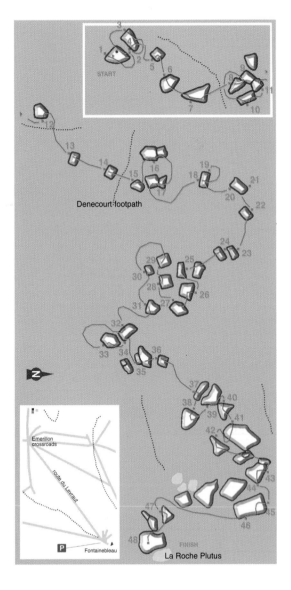

Denecourt footpath

Emerillon crossroads

route du Levraut

P Fontainebleau

FINISH

La Roche Plutus

Gorges du Houx

CIRCUITS	
Off-circuit	**x**

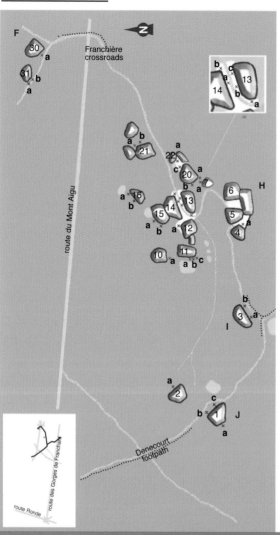

Near the carrefour de Franchière (Franchière crossroads) you will find one of the new climbing venues. In the line-up are about thirty routes from 5 to 7c+ of all styles, in a quiet and shady spot which is about a twenty-minute walk from the carpark.

Particular mention must be made of the most impressive problem of the area: Inaccessible absolu, a 7c with wild exposure, which has only been soloed a few times.

Gorges du Houx
hors circuit

Opposite: Transition.

Below:
Marc'O Montchaussé
cruises Gargantoit, strong
arms essential.

OFF-CIRCUIT

boulder	route	grade	name
1	a	5c	
1	b	6c	J1
1	c	6a+	J2
2	a	6c	J.J. dalle
3	a	6a	
3	b	6a	
4	a	7a+	Gargantoit Sitting start 7b+
7	a	6b+	
10	a	6a	
11	a	7b+	Raidemption
11	b	7b+	
11	c	6c	
12	a	6c	Transition
13	a	6c	
13	b	6b+	
13	c	7b	Soirée cubaine
14	a	5a	
14	b	6a+	
15	a	7a	Ligne de mire Direct
15	b	5b	
16	a	6b+	
16	b	6b+	Tempo
20	a	6b	
20	b	5b	
20	c	7a+	L'extrémiste Lefthand finish 7b
21	a	6a	
21	b	6c	
22	a	5c	
30	a	7c	L'inaccessible absolu
31	a	7a	Objectif Lune
31	b	7c+	De la Terre à la Lune

Le Calvaire

CIRCUITS

Orange AD ❑

Selected problems:

- **Traverses**
1 : 6b+ (15 m)
2 : 6c+ (15m)
2° finish by 3 : 7c (15m)
1° and 2 : 7b
2° finish by 7 : 7a

- **Boulders**
6 : Applat du gain, 8a+
5 : 7b
3 : 6c+
4 : 7a
7 : 5a (very first problem)
8 : 6c

This is a huge overhang. Its shape in the form of a big awning has made this a popular choice of climbing venue when it's raining or is very hot. There are numerous traverses and girdles which provide more than fifty metres of athletic climbing, with no real opportunities for resting, but often on excellent holds (watch out for some of the flakes, they are not completely trustworthy).

There is also an orange circuit close by with about thirty interesting routes.

Finally, to the left of the huge band of overhangs, you will find one of the most difficult problems in the forest which answers to the name of L'applat du gain. A spotter is vital for these three amazing moves.

It's worth making a ten metre detour to the croix du Calvaire (Calvaire cross) to see the view over Fontainebleau.

Following page: Alain Ghersen
on the first ascent of L'applat du gain.

Words from a Bleau pioneer

It is now more than ten years since I lived in Paris, but there are certain indelible memories which are still with me.

Lonely dawn starts at five in the morning, in order to have the best conditions for good friction; mainly because from springtime onwards the heat makes conditions less favourable.

I also remember how cold it was when I was working on L'applat de gain at dawn in mid-winter in order to get more grip from the holds and which ultimately enabled me to succeed on this problem.

On my return to the capital, I relived these climbs as though they were mountain routes, because the dawn starts and unusual hours made me feel as though I was back in the mountains. It was only the length of the routes that was different, underlining the almost comical fact that I was pushing myself to the limit on something so small.

Bleau will always be associated with carefree days and the birth of a passion which still burns within me.

Alain Ghersen

EXTREMES OF YOUR DREAMS ... EXTREMES OF YOUR DREAMS ...

Bouldering is nearly more than a century old, so it seems appropriate to give a brief summary of the routes which were landmarks of their time. Since the first grade four was done in the second decade of the last century, standards have been continually pushed forward until today we are on the verge of grade nine. We will undoubtedly see the breakthrough into that grade this century.

We have deliberately ruled out any idea of an exhaustive catalogue (there are nearly two hundred boulders recorded within the grades we have listed) and selected the best quality routes.

We have laid the threshold for extreme climbing at the portals of 7c because it seems that it is the gap between 7b and 7c which is the determining factor in opening the door to the highest level of climbing.

For each of the problems, we use grades which have been the subject of wide consultation and reflect as far as possible the true grade of the climbs. In some cases, we have mentioned the existence of a variation to a problem where the variation is particularly outstanding. The variation may alter the grade up or down as the case may be.

For example, L'ange naïf in area 95.2 of the forest goes at 7c+, which was the original grade of the problem, but there is a 7a+ variation using other holds, which in the table overleaf is marked as V7a+.

A few key moments of the century:

1914: Prestat, the first grade four, at Bas Cuvier

1934: L'Angle Allain,the first grade five, at Cuvier Rempart

1946: Marie Rose, the first grade six, at Bas Cuvier

1953: La Joker, the upper limits of grade six, at Bas Cuvier

1960: L'Abattoir, the first grade seven, at Bas Cuvier

1983: L'Abbé Résina, the upper limits of grade seven at Bas Cuvier

1984: C'était demain, the first grade eight, at Cuvier Rempart

1999: 8b/8b+ is confirmed as the landmark grade for climbing at its highest level.

La Pierre philosophale, an 8b in ten parts.

AREA	NAME OF PROBLEM	TECHNIQUE	GRADE
Rocher du mauvais passage	Peter Pan	Dyno	7b+
JA Martin	L'étrave	Arête	7b+
Bas Cuvier	Coup de feel	Wall	7b+ (V 8a+ without the edge)
L'étrave	Arête		7b+
Bas Cuvier	Carnage	Overhanging wall	7b+V 7c (V l'Abbé Résina finish)
Drei Zinnen	Chat perché	Overhanging wall	7b+
Franchard Sablons	Le modulor	Overhanging wall	7b+
Gorges du Houx	GarganToit	Roof	7a+ V 7b+ (V sitting start)
Fosse aux Loups	Super bouffon	Wall	7b+
Cuisinière	Reine des bois	Arête	7b+ exposed
Franchard Isatis	Mur des lamentations/12bis	Wall	7b+
Franchard Isatis	Surprise	Overhanging wall	7b+
Cul de chien	Arabesque	Roof	7b+
Gorge aux chats	Rubis sur l'ongle	Overhanging wall	7b+
Dame Jeanne	Plus que parfait	Arête	7b+
Gréau	Conquistadores	Wall	7b+
Cuvier Rempart	L'émeraude	Slab	7b+
Bas Cuvier	Aérodynamite	Dyno	7c
Bas Cuvier	Ange gardien	Slab	7c
Bas Cuvier	Abbé Résina	Overhanging wall	7c
Bas Cuvier	Infidèle	Arête	7c
Bas Cuvier	Hypothèse	Wall	7c
Cul de Chien	Eclipse	Wall	7c
Drei Zinnen	Cocoon	Overhanging wall	7c
Cuvier Rempart	Baisers volés	Slab wall	7c
Cuvier Rempart	Tristesse	Wall	7c
Cuvier Rempart	Noir désir	Overhanging wall	7c V 7c+ (V righthand finish) sitting start
Cuvier Rempart	Michel ange	Overhanging wall	7c
Cuisinière (South edge)	Tailleur de mensonges	Wall	7C
Cuvier Rempart	Big boss	Overhanging wall	7c
Merveille	Dalle de fer	Slab	7c
Éléphant	Coup de lune	Overhanging wall	7c
Eléphant	Gargamel	Wall	7c
Eléphant	Envie d'ailes	Overhanging wall	7c
Franchard Isatis	Arrache cœur	Roof	7c
Franchard Isatis	Gnossienne	Wall	7c
Franchard Isatis	Gymnopédie	Wall	7c
Franchard Isatis	Super joker	Wall	7c
Franchard Isatis	Alta	Overhanging wall	7c
Franchard Isatis	Métropolis	Overhanging wall	7c exposed
Buthiers	Flagrant désir	Wall	7c
Mont Ussy	Art'rete	Arête	7c
Cornebiche	Pyramidale	Slab	7c
Franchard Cuisinière	Maudit manège	Overhanging wall	7c exposed
Franchard Cuisinière	Atomic power	Wall	7c
Franchard Cuisinière	Toute peines confondues	Overhanging wall	7c roped
Gorges Houx	Inaccessible absolu	Wall	7c exposed
Bois Rond	Lucky Luke	Wall	7c
Roche aux Sabots	Sale gosse	Overhanging wall	7c V 7c+ (V sitting start)
Gréau	Mégalithe	Arête	7c

AREA	NAME OF PROBLEM	TECHNIQUE	GRADE
95.2	Futurs barbares	Wall	7c+
95.2	Ange naïf	Overhanging wall	7c+ V 7a+ (V keeping right)
Gorges d'Apremont	Marginal	Wall	7a+ V 7c+ (V in the middle of the wall)
Apremont	Psychose	Arête	7c+ exposed
Boissy aux cailles	Evidence	Overhanging wall	7c+
Cul de chien	L'œil de la Sybille	Roof	7c+ (sitting start)
Rocher Cassepot	Synapses	Wall	7c+
Bas Cuvier	Antithèse	Wall	7c+
Bas Cuvier	Balance	Overhanging wall	7c V7c+ (V keeping to the left)
Cuvier Rempart	Big golden	Overhanging wall	7c+
Cuvier Rempart	Haute tension	Wall	7c+ V 8a (V going straight up)
Cuvier Rempart	Fourmis rouges	Overhanging wall	7c+
Cuvier Rempart	T Rex	Overhanging wall	7c+ V 8a (sitting start)
Gorges du Houx	De la terre à la lune	Overhanging wall	7c+
Drei Zinnen	Matière grise	Wall	7c
Franchard Cuisinière	La chose	Overhanging wall	7c+ V 7b+ (V keeping to the left)
Franchard Isatis	Vin aigre	Dyno	7... to 7c+ depending on your height
Gréau	Plein vol	Slab	7c+
Rocher Saint Germain	The bloc	Overhanging wall	7c+ V 8a (V sitting start)
Rochers de Bouligny	Les beaux quartiers	Overhanging wall	6c+ V 7c+ (V without the arête)
Buthiers	Mysanthropie	Overhanging wall	8a
Cuvier Rempart	Atrésie	Overhanging wall	8a
Apremont (secteur Marginal)	Emprise	Overhanging wall	8a
Buthiers	Partage	Arête	8a
Gorges aux Chats	Gospel	Wall	7c V8a (V without the foot pocket)
Cul de Chien	L'âme de fonds	Roof	8a (sitting start)
Cul de Chien	L'intégrale	Roof	8a (sitting start)
Bas Cuvier	Digitale	Wall	8a
Cuvier Rempart	C'était demain	Wall	8a
Merveille	Merveille	Arête	8a
Envers d'Apremont	L'apparement [1]	Overhanging wall	8a
[1] this problem is ten metres from "Pierre Philosophale" (the old N° 40 of the Farine red circuit)			
Franchard Cuisinière	Duel	Slab	8a
Franchard Cuisinière	Karma	Overhanging wall	8a
Franchard Cuisinière	Hale Bopp	Dyno	7... to 8... depending on your height
Roche aux Sabots	Déviation	Wall	8a
Vallée de la Mée	Surplomb	Overhanging wall	8a+ V 7c (V traversing from the blue circuit)
Eléphant	Partenaire particulier	Wall	8a+ (start standing on a rock or two mats on top of each other)
Boissy-aux-Cailles	Hip Hop	Wall	8a+ (V 8b+ sitting start)
Bas Cuvier	Golden feet	Slab	7c+ V8a+ (V without using the edge)
Cul de chien	Total eclipse	Roof	8a+ (sitting start)
Calvaire	Applat du gain	Overhanging wall	8a+
Cuvier Rempart	Khéops	Arête	8b
Cuvier Rempart	Fat man	Roof	8b
Dame Jeanne	Unforgiven	Wall	8b
Envers d'Apremont	Pierre philosophale	Roof	8b
Franchard Isatis	Insoutenable légéreté…	Roof	8b+ (the + remains to be confirmed)

Problems on which the crucial hold has broken

Gorges d'Apremont	L'alchimiste	Dévers	originally 8b
Bas Cuvier	Coup de feel	Mur	originally 8a+

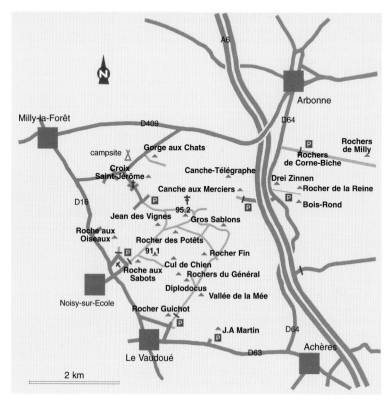

Les Trois Pignons.

Access
Because of the many access points to this area, the climbing areas in the Trois Pignons part of the forest are described according to where they are in relation to the main car-parks near Arbonne (in the north-east), Noisy/Croix Saint Jérome (in the west), Noisy/cimetière (in the south-west) and finally Vaudoué (in the south).

You only need blue skies above the white sand of the Trois Pignons area to imagine yourself somewhere else on the planet other than at the gates of Paris.

Milly-la-Forêt, Arbonne, Le Vaudoué, Noisy-sur-Ecole ... these picturesque villages are scattered around the edge of the hundreds of square metres of a forest which nature has generously endowed with sandstone boulders.

The landscape, the rocks, the sand and the trees make this one of the most popular areas, enjoyed equally by climbers, walkers, cyclists, riders or those who simply come to meditate.

However the forest is a victim of its own success, as it is suffering from an excess of popularity especially on sunny days. But there are certain places, away from the car-parks, where you can escape from the crowds.

From the wilderness of Gros Sablons to the more accessible areas such as the Roche aux Sabots, from the magic little corner of 95.2 to the sands of Cul de Chien, from the marbled rocks of La Vallée de la Mée to the exotic Roche aux Oiseaux, everyone, whether they be beginner or expert climber, will find something to satisfy their appetite at the Trois Pignons.

LES TROIS PIGNONS The origins of a wilderness ... a glance at the past

"Not the Trois Pignons again!" I hear you exclaim, because you have read so many descriptions and of so many routes of this part of "Bleau". But I am inviting you to come with me to discover "the most beautiful and the most intriguing area of the forest", in order to focus your mind on an unrecognized and neglected point: which are the best rocks to climb on.

"But why? I hear some of you say. Why tell everyone about it and fill this last refuge of tranquillity with hordes of climbers!" Put your minds at rest.

Firstly, the Trois Pignons will always be 2 or 3 hours walk from the station ... Secondly, from a climbing point of view, the Trois Pignons are really only of secondary value ...

"What, I hear you cry, number them, order them, put up maps, what sacrilege!" Such reasoning would lead you to condemn the work of Denecourt ... and to want to conserve the charm of this or that particular corner for a small group of connoisseurs is surely elitism of the first order?

Only ten years ago, one approached the Trois Pignons area with a certain amount of trepidation, for who has not at one time or another lost their way in this vast landscape? ... The huge pine trees have been ravaged either by fire or by deforestation which goes beyond the bounds of good sense. ... Those who knew the Trois Pignons area several years ago, cannot come here now without remembering with bitterness and regret, what this sea of trees was like then; they cannot forget the knee-deep mossy cushions which they sank into ... But after the years 43, 44, 45, apart from a few wooded copses, it became a desert, of bare sand, charred wooden stumps ...

Extract from an article written in 1948 by Maurice Martin in *Le Bleausard*: "Escalade et Trois Pignons".

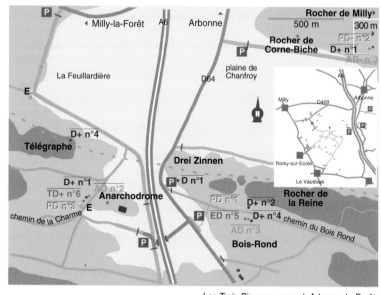

Les Trois Pignons, around Arbonne-la-Forêt.

Calm and serenity in the Bois-Rond.

Chloé on a technical arête .

Bois-Rond

CIRCUITS

Orange AD ●
Blue D+ ●
Red ED- ●

If you were to use two words to describe this place, they would undoubtedly be calm and serenity; if it was not for the motorway and its noise pollution, particularly when a westerly wind is blowing. The circuits radiate out from the middle of a peaceful wooded spot which gives the climbing, pleasant though it is anyway, that extra bit of character. The grade of the routes, generally speaking of a reasonable standard, allows climbers the opportunity to build up a good technical repertoire and to taste for themselves the pleasures of the various traverses, of which there are many within the circuits here.

Bois-Rond

Sébastien Frigault, on De la terre à la lune (From the earth to the moon) *(Gorges du Houx).*

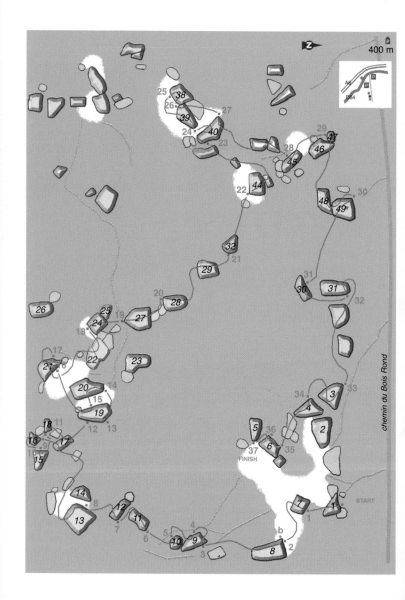

400 m

chemin du Bois Rond

ORANGE CIRCUIT

route	boulder	grade
0	1	2c
1	7	3a
2	8	3b
2b	8	2c
3	9	3c
4	9	3b
5	10	3b
6	11	3b
7	12	2c
8	13	3c
9	16	2c
10	15	3a
11	18	3b
12	19	3a
13	19	3a
14	20	3a
15	19	3a
16	21	3b
17	21	3b
18	24	2c
19	27	3b
20	28	3b
21	32	2c
22	44	2b
23	40	4a
24	39	3a
25	38	3b
26	39	3b
27	40	3b
28	45	3a
29	47	3a
30	49	3c
31	30	3a
32	31	4a
33	3	3a
34	4	3b
35	6	3b
36	6	3b
37	5	3a

Bois-Rond

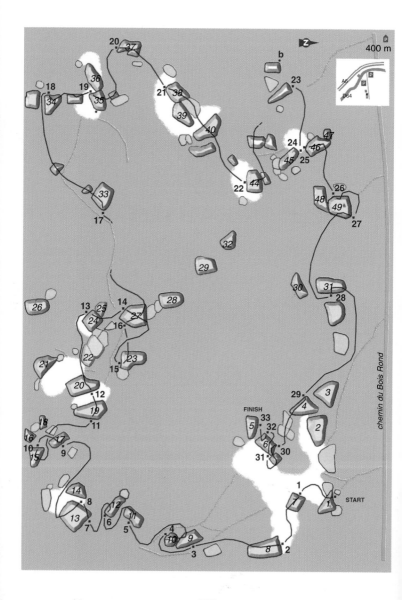

The phantom meteorite

This story is a good example of postwar bleausard humour. It was first told by Robert Paragot, who was big on talent as well as spirit. As an illustration of this, here is the story of the strange practical joke which he used to play on his friends the day after a drinking session in the various bivouacs around Cuvier Rempart. The yellow circuit starts on a boulder perched on a pedestal nicknamed the Meteorite. He would climb the boulder, wait until someone else had started up it, then move to the other side and push as hard as he could on the big heavy block, thus making it rock gently. Enough, anyway, to make the climber feel as though he was still under the influence and quickly go to have a lie down. Of course he did not tell the unsuspecting climber about it until later and then he too, having been let into the secret could go on to play the trick on others himself. However, some people never found out; and perhaps they will discover by reading it here more than forty years later. Try it if you have the chance, it still works.

route	boulder	grade
BLUE CIRCUIT		
0	1	4b
1	7	5b
2	8	5c
3	9	4c
4	10	4b
5	11	4b
6	12	4c
7	13	4c
8	14	4b
9	17	5a
10	15	4c
11	19	4b
12	20	4c
13	24	4c
14	27	4c
15	23	4b
16	27	4c
17	33	5a
18	34	4a
19	35	5a
19b	35	4b
20	37	4b
21	38	4c
22	44	4c
23b	41	4c
23	42	4b
24	45	5b
25	46	5b
26	49	4c
27	49	4c
28	31	5b
29	4	4b
30	6	5a
31	6	5b
32	6	4a
33	5	5a

Bois-Rond

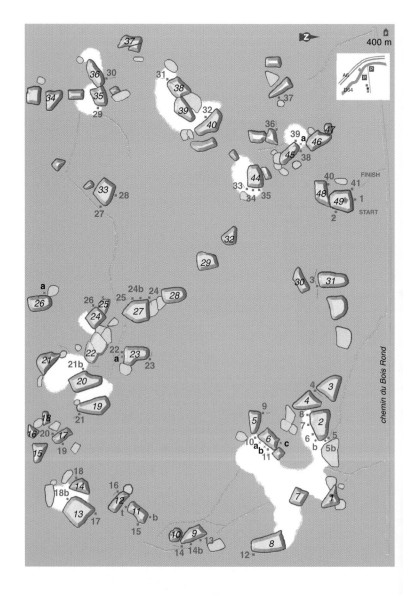

RED CIRCUIT

route	boulder	grade	name	route	boulder	grade	name
1	49	5b		20	17	6a	Ponction lombaire
2	49	6a		21b	20	7a	Le tourniquet du 93.7 *Girdle traverse of the boulder*
3	31	6a					
4	3	6b		21	19	5b	
5b	2	6c	Modokasi	22	23	6a	Le meilleur des mondes
5	2	6c	Kasimodo	23	23	6a+	La théorie des nuages
6b	2	5b+	Mur du rouge	24b	27	7a	
6	2	6a	Silver lago	24	27	5c	
7	2	6a	Little shakespeare	25	27	6a	
8	2	5b	Hamlet	26	24	5b	Razorback
9	5	6a	Friction et réalité	27	33	6a	Gilette pare dalle
10	6	5c	Objectif grand angle	28	33	5c	
11	6	6a	Planète morphos	29	35	6c	Aero beuark
12	8	6a+	Haute calorie	30	36	6b	Super vista
13	9	5c	Glasnot	31	38	5b	
14b	9	5a	Point d'équilibre	32	40	6c	
14	9	6b	Regard de statue	33	44	5c+	L'otan en emporte le vent
15b	11	6a	Les grattons laveurs	34	44	6c	Galla lactique
15t	11	6b	Morphotype	35	44	6c	Constellation des amoureux
15	11	5c	L'amie dalle	36	43	5b	
16	12	5c	L'attraction des pôles	37	42	5c+	Le long fleuve tranquille
17	13	5c		38	45	6b+	Le vélo de max
18b	13	6c+	La Michaud	39	45	5c	L'appui acide
18	14	6c		40	48	5c	
19	17	6a	Prise de becquet	41	49	5c	Fritz l'angle

Bois-Rond

off-circuit

OFF-CIRCUIT

route	boulder	grade	name
a	6	7c	Lucky luke
b	6	7b	Sensation
c	6	7a	Jo Dalton
a	23	7a+	Spyder bloc
a	25	7a+	Bande passante *G>D (L>R) traverse*
a	26	7b	Les plats *G>D (L>R) traverse*
a	45	7a	Le Boudha peste *High level G>D (L>R) traverse*

Chalk, the little bag of courage.

Canche aux Merciers

CIRCUITS

White children's circuit	❏
Yellow PD-	❏
Orange AD	🔵
Blue D+	⚫
Red TD+	🔴
Telegraph blue	❏

Not so very long ago this area had a bad reputation for being left in a mess because the army often stayed here while on exercise.

Fortunately the cartridge cases and other munitions gradually disappeared and now climbers like to come here with their families to do the many beginners' circuits. The rock here is particularly well endowed with holds, rendering the climbing slightly less aggressive than elsewhere. But watch out for the polished foot holds, which make success uncertain and the grades surprisingly difficult.

The fashion for traverses during the eighties led to the exploration of a yet undiscovered dimension of climbing in this area and the small size of the boulders was for once an advantage in the development of these new horizontal climbing games.

Bernard Théret begins a friction section.

THE TRAVERSES

L'iceberg.

When climbers tired of verticality, they invented a new game which took them into the horizontal plane and meant the mastery of new techniques and new moves. Traversing became a very "in" thing to do in the nineties and more than a thousand new traverses of all grades were put up in the forest.

Traverse grading
Every grading system is specific to itself. It is as well to bear in mind that the traverse grading system, takes into account a certain number of criteria. You have successfully completed a traverse when you have linked the starting and finishing points without falling or resting with your feet on the ground.

Le Derviche tourneur.

Traverse grading criteria:
• The intrinsic difficulty of the most difficult moves.
• The notion of linking together several moves (7 on the shortest traverse and more than 60 on the longest).
• Whether or not there are any natural resting points.
• The length of time it needs to be worked on before achieving success.
• The uncertainty of certain moves: holds where friction is all-important, moves which are difficult to do at all.
• Morphological criteria: distance between holds and their layout.
• Cross-referencing with other traverses to achieve a uniform standard.

By way of conclusion
Traverse grading is not comparable with bouldering grades and even less so with crag climbing grades. This hybrid grading system is mid-way between bouldering grades, which by definition are very precise because they are based on a short explosive effort and crag climbing grades which involve considerations of stamina.
In any case, the routes are always graded by the first ascensionist and the grade is then confirmed by those who repeat the route.

L'iceberg.

DREAM TRAVERSES... DREAM TRAVERSES... DREAM TRAVERSES... DREAM TRAVERSES...

CLIMBERS	AREA	NAME	LOCATION	GRADE	DIRECTION	LENGTH IN METRES	NUMBER OF MOVES
BEGINNING	Bas Cuvier	Ballade	problem on orange 33	3a	G>D (L>R)	5	15
	Bas Cuvier	Voyage	orange 31	5a	G>D (L>R)	6	12
	Rocher fin	Cool bloqueur	red 25	5a	G>D (L>R)	10	20
	Elephant	Odyssée des trous	green 5	5b	D>G (R>L)	6	10
	Beauvais est	Soleil cherche futur	red 4	5c	G>D (L>R)	5	15
	Dame jeanne		red 26	5b	G>D (L>R)	7	15
	Bas Cuvier	Crampes	red 13	6a+	D>G (R>L)	6	12
	Bas Cuvier	Longue marche	red 14	6b+	G>D (L>R)	12	17
	Bas Cuvier	Derviche	blue 27	5b	D>G (R>L)	4	7
	Dame Jouanne	Pontet bas	black 18	6a+	D>G (R>L)	6	15
	Dame Jouanne		red requin start	6a+	D>G (R>L)	7	15
CRUISING	Beauvais est	Crawl en mer noire	black 29	6c	D>G (R>L)	13	20
	Beauvais est	Le confit de canard	red 11	5b	G>D (L>R)	12	13
	Elephant	Ras de sol	black 40	6b+	D>G (R>L)	9	15
	Rocher Canon	L'académicienne	off to the side (blue footpath)	6c+	G>D (L>R)	10	20
	Rocher Canon	Levitation	red 44	7a	G>D (L>R)	6	12
	Eléphant	Traversée des dieux	black 15	6c+	G>D (L>R)	12	20
	Eléphant	Bout du monde	on the flat area off to the side	7a	D>G (R>L)	12	15
	Bas Cuvier	Kilo de beurre	red 41	7a+	G>D (L>R)	15	25
SERIOUS	Bois-Rond	Le tourniquet...	red 21b	7a+	G>D (L>R)	25	30
	Beauvais est	La magie noire du derviche	black 13	6c+	G>D (L>R)	10	18
	Canche	Double face	red 25	7a	D>G (R>L)	8	15
	Canche	Ni vieux ni bête	Anarchodrome sector	7a+	D>G (R>L)	13	35
	Canche	Coup bas	red 15b	7a	G>D (L>R)	8	15
	Roche aux Sabots	Rumsteack en folie	red 31	7a	G>D (L>R)	20	30
	Roche aux Sabots	Tourniquet	yellow 1	7a	D>G (R>L)	15	25
	Franchard Cuisinière	Descente aux enfers	black 4	7a	G>D (L>R)	4	10
	Cuvier Rempart	Johannis	above Big boss	7a+	D>G (R>L)	7	12
	Cuvier Rempart	Le bivouac	Trivellini black 22	6c	G>D (L>R)	5	8

CLIMBERS	AREA	NAME	LOCATION	GRADE	DIRECTION	LENGTH IN METRES	NUMBER OF MOVES
	Franchard Isatis	L'intégrale	red 5	7a+	G>D (L>R)	12	20
	Calvaire	La totale	Calvaire roof	7a	G>D (L>R)	20	35
	Buthiers	Petite sirène	facing Robinson Inn	7a+	D>G (R>L)	6	12
	Franchard, route Ronde	Petit homme	west crossroads	7b+	G>D (L>R)	12	15
	Cuisinière	Eclipse	facing white 45	7b+	D>G (R>L)	9	15
	Cuvier Rempart	Swell	before la Merveille	7b+	D>G (R>L)	7	15
	Cuvier Rempart	Les pieds nickés	Duroxmanie sector	7c+	G>D (L>R)	8	12
	Bas Cuvier	Banlieue nord	on the other side of blue 21	7b+	G>D (L>R)	8	16
	Buthiers	Mygale	tennis sector	7b+	G>D (L>R)	15	25
FANATICAL	JA Martin	Jardin secret	route du Rocher Caillaud	7b+	G>D (L>R)	12	15
	Rocher Canon	Trois graines	in the west of the area	7b+	D>G (R>L)	15	25
	Rocher Canon	Vagabond des limbes	problem on red 44	7b+	G>D (L>R)	12	24
	Eléphant	Monsieur plus	black 24	7b+	D>G (R>L)	9	13
	Cuvier Rempart	Les petits anges	Carré d'as (four acres)	7b+	G>D (L>R)	12	25
	Franchard Sablons	Trainée de poudre	red 5	7c	G>D (L>R)	5	7
	Rocher Saint Germain	La cité perdue	off to the side	7c+	D>G (R>L)	12	16
	Rocher Saint Germain	Double croche	Danse sector…	7c+	G>D (L>R)	6	10
	Rocher Saint Germain	Danse de printemps	Danse sector…	7b+	D>G (R>L)	12	20
	Rocher Canon	Crescendo	red 40	7c+	D>G (R>L)	12	25
	Cuvier Rempart	Massacre…	close to black 1	7c	G>D (L>R)	10	15
	Franchard Sablons	Voltane	Chemin des Epines	8a	D>G (R>L)	12	20
	Franchard Isatis	Iceberg	red 55	8a	D>G (R>L)	20	25
	Franchard Cuisinière	Laisons futiles	on the other side of white 44	8a	D>G (R>L)	9	12
	Bas Cuvier	Obsession	black 6	7c+	G>D (L>R)	10	20
TOP FLIGHT	Bas Cuvier	Mouvement perpétuel	blue 11	8b	D>G (R>L)	15	40
	Rocher Saint Germain	Sonate d'automne	Danse de printemps	8b+	D>G (R>L)	5	25
	Rocher Canon	Légende	problem on red 44	8a	G>D (L>R)	16	37
	Buthiers	Coccinelle	tennis sector	8a	G>D (L>R)	7	12
	Canche	Colonne durutti	Anarchodrome sector	8a	G>D (L>R)	20	45

DREAMING OF TRAVERSES... DREAMING OF TRAVERSES... DREAMING OF TRAVERSES... DREAMING

Canche aux Merciers
circuit orange

ORANGE CIRCUIT route	boulder	grade
0	2	2c
1	2	3b
2	3	3a
3	1	3b
4	4	3a
5	6	2c
6	7	3b
7	10	4b
8	13	3a
9	14	3b
10	15	2c
11	16	3a
12	20	2c
13	22	3a
14	29	3a
15	30	3c
16	31	3a
17	32	4a
18	51	2b
19	51	3b
20	53	3c
21	56	2c
22	57	3c
22b	57	2b
23	58	3a
24	59	2c
25	60	2b
26	61	3b
26b	61	4a
27	70	1c
28	72	2a
29	73	3c
30	74	3a
31	75	2b
32	76	4b
33	77	3b
34	78	2a
35	79	3b
36	71	2c
37	47	1a
38	46	4a
39	45	3b
40	39	3a
41	38	3c

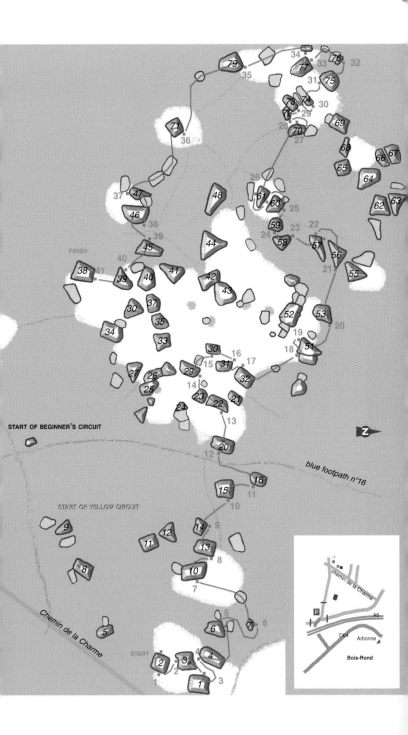

FINISH

START OF BEGINNER'S CIRCUIT

START OF YELLOW CIRCUIT

blue footpath n°16

Chemin de la Charme

START

chemin de la Charme

A6

D64

Arbonne

Bois-Rond

Canche aux Merciers

blue circuit

A touch of winter on the very technical circuit at La Canche.

BLUE CIRCUIT

route	boulder	grade	route	boulder	grade
1	2	4c	22b	53	4b
2	3	5a	23	56	4c
3	1	4b	23b	56	3c
4	4	5a	24	55	3c
4b	4	4a	25	62	5a/4a
5	10	4a	26	64	4b/6b
6	11	4a	27	65	5b
7	12	4c	27b	65	4b
8	13	5a	28	69	4b
9	15	3c	29	75	4b
10	22	4c	30	75	3c
10b	22	4a	31	77	5a
11	24	5b	32	79	4b
12	27	3b	33	48	4b
12b	27	3c	34	46	4b
13	34	3c	34b	46	4b
14	33	4b	35	45	5a
14b	33	5b	36	40	3c
15	28	4c	37	41	3b
16	29	5a	38	42	4b
16b	29	4b	39	43	4c
17	23	5a	39b	43	4a
18	31	4a	40	33	4a
19	32	5b	41	37	4b
20	50	4b	42	39	5a
21	51	3c	44	38	5b
22	52	4b	44b	38	4b

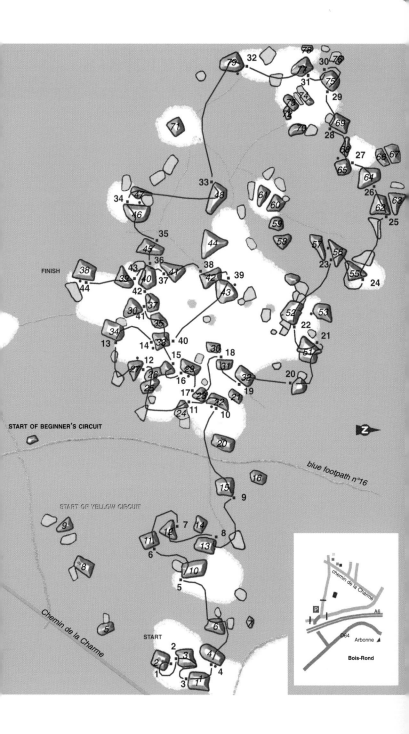

FINISH

START OF BEGINNER'S CIRCUIT

blue footpath n°16

START OF YELLOW CIRCUIT

START

Chemin de la Charme

chemin de la Charme

A6

D64   Arbonne

Bois-Rond

Canche aux Merciers
red circuit

RED CIRCUIT

route	boulder	grade	name	route	boulder	grade	name
1	8	5a	Départ – Ca dérape sec	17	79	5c	Vous avez dit gros bœuf
2	5	5c	Les nineties	18	79	5c	Equilibriste
3	2	5c	L'autoroute du Sud	19	46	5a	Beau pavé
3b	2	5c		20	46	6a	Okilélé
4	1	4c	La débonnaire	21	45	5a	Triste sire
5	3	5c	Maurice Gratton	22	45	5c	Grande classique
6	3	6a	La goulotte à Dom	23	40	5b	Lune rousse
7	10	5b	Le croisé magique	24	40	5c	Rève de chevaux blancs
8	13	5c	Par Toutatis	25	38	5c	La conti
9	21	5b	Le beau final	26	38	6a	Uhuru
9b	22	5c	variante	27	39	5c	L'air de rien
10	31	6a	Bobol's come back	28	40	5b	L'hésitation
11	52	6a	Pas pour Léon	29	36	6b	Les doigts d'homme
12	52	6b+	Gueule cassée	29b	36	6c	Kaki dehors
13	52	6a	Jeu de jambes	30	34	5c	La femme léopard
13b	52	5c	Le piston	31	34	5b	Hatari
14	54	5c	Sortie des artistes	32	33	6b	Glycolise
15	60	6a	L'enfer des nains	33	26	4c	Récupactive
15b	60	7a	Coup bas	33b	26	5c	Arrivée – Gros os
16	77	6b	Chouchou chéri				

Canche aux Merciers
off-circuit

OFF-CIRCUIT

route	boulder	grade	name	route	boulder	grade	name
a	3	7a+	Infusion du soir	b	52	8a	Jacadi
a	33	7a	Crise de l'énergie *Low traverse*	c	52	8a	Saut de puce *Crack*
a	35	7a		a	57	6c	*D>G (R>L) traverse*
a	38	7a	Double face *(7b keeping low)* *G>D (L>R) traverse*	a	61	7b	*D>G (R>L) traverse*
a	42	7b	P'tit bras *D>G (R>L) traverse*	a	68	7b	Séance friction *D>G (R>L) traverse*
a	43	6b	Les bons plats *D>G (R>L) traverse*	A		7a+	Ni vieux ni bête *D>G (R>L) traverse*
a	44	7b	*G>D (L>R) traverse*	B		7c	Soléa pour Valérie *G>D (L>R) traverse*
b	44	6c+	Le nez *Roof*	C		8a	La colonne Durruti *G>D (L>R) traverse*
a	52	7b+	Rage dedans				

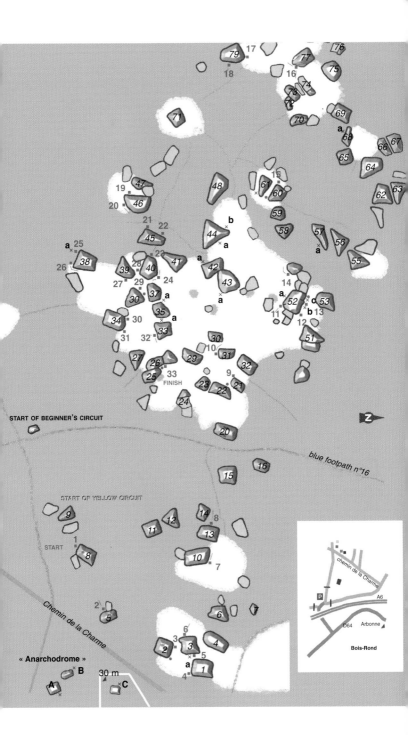

START OF BEGINNER'S CIRCUIT

blue footpath n°16

START OF YELLOW CIRCUIT

START

Chemin de la Charme

« Anarchodrome »

30 m

FINISH

chemin de la Charme

A6

Arbonne

D64

Bois-Rond

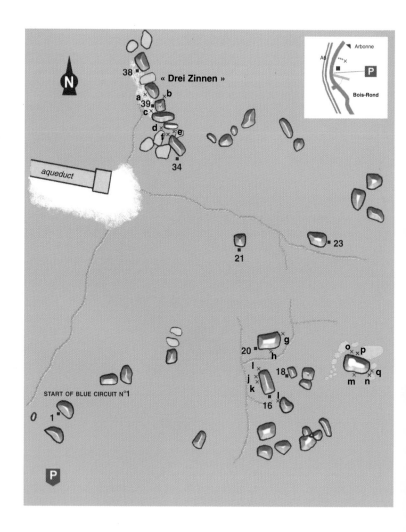

« Drei Zinnen »

aqueduct

START OF BLUE CIRCUIT N°1

Drei Zinnen

CIRCUITS

Blue D ☐

Off-circuit ✗

The three towers ... These boulders, perched high on the hillside, are named after the famous Drei Zinnen or Tre Cime in the Dolomites. The motorway cuts through the forest here and its noise and pollution is a constant background presence. This historic area enjoyed something of a renaissance at the end of the nineties thanks mainly to the establishment of several major new lines which are amongst the best in the forest. Here there is the opportunity to be at one with an untracked wilderness and to witness for yourself the possible trends of this third millenium: a return to bold climbing and new conventions such as sitting starts and the absence of route marking.

Jean-Pierre Bouvier shows how it's done on
Le désert des Tartares.

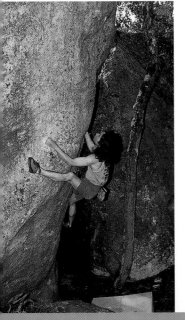

BLUE CIRCUIT

route	grade	name
a	7c	Matière grise
b	7c+/8a	Désert des tartares
c	7a+	Sans le baquet
d	6c	
e	6b+	
f	6c+	
g	5c	
h	6b+	Traversée
i	7a+	La mer des larmes
j	6b	L'exterminateur d'écailles
k	7b+	Chat perché
l	7b+	Close contact *Sitting start*
m	7b+	*Sitting start*
n	7b+	Cocoon
o	7b+	Bifurcation (left) *Sitting start*
p	7a+	Diversion (right) *Sitting start*
q	6a+	*Bold exit*

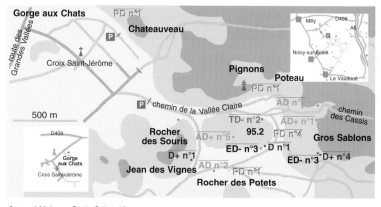

Around Noisy – Croix Saint-Jérome.

Dawn breaks out in early light over a shadowed landscape

La Gorge aux Chats

CIRCUITS

Selected problems:

Routes below 5a   ✗
Routes from 5a to 6c+ ✗
Routes of 7a and above ✗

Situated on the edge of the Trois Pignons forest, the Gorge aux Chats area is full of charm ("chat" being a diminutive of châtaignes (chestnut tree) and not the furry four legged animal:"chat" is also the French word for "cat".) It is popular because of its peaceful situation and because of one particularly superb problem right on the summit of the hill (pignon), which is called *Rubis sur l'ongle*.

Several circuits were created, then permanently removed because of parking problems. Today climbing is once again permitted. The problems selected are an assortment of the most difficult ones, regardless of grade.

Being exposed to the wind, the boulders dry very quickly after rain. Which is one of the reasons climbers like to come here. It is also a wonderful viewpoint over the surrounding villages.

Aesthetic dyno on the ochre rock

La Gorge aux Chats
selected problems

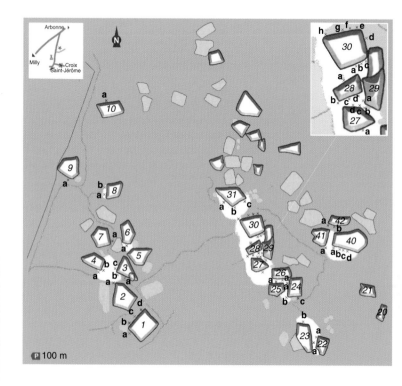

Laurent Laporte resting (Cuisinière).

SELECTED PROBLEMS

boulder	route		grade	name		bloc	voie		cotation	nom
1	a	✗	5a			27	c	✗	7a	Pierre vicieuse
1	b	✗	4c			27	d	✗	5b	Le cyclope
1	c	✗	6a			28	a	✗	6a+	
1	d	✗	4a			28	b	✗	4b	
2	a	✗	3c			28	c	✗	8a	Gospel
3	a	✗	5c			28	d	✗	7b+	Rubis sur l'ongle
3	b	✗	5c			29	a	✗	6b	Travaux forcés
3	c	✗	5b			30	a	✗	5c	
4	a	✗	6a			30	b	✗	6b	
4	b	✗	7a+	Le pare dessus		30	c	✗	6b	
6	a	✗	3c			30	d	✗	6b	
7	a	✗	4b			30	e	✗	4b	
8	a	✗	5b			30	f	✗	4c	
8	b	✗	5c			30	g	✗	5c	
9	a	✗	4b			30	h	✗	4a	
10	a	✗	4a			31	a	✗	4b	
22	a	✗	6b			31	b	✗	6a	
23	a	✗	3b			31	c	✗	3c	
23	b	✗	6b			40	a	✗	6a	
24	a	✗	3c			40	b	✗	6a	
24	b	✗	6b			40	c	✗	6a	
24	c	✗	7a	Ca pelle au logis		40	d	✗	6b	*D>G (R>L) traverse*
25	a	✗	4a			41	a	✗	4a	
26	a	✗	6b			42	a	✗	4c	
27	a	✗	5c			42	b	✗	6b	
27	b	✗	5c							

95.2

CIRCUITS

Yellow PD+	❑
Blue D	●
Red TD-	●
White ED-	◐
Off-circuit	✗
Off-site	★

Situated right in the very heart of the Trois Pignons forest, area 95.2 represents the quintessence of bleausard climbing. In the middle of nowhere, a small hill suddenly appears as if by magic. Its sandy slopes, which evoke the thought of beaches and horizontal as opposed to vertical pleasure, are covered with boulders of all shapes and sizes. However during the fifties and sixties, each rock was painted with small coloured arrows with one thing in mind: edging.

On good winter days, this little hill is crowded with those making the most of the sunshine and maximum friction.

Erosion could become a problem here: watch where you walk and climb and try and keep to the paths, so that future generations will also be able to enjoy the beauty of this place.

Steel fingers are "de rigueur" on Les futurs barbares.

OF HANDS AND FEET

You would think that strength would be the most important quality necessary for bouldering. But that would be to forget about balance, which is equally fundamental, especially on arêtes and slabs which are part of the essential bleausard art and on which athleticism is not necessarily a prerequisite for success. Understanding is doing. We have suggested the following problems; they are representative cross-section of all that is best within all the grades and will no doubt help you to gain some perception of the other key word in bouldering: the subtlety of footwork.

Grade five
At Apremont, La science friction, red n°34 (5c) and *La balafre*, salmon n°24 (5b)
L'arc de cercle (red bis n°12), at 91.1 (5b)
Black n°1 at Buthiers, Canard sector (5b)
N°1 and n°12 on the black circuit at Puiselet (5b)
La pryamide at Rocher Gréau (5b)
Red n°1 in the Vallée de la Mée
La piscine, black n°4, at Gros Sablons (5c)
La dalle Icare, red n°6 at Chamarande (5a)

Grade six
Le pilier légendaire, black n°33, at the Eléphant (6c)
Le pilier Droyer (on the other side of Mur de la mort) at the Eléphant (6c+)
La super fresque, black n°27, at Buthiers (6c)
White n°48 at Franchard Cuisinière (6b)
Coup de blues, black n°4, at Beauvais est (east) (6c)
Le carré d'as (n°30, finishing point of black Trivellini circuit) at Cuvier Rempart (6c)
Black n°22 at Dame Jeanne (6a)
Red n°12 at 91.1 (6a)
White n°50 at Isatis (6b)
La Stalingrad (white n°15) on the white circuit at Bas Cuvier (6b)
Red n°32 at Bas Cuvier (6a)
La Tarentule (white n°13) at Gorges díApremont (6c)
Start of the red circuit at J.A. Martin (6c)
Red n°3 at Rocher Guichot (6b)
L'Everest, white n°22, at 95.2 (6a)
Le dé à coudre, black n°46, at Cuvier Rempart (6c)
L'oeuf, black n°25 at Petit Bois (6c)
L'étrave à sucre, black and white n°.4b, at Beauvais est (east)

Grade seven
L'émeraude at Cuvier Rempart (7b+)
La super forge (7a) and *La super Prestat* (7b+) at Bas Cuvier
Le sourire de David (7a) and *La dalle de fer* at La Merveille (7c)
Monument dalle, black n°26, at Dame Jeanne (7a)
La dalle d'Alain, 2 metres to the left of sky blue n°24 at Gorges d'Apremont (7a+)
Calamity Jane (7b) and *Cosa nostra* (7c) at Dame Jeanne d'Avon
La diagonale on the other side of n°31 on the black circuit at the Eléphant (7a+)
Plein vol at Rocher Gréau (7c+)
Onde de choc, opposite salmon n°30 (7b)
Le dernier angle, towards the Rocher aux Sabots (7c)
La figure de proue at the Eléphant (7a)
Danse avec les loups, white n°32b, at 95.2 (7a)
Excalibur, black n°3, at Franchard Cuisinière
L'angle parfait, white n°23 (7a+), and *L'angle plus que parfait* (7b+) at Dame Jeanne
A l'impossible (red and white, to the left of red n°24) at Roche aux Sabots (7a+)

Grade eight
Duel at Franchard Cuisinière (8a)
Partage at Buthiers Malesherbes (8a)
La merveille at La Merveille (8a)
Khéops at Cuvier Rempart (8b)

95.2

Even darkness does not deter the incorrigible bleausards.

BLUE CIR-CUIT		
route	boulder	grade
1	2	4b
2	1	4b
3	7	4c
4	3	3c
5	8	4c
6	9	4c
7	11	3b
8	16	5a
9	10	4b
10	15	4b
11	25	3c
12	16	4b
13	22	4c
14	23	3c
15	35	4b
16	36	5b
17	39	4b
18	41	3c
19	38	4c
20	37	4b
21	38	3c
22	33	3b
23	32	4b
24	31	4b
25	29	4a
26	28	3c
27	28	4a
28	30	4c
29	60	4b
30	61	3c
31	62	3c
32	64	4b
33	65	4b
34	67	4c
L'ectoplasme		
35	65	5a
36	66	3c
37	68	3b
38	68	5a

95.2

Everything in balance on the slabs at 95.2.

RED CIRCUIT		
route	boulder	grade
1	56	4a
2	56	4b
3	55	4c
4	54	4b
5	53	4c
6	51	4c
7	49	4b
8	48	3c
9	50	4c
10	46	4c
11	45	5b
12	44	4b
13	42	4c
14	43	4b
15	38	4c
16	37	5a
17	36	5c
18	20	4a
19	21	5b
20	12	4c
21	13	4c
22	19	5b
23	22	4b
24	23	4b
25	24	5a
26	17	4b
27	9	5b
28	2	5a
29	2	5a
30	7	4b
31	1	4b
32	5	5a
33	16	4c
34	15	5a
35	26	4c
36	27	4a
37	28	5a
38	28	4c
39	29	4b
40	33	4c
41	34	4c
42	32	5a
43	62	5b
44	64	5b
45	63	5b
46	64	4c
47	67	5c

95.2

white circuit and off-circuit variations

WHITE CIRCUIT

route	boulder	grade	name	route	boulder	grade	name
1	5	5b	Le kilo de beurre	21	55	5a	
2	6	6b	La Poincenot	22	56	5b	
			7a without the chipped hold	23	56	5b	
3	7	5c		24	67	5c	
3b	7	7a+	Le bloc à Bertrand	24b	67	6b	
3t	7	7a+		25	67	6a	
4	13	6a		26	65	5b	
5	13	6b		27	64	5b	
6	13	5a		28	63	4c	
7	36	6a		28b	63	7a	
8	38	5b		29	33	5c	
9	38	5b		29b	33	7a	Miss KGB
10	38	6a		30	33	6a	
10b	38	6b		30b	33	7a+	Mister proper
11	41	5c		31	33	5c	
11b	41	6b+		31b	33	7a	Tarte aux poils
12	42	5c		32	28	7a	La fosse aux ours
13	43	5b		32b	28	7a	Danse avec les loups
14	48	5a		32t	28	7a	
15	50	5a		33	29	5c	
16	50	5b		34	26	5c	
17	51	5c		35	14	5b	
18	51	6b		36	4	5b	
19	52	6a		37	4	5c	*Direct variation 6b*
20	54	5b					

OFF-CIRCUIT VARIATIONS

boulder	route	grade	name
5	a	7a+/ 7c+	L'ange naïf *Grade depends on technique used*
12	a	7b+	Le médaillon
40	a	7a+	Le p'tit toit
67	a	7c+	Futurs barbares
68	a	7b+	Absinthe
69	a	7a	Pierre précieuse (Yaniro)
69	b	7a+	*The arête on the left*

OFF-SITE

route	grade	name
A	7a	Oxygène / Oxygène actif *D>G (R>L) traverse/there and back*
B	7b	Yogi
C	7b	Prouesse
D	7a+	Extraction terrestre
E	7a	Surplomb du bivouac

This circuit is very representative of climbing in the seventies and is still used as a reference for climbing at Fontainebleau. The climbing is on slabs and it is subtlety of footwork that is required here, in the wide and open setting which is peculiar to this area.

As in other areas, but more particularly here, the delicate problem of erosion raises its head. Which is why you will find many parts which are obviously looked after by the ONF, CO-SI-ROC and climbers who are anxious to preserve the longevity of their playground.

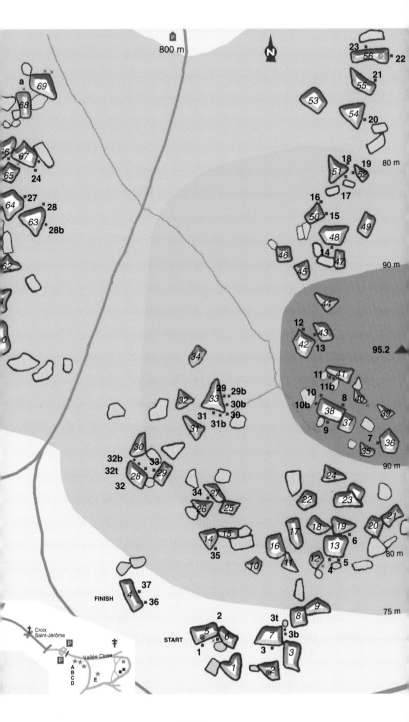

Rocher des Potêts

This area is rather eclipsed by the proximity of the more popular 95.2. Which is why it is very quiet and therefore perfect for those who want to make their climbing début without an audience. The boulders are small and the range of moves required on the problems is not great, making it an ideal beginner's area. On one of the boulders you can see the traces of paintings on the rock, relics of a distant past.

Rocher des Potêts

yellow circuit

orange circuit

YELLOW CIRCUIT

boulder	grade	name	boulder	grade	name	boulder	grade	name
0	2b	Départ	15	2a		30	1c	
1	2b	Le colimaçon	16	2b		31	2b	La piscine
2	2b	L'escargot	17	2a		32	3a	L'interminable
3	2a		18	2b		33	2b	
4	2b		19	2c	Le dièdre caché	34	2c	La Yosemite
5	2c	Le cube	20	2a	Le passage cahotique	35	2a	
6	2a	La politesse	21	2b	Le jardin botanique	36	2c	
7	3a	L'impolitesse	22	2c	La JCB	37	2c	La réflexion
8	2b		23	2a	La GB	38	3a	
9	2a		24	2a	La Vallot	39	2a	
10	2a	Paul Valéry	25	2a	L'adhérence	40	2a	
11	2c	Le TCF	26	2b		41	1c	
12	2c		27	2c		42	2c	Souvenir
13	2b	L'oublié	28	3c	La droite			
14	2b		29	2a				

ORANGE CIRCUIT

boulder	grade	boulder	grade	boulder	grade	voie	cotation
Départ	2b	9	2c	20	4b	31	2b
1	2c	10	3b	21	2c	32	2c
2	2b	11	3c/5b	22	2c	33	3b
3	1c	12	4a	23	1c	34	2c
4	3b	13	3a	24	2b	35	3b
5	3b	14	2c	25	3c	36	4a
5b	3b	15	4b	26	2b	Le grand K	
6	4a	16	2b	27	3a	36b	4a
7	3c	17	4a	28	2c		
8	4b	18	3b	29	2a		
La casquette		19	2c	30	3b		

Les Gros Sablons

CIRCUITS

Orange AD+ (n°1) ⬤
Orange AD (n°2) ❑
Blue D+ (n°4) ❑
Black ED- (n°3) ●

A wonderful spot right in the very heart of the Trois Pignons forest. Deciding to come here is very like leaving for a mountain route, in that there is the same element of delicious uncertainty. Each of these huge rocks requires great mental control; on reaching the finishing holds it is not uncommon to feel a certain characteristic tension in the pit of your stomach. Coming here is like making a pilgrimage and this is where, more than anywhere else in the forest, climbers attempt to push the limits of climbing into another dimension. There are not many very hard routes; but a large majority of the problems are played out between earth and sky, far from anything and everyone. Certain problems in the anthology, such as *La fissure de la Liberté* are worth the visit in themselves. It is in places such as these where the word "liberty" takes on its true meaning.

Reaching for the light.

Les Gros Sablons

orange circuit

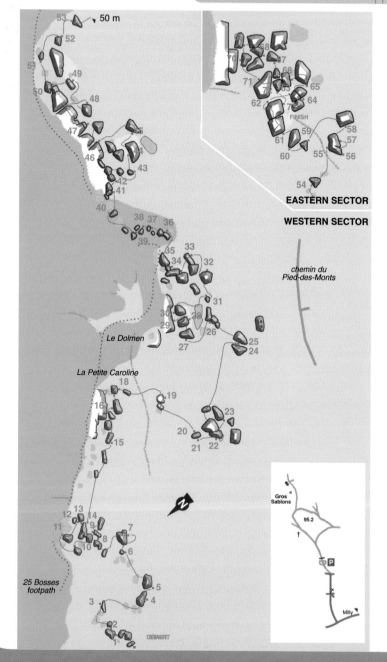

50 m

53
52
51
50
49
48
47
46
43
42
41
40
38 37 36
39
35 33
34 32
31
30 28
29 26
27
25
24
Le Dolmen
La Petite Caroline
18
16 19
15
23
20
21 22
13
12 14
11 9
8 7
10 6
5
3 4
2
1
DÉBART

EASTERN SECTOR

WESTERN SECTOR

68
70 67
66
71 65
64
62 FINISH
61 59 58
60 55 57
54 56

chemin du
Pied-des-Monts

25 Bosses
footpath

Gros
Sablons

95.2

P

Milly

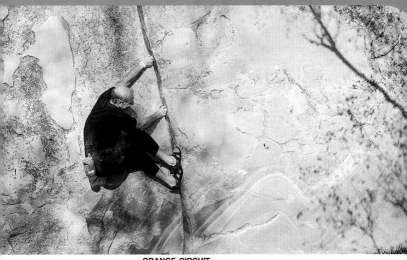

Homage to Hans Dülfer, inventor of the layback.

Another circuit dating from the fifties which was created as a test of fitness for climbers training for the alps. It winds its way along the length of the Gros Sablons plateau, passing through some lovely places. You will be able to cast your eye over some particularly impressive problems on the black circuit and finally, at the end of the day, have a wonderful view of the sunset over the Trois Pignons.

ORANGE CIRCUIT

route	grade	name	route	grade	name
1	4a	*4b variation*	37	2c	*2c variation*
2	3c	*3b variation*	38	2c	
3	3c		39	2c	
4	3c		40	3b	
5	4b	*2b variation*	41	3c	*2c variation*
6	3c		42	3c	
7	3b		43	3b	
8	3c		44	3a	La balade
9	2c	*3c variation*	45	3a	
10	3c	*2c and 3a variations*	46	3a	
11	4a		47	3c	*3c variation*
12	3b		48	3a	*3c variation*
13	3a		49	2c	La salle à manger
14	3c		50	3a	*3c variation*
15	3c	*3c variation*	51	2b	
16	2c	*3a and 4a variations*	52	3a	
17	2c	La petite Caroline	53	3c	
18	2c	La petite Caroline *Down climb*	54	4a	Le fer de lance
19	3a		55	2c	
20	2b		56	3b	
21	3a		57	3c	*3c variation*
22	3c	*4a variation*	58	3c	
23	3c		59	3c	
24	3c	*3c variation*	60	4a	*3c variation*
25	3c		61	2c	*3c variation*
26	3a		62	4b	
27	2c		63	3a	*3c variation*
28	4a		64	4b	Le coup de sabre
29	3c		65	3b	
30	4a	La petite piscine *3c variation*	66	3b	*3c variation*
31	4a	Le surplomb de la vipère	67	3b	
32	3c		68	2c	*3c variation*
33	2c	La tour de Pise	69	3a	*3c variation*
34	3a		70	3a	*3c variation*
35	3a		71	3c	*3c variation*
36	4a	La main haute *3b variation*	72	3b	
			73	3a	Les trous du gruyère

Winter sunlight at Gros Sablons.

Les Gros Sablons

black circuit and off-circuit

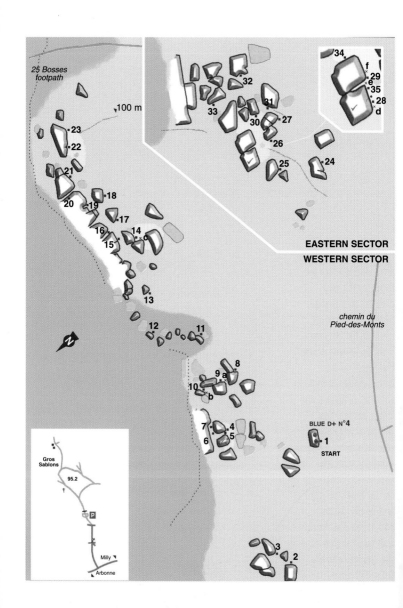

25 Bosses footpath

100 m

23
22
21
20 19 18
17
16 14 c
15
13

12 11

34
f
29
e 35
28
d

32
33 31
30 27
26
25 24

EASTERN SECTOR
WESTERN SECTOR

chemin du Pied-des-Monts

8
9 a
10
b

7 4
6 5

BLUE D+ N°4
1
START

Gros Sablons
95.2
P
Milly
Arbonne

3
2

BLACK CIRCUIT AND OFF-CIRCUIT

route	grade	name
1	6b	La popo
2	5c	La mandarine
3	5b	La râpeuse
4	5c	La piscine
5	6a	L'expolivet
6	4c	La toile cirée
7	5b	L'oubliée
8	4c	La tête
9	5b	Les jambes
10	5b	La colique
11	5c	La main basse
12	5c	La brosse à dents
13	5b	L'iguane
14	5c	Le mobile
15	5c	L'anti-Lerch
16	5c	La magnésie
17	5c	Le croque-monsieur
18	7a	La didi
19	5b	La fusée
20	4c	Le treuil
21	5c	Le bivouac
22	6a	L'Everest
23	6b	Le suppositoire
24	6a	La patinoire
25	5c	Le hachoir
26	5b	La Bérézina
27	4c	La possible
28	5c	L'escalier
29	5b	L'angle gauche
30	5b	Les chauves-souris
31	5b	Les parallèles
32	5a	
33	5b	L'ordure
34	6b	Bande première
35	6b	La pipicaca
35b	6b+	La fissure de la Liberté
a	7a	L'œil du cyclone
b	7b	Dix sur dix
c	7a	Casus Belli
d	7a	La rampe
e	7a	L'arête
f	7a	L'évasion

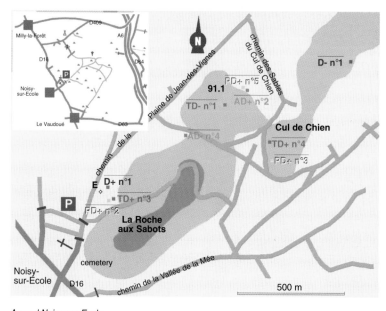

Around Noisy-sur-Ecole.

The surplomb du tiroir.

La Roche aux Sabots

CIRCUITS

White children's circuit	❑
Yellow PD+	●
Blue D	●
Red TD+	●
Red and white ED	○

(routes marked but not numbered)

Off-site	★

This area is often called the Bas Cuvier of the Trois Pignons because there are so many routes in such a small area. The proximity of the car-park, the crowds, which can sometimes be impressive, all serve to accentuate this comparison. But this is where the similarity ends, as the type of climbing is totally different. Here, the emphasis is on a more gymnastic style and the circuits of all grades offer a wide variety of such problems.

All the circuits are interesting and link sequences of moves which will help you to improve your technique, particularly at the TD and D grades. The D circuit is one of the best blues in the forest. On the location map there are two very hard routes marked and *Dernier angle* is generally agreed to be one of the most superb arêtes in the forest.

This is one of the most popular areas, you can climb at leisure in the shade of the tall trees in the heat of summer. Although these same trees make climbing more difficult after rain, when the rock takes longer to dry.

THE SURPLOMB DU TIROIR

This boulder has been very popular since the beginning of the eighties, when a new route starting from a prone position under the roof led to the creation of numerous test pieces, some of the most original of which are listed below.

Sleight of hand
1 *L'angle Ghersen* : 6b+
2 *Rien de bon* : 6a+ (problem also nicknamed *Le tiroir* (The drawer), because of the quality of the crux hold)
4 *Jete-toit* : 6c
b *Sphincter* : 7a (start under the overhang)

b3 or b4 *Sphincters toniques* : 7a+
a 4 *L'oblique* : 7a
5 finishing on red 24: 6c+ traverse
5 finishing on 2: 6b traverse

Superb problem combinations
• Combine the start of 5 then 1; descend 2 to finish on 4: 7b traverse
• Start b, traverse and go up n°1, descend 2, go up 3 and traverse to join 5, the finish with 4: 7c traverse

---

La Roche aux Sabots

blue circuit

yellow circuit

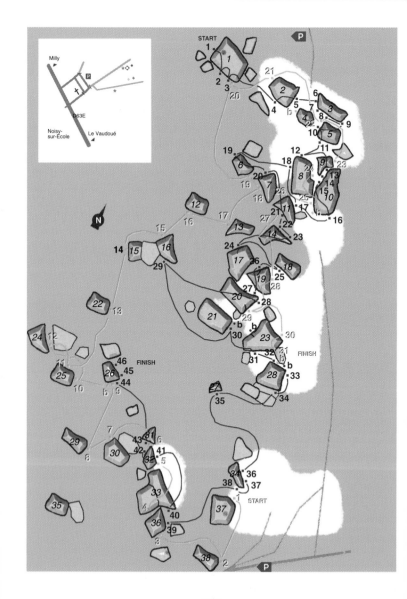

BLUE CIRCUIT

route	boulder	grade
1	1	4b
2	1	4b
3	1	4b
4	2	4b
5	2	4a
6	3	4c
7	3	4a
8	3	3b
9	3	4b
10	5	3c
11	5	3b
12	8	5a
13	10	3b
14	10	4a
15	10	4a
16	10	4c
17	11	5b
18	8	4b
19	6	4b
20	7	4a
21	11	4a
22	14	4a
23	14	5a
24	17	4c
25	18	3c
26	19	4c
27	20	4c
28	20	3c
29	16	5a
30	21	3b
30b	21	5a
31	23	3b
31b	23	4b
32	28	4b
33	28	4b
33b	28	4b
34	28	4a
35	27	3c
36	34	4b
37	34	4a
38	34	3c
39	35	3c
40	33	4c
41	32	3c
42	32	4a
43	31	4a
44	26	4a
45	26	4c
46	26	4b

I t is difficult to find enough adjectives to describe what this trail has to offer. Unbeatable is undoubtedly the one which fits best. The (confirmed) beginner will love it, the regular visitor will enjoy repeating the circuits which the passage of time has not dated.

The sweeter the fall.

YELLOW CIRCUIT

route	boulder	grade
1	37	2c
2	38	3a
3	36	2b
4	33	1c
5	32	3a
6	31	2c
7	30	3b
8	29	2c
9	26	3b
9b	26	3b
10	25	1c
11	24	2a
12	24	3a
13	22	2c
14	15	2c
15	16	3b
16	12	2b
17	13	2b
18	7	1c
19	6	2c
20	1	2c
21	2	2c
21b	4	3a
22	5	2c
23	9	2c
24	8	3a
25	10	3b
26	11	3a
27	14	2b
28	19	2b
29	20	2a
30	23	3b
31	28	2b
31b	28	3a

La Roche aux Sabots

red circuit

red and white circuit

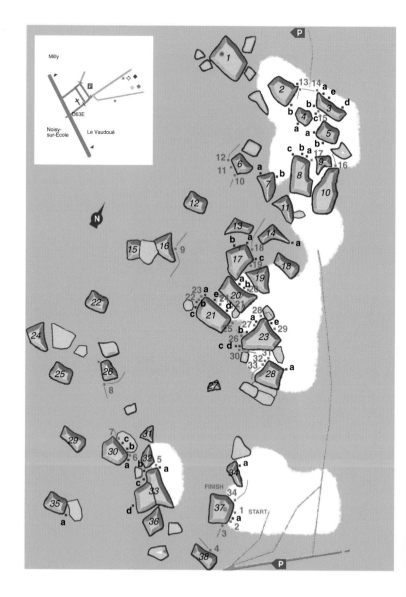

RED AND WHITE CIRCUIT

boulder	route	grade	name
— black squares on the map = routes marked but not numbered			
2	a	7a+	C'est assis, mais c'est tassé
2	b	7c	Le poil de la bête Low level D > G (R > L) traverse
3	a	6b	
3	b	7a	Lime à ongles
3	c	7b	La bas-bas cool Low level G > D (L > R) traverse
3	d	7a	Prima G > D (L > R) traverse – red 14 finish
3	e	6b	
4	a	6b	D > G (R > L) traverse
5	a	6b	Silence, on tourne G > D (L > R) traverse
5	b	7b	Lucifer
7	a	6c	Anglomaniaque Start on blue n°20
7	b	7a	Jeux de toit 7b variation
8	a	8a	Déviation
8	b	6b	Le bond de l'hippopotame
8	c	6c	Le flipeur
14	a	6b	Chapeau chinois
17	a	7a	Angle
17	b	6b	L'inversée satanique Direct variation 6c+
17	c	6b+	Angle
20	a	7a	Amanite dalloïde
20	b	6c	Bazooka jo
21	a	6b+	Angle Ghersen
21	b	7a+	Sphincters toniques On the hands

boulder	route	grade	name
21	c	7c	Pets O2 max Combination of routes on the main face
21	d	7a+	A l'impossible
21	e	7b	Ongle jo
23	a	7a	Jet set
23	b	7b	Jack's finger
23	c	7a	Les yeux
23	d	7b	D > G (R > L) traverse, finish with red 28, 7c
23	e	7b+	Le parallèlogramme
28	a	6c+	Rumsteak en folie
30	a	7a	Achille Talon
30	b	7b+	100 % pulpe
30	c	7a	Jus d'orange
33	a	7c	Sale gosse Sitting start 8a
33	b	7a	Gravillon Overhanging corner
33	c	7a	Graviton
33	d	7b+	Vieille canaille G > D (L > R) traverse
34	a	6c+	Surplomb des frelons D > G (R > L) traverse
35	a	7a+	Partie de jambes en l'air D > G (R > L) traverse
37	a	7a	Le tourniquet Girdle traverse of the boulder

OFF-SITE

	A	7c	Miss world G > D (L > R) traverse
	B	7c	Le dernier angle Arête

RED CIRCUIT

route	boulder	grade	name
1	37	6a	Le saute-montagnes
2	37	6a	Le coup de genoux
3	37	6a	Le surplomb à coulisse
4	38	5b	La dalle de cristal
5	33	5b	Le passage à tabac
6	30	5c	Le porte à faux
7	30	4c	Le mur Badaboum
8	26	5b	Beauf en daube
9	16	5b	Little Crack
10	6	5c	Danger majeur
11	6	5c	L'arrache-moyeu
12	6	5b	L'angle à Gilles
13	2	5b	Red one
14	3	6b	L'angle de la pierre ôtée
15	3	6a+	Coup de patte
16	10	5b	Le mode d'emploi
17	8	5a	Vol au vent

route	boulder	grade	name
18	17	6a+	Le mur à Robert
19	17	6a+	les joyeuses de Noël
20	20	5b	Passage à l'acte
21	20	5b	Mine de rien
22	21	6a+	Le tiroir/Rien de bon
23	21	6a	Bon à rien
24	21	6a	Les grattons belliqueux
25	21	6b+	L'angle à Jean-Luc
26	23	5a	Le goût du jour
27	23	5c	Crosse en l'air
28	23	6a+	Service compris
29	23	6b	Le mur à Michaud
30	23	5b	La barquette de beurre
31	28	5b	Servir frais
32	28	5c	Le pain total
33	28	5c	Le théorème de Pascal
34	37	6a	L'auriculaire - Toit aux frelons

Le Cul de Chien

CIRCUITS

Yellow PD	❏
Blue D	●
Red TD+	❏

Another mystery in the forest: how did this boulder, in the shape of a dog's head, appear out of nowhere? Legend has it that a monster from the past ended up in this vast wilderness and was devoured by predators, who left its fossilised remains scattered throughout the forest. It is one of the most magical places of the forest, where you would almost be happy just to go and meditate. But the climber within us needs his fill of rock and there is enough here for us to have a feast.

Le Joker is the route on the famous Toit du Cul de Chien which, at grade seven's door, has moves which take you into seventh heaven. Further on another roof ("L'Autre toit"), is in another world, that of the highest grade. You will find details of both routes in the following pages.

Surreal light plays on the most famous boulder in the forest

Hung up on my overhang

This is based on the wild desire to have a go at a problem which was considered to be one of the most representative of its time in terms of difficulty and boldness. This famous roof gives climbing of three different angles: the start: vertical; the crux: a horizontal roof; and the finish: back to the vertical. It should definitely be possible for three people to be climbing the route at the same time. No sooner said than done and this mythical problem became, for a few minutes in time, the scene of a curious merry-go-round which must have made a profound impression on the many climbers who every Sunday expected to see an ascent of this amazing route. On this particular day, they could marvel to their hearts content. Imagine five climbers one after the other. As one person left one section of the route, another took his place and in the space of five minutes there were some twenty ascents. The hardest part was, once on the summit getting down quickly enough to be ready to go again straight away.

Le Cul de Chien

blue circuit

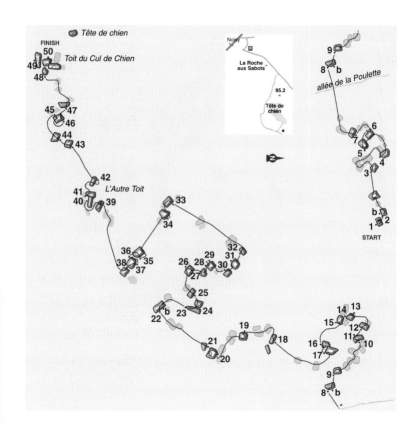

Thierry Plot on Eclipse.

BLUE CIRCUIT

route	grade	route	grade
1	3b	25	3c
2	2b	26	4a
2b	3c	27	3c
3	4a	28	3b
4	3c	29	4c
5	4a	30	3c
6	4b	31	3c
7	4a	32	3c
8	3b	33	4c
8b	5a	34	4c
9	3c	35	4b
10	4a	36	4b
11	3c	37	5a
12	3c	38	4b
13	4a	39	3a
14	4a	40	3c
15	3c	41	3b
16	4a	42	4c
17	4b	43	4b
18	4c	44	3c
19	3b	45	4a
20	4a	46	4a
21	4a	47	4a
22	4b	48	4b
22b	4a	49	3c
23	3c	50	4b
24	4a		

The famous Cul de Chien roof, bold and unforgettable.

L'AUTRE TOIT

A potted history

There were ten years between the first ascent of the first route on "L'Autre toit", which used a chipped hold, and an ascent of the same route without the chipped hold, at the same grade. Which is further proof, if more is needed, of the futility of the chipped hold. It's just patience … Since then, numerous routes and linked problems have been done on this extraordinary overhang, one of the best known at Fontainebleau.

Les passages

1 *Arabesque :* 7b+ (the original route)
2 *La nouvelle vague :* 7b+ (the same problem without using the chipped hold)
3 *Eclipse :* 7c
4 *The Maxx :* 8a
5 *Jack in the box :* 8a+
6 *L'œil de la Sybille :* 7c+
a1 *L'intégrale :* 8a (start at the bottom and finish on *Arabesque*)
a2 *L'âme de fond :* 8a (start at the bottom and finish on *Nouvelle vague*)
a3 *Totale éclipse :* 8a+ (start at the bottom and finish on *Eclipse*)

ECLIPSE

Location:
Cul de Chien, l'Autre toit.

Grade: 7c.

Style:
three moves; in two words: sensitive and relaxed.

Climber:
Christophe Laumône.

It was only very recently that this problem had a first ascent by Stéphan Denys, overshadowed although it rightly was by the horizontal climbing specific to the Autre toit du Cul de Chien. However, now it is a great classic and the relaxed technique needed to do it is described by Christophe Laumône.

Technique
Place the left hand on a tiny line of edges, the left foot well hooked in the big hole, bring the right foot carefully up onto the big ramp to balance yourself and to enable you to reach a flat hold with your right hand pinching it as much as possible.

Place the left hand in the crack, hooking with the tip of the left foot to enable you to take your right foot out of the hole.

Take both feet off the rock, both hands braced allowing you to make this spectacular but easy move.

Place the inside edge of the left foot on the left side of the crack.

With the right foot holding you in balance, most of your weight is now on your left hand and the next move involves standing up straight on the left foot, at the same time thinking as much about lifting the body as about the finishing hold.

Once this move is begun, the finish follows, without real effort, because the edge you are going for is very good and the right hand falls on to it naturally. That is called a gentle dyno.

91.1

CIRCUITS

Yellow PD+ (n°5) ❏
Orange AD (n°4) ❏
Orange AD (n°2) ●
Red TD+ (n°4) ●

Area 91.1 is midway between the car-park and the sands of the Cul de Chien and is a good alternative for those who prefer slabs of all kinds. A quiet area abundantly supplied with good routes of all grades which has nothing uncivilised about it except its name, 91.1 metres, which is singularly at odds with the beauty of the surroundings. On each circuit, the requirements are the same: balance, coolness and precision, on a very distinctly coloured sandstone where the friction requires a special understanding. And still this sandy wilderness continues to delight the senses.

On the elusive incuts of the red circuit

91.1

orange circuit

ORANGE CIRCUIT

route	boulder	grade
1	58	3a
1b	58	3c
2	57	3c
3	56	3c
4	55	4a
5	54	3c
6	53	3a
6b	53	3c
6t	53	4a
7	52	3c
8	51	3b
9	51	3c
10	50	3b
11	47	4a
12	48	4a
13	45	3c
14	44	3a
15	43	4a
16	42	2c
17	40	2c
18	8	4c
19	7	3a
20	6	3b
21	6	3b
22	30	3b
23	33	4a
24	31	3c
25	32	4b
26	38	3c
27	35	4a
28	36	3a
29	37	3c
30	26	3c
31	25	3b
32	23	3a
33	22	2c
34	19	3a
35	16	3b
36	17	2b
37	21	3a
38	14	3c
39	13	3a
40	12	3b
41	14	3b
42	3	3b
43	3	3b
44	5	3b
45	4	3c
46	4	4b
47	1	4b

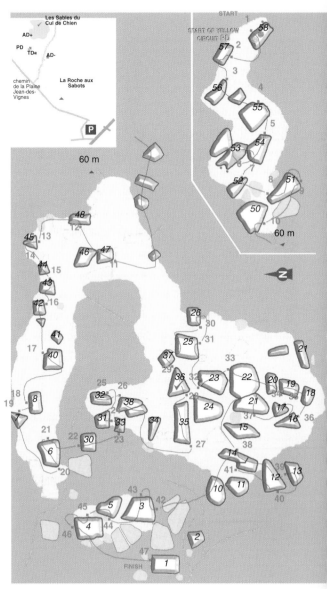

Les Sables du Cul de Chien

AD+
PD
TD
AD-

chemin de la Plaine Jean-des-Vignes

La Roche aux Sabots

60 m

START

START OF YELLOW CIRCUIT PD

60 m

FINISH

91.1

red circuit

off-circuit

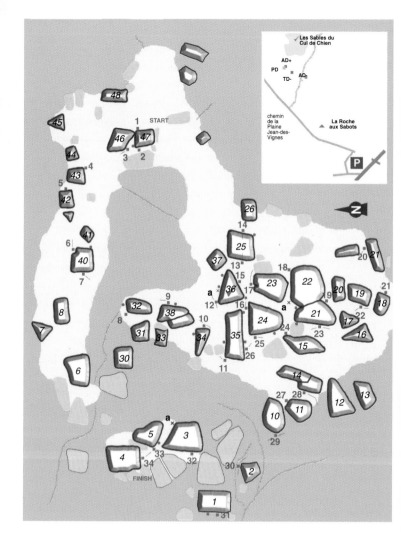

To be able to climb on nature's miracles is surely one in itself.

RED CIRCUIT AND OFF-CIRCUIT

route	boulder	grade	name	route	boulder	grade	name
1	47	4c		17	23	4c	
2	47	5b		18	22	5a	
2b	47	6b		19	21	5a	
3	46	3c		20	21	4b	
4	43	4a		21	18	4a	
5	42	4b		22	19	4c	
6	40	4b		23	21	5b	
6b	40	5c		23b	21	5c	
7	40	5b		23t	21	6a	
8	32	4c		24	15	4c	
8b	32	6a	Le Flipper	25	24	4c	
9	38	5a		25b	24	5a	
9b	38	5c		26	35	4c	
10	34	4b		26b	35	6a	*G<>D (L<>R) traverse*
10b	34	5c		27	11	4c	
11	35	4b		28	14	4b	
11b	35	4b		29	10	5b	
12	36	5c		30	2	5b	
12b	36	5c	L'arc de cercle	31	1	4b	
12t	36	6a	Le Grand dièdre	31b	1	5a	
13	25	4c		32	3	5a	
14	25	6a	La Goulotte	33	5	4c	
14b	25	5a		33b	5	6b	
15	36	5b		34	4	5c	
15b	36	5a		a	36	7a	Les pieds nickelés
16	24	5b		a	3	6c	*Traversée G<>D*
16b	35	5c		a	23	7a	Le Sur Plomb

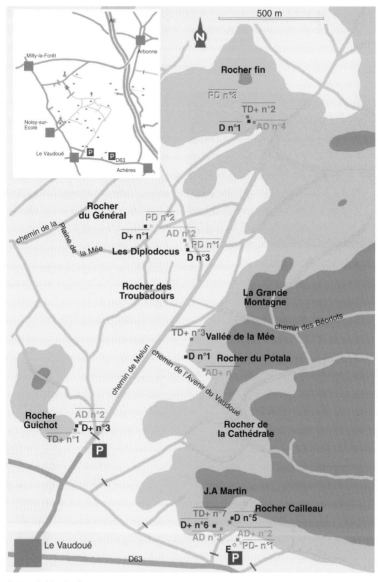

Autour du Vaudoué.

Rocher Guichot

CIRCUITS

Yellow AD- ●
Blue D ●
Red TD+ ●

Area 91.1 is midway between the car-park and the sands of the Cul de Chien and is a good alternative for those who prefer slabs of all kinds. A quiet area abundantly supplied with good routes of all grades which has nothing uncivilised about it except its name, 91.1 metres, which is singularly at odds with the beauty of the surroundings. On each circuit, the requirements are the same: balance, coolness and precision, on a very distinctly coloured sandstone where the friction requires a special understanding. And still this sandy wilderness continues to delight the senses.

The Denecourt tower honours the man who created the first footpaths.

The forest in all its finery.

Rocher Guichot

yellow circuit

blue circuit

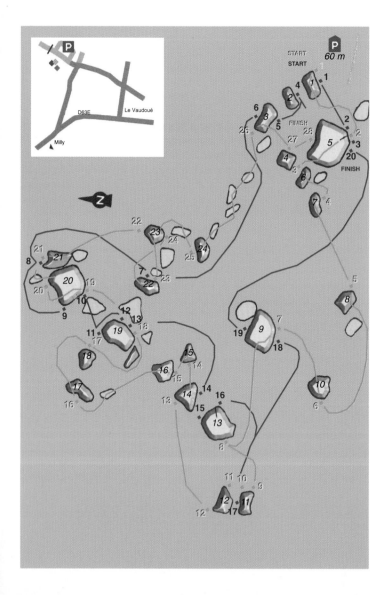

BLUE CIRCUIT

route	boulder	grade
1	1	4a
2	5	4c
3	5	4b
4	2	4a
5	3	4c
6	3	5a
7	22	4a
8	21	4c
9	20	5a
10	20	4a
11	19	4b
12	19	5b
13	19	5a
14	14	4c
15	13	4c
16	13	4c
17	11	5a
18	9	5b
19	9	4c
20	5	5a

YELLOW CIRCUIT

route	boulder	grade
1	1	2c
2	5	2b
3	6	2b
4	7	2b
5	8	2a
6	10	3a
7	9	3a
8	13	2a
9	11	3a
10	11	2b
11	12	2c
12	12	2b
13	14	3a
14	15	3c
15	16	2b
16	17	2c
17	18	2b
18	19	3c
19	20	2b
20	20	2b
21	21	2c
22	23	2a
23	22	3c
24	23	3b
25	24	2a
26	3	3a
27	4	2b
28	5	3b

Rocher Guichot

red circuit

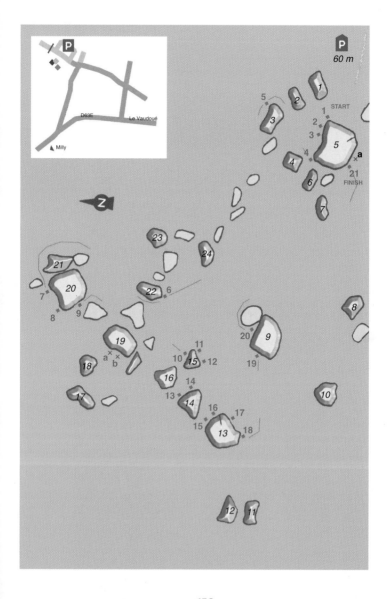

AROUND VAUDOUE

RED CIRCUIT AND OFF-CIRCUIT

route	boulder	grade	name
1	5	5b	
2	5	6a	
3	5	6b	
4	5	6b	
5	3	6b	
6	22	6a	
7	20	6b	
8	20	5c	
9	20	5b	
10	15	5c	
11	15	6a	
12	15	5b	
13	14	5c	
14	14	5b	
15	13	6b	
16	13	6b	
17	13	6c	
18	13	5b	
19	9	6a	
20	9	6b	
21	5	6a	
a	5	8a	*D>G (R>L) traverse*
a	19	7c	Mayonnaise de passion *D>G (R>L) traverse*
b	19	7c+	L'univers des arts *D>G (R>L) traverse, finish on the overhang*

The colours of the forest ...

... purple or green.

Le Diplodocus

CIRCUITS

Yellow PD
Orange AD
Blue D

The evocative name of this area should be enough to stimulate the imagination of even the most blasé amongst us. How on earth did a diplodocus come to be fossilised here, thereby allowing us to play on his back today? At the same time we will never be able to explain the presence of the rocking-stone (a boulder perched precariously on a rocky pedestal) of which there are several examples in the forest. How did they get there? How long ago?

On either side of this giant rock are its family and it is a delight to see such amazingly shaped sandstone boulders grouped together in this setting. Unfortunately the rock has become very polished by generations of climbers. The Diplodocus rock itself, is high and committing; there is a fixed belay on the summit.

Snow on the little summits of Fontainebleau (Larchant).

Le Diplodocus

yellow circuit

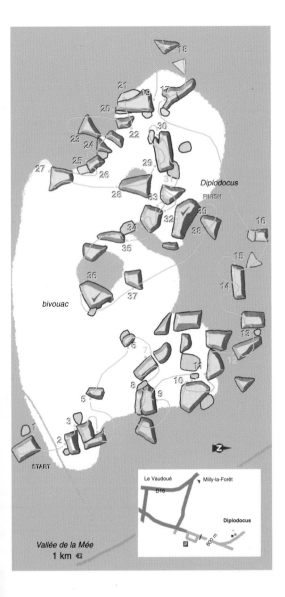

route	grade
YELLOW CIRCUIT	
1	3b
2	2b
3	2b
4	1b
5	2b
6	2c
7	3a
8	2b
9	2b
10	2b
11	2b
12	3b
13	3a
14	2c
15	2c
16	2b
17	2c
18	1c
19	2c
20	3a
21	2c
22	2c
23	3a
24	2b
25	2b
26	2b
27	2b
28	2b
29	2c
30	3a
31	2c
32	2c
33	2c
34	3a
35	3a
36	2c
37	2b
38	2b
39	3b

On the Diplodocus monsters.

Le Diplodocus

orange circuit

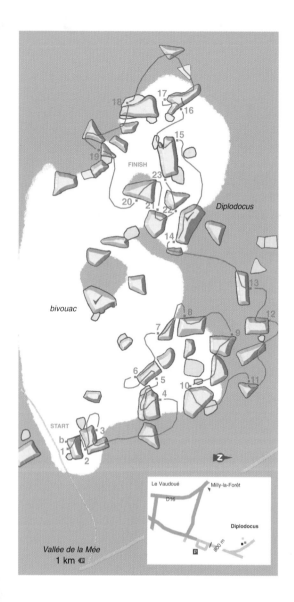

FINISH

Diplodocus

bivouac

START

Vallée de la Mée
1 km

Le Vaudoué   Milly-la-Forêt

D16

Diplodocus

800 m

ORANGE CIRCUIT

route	grade	name
1	3a	La lulu
1b	2c	Le bout du Simon
2	3b	Le premier jeu
3	3c	L'angle désaxé
4	2c	La crèmerie
5	4a	L'épicerie
6	2c	La culottée
7	3c	La S.P.A
8	3b	Le fusible
9	3a	Fer à cheval
10	3a	Le fou
11	2b	Micro sillon
12	3b	Le marteau
13	3c	Le coryza fou
14	3c	Pilier rouge
15	3a	La Onze traction
16	3a	Le nain jaune
17	3b	La ricorée
18	2c	Surplomb du croissant
19	3a	Le brelan d'as
20	2c	La couleuvre
21	3c	Le 4ème réflexe
22	3a	Fissure de la Pres'toi
23	4b	La torniol

An exposed grade five (La Padôle).

Le Diplodocus

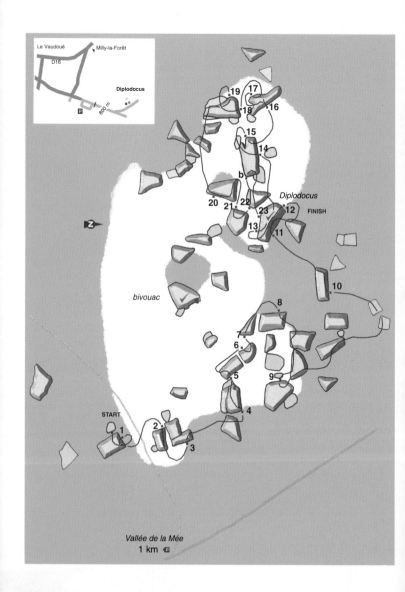

BLUE CIRCUIT

route	grade
D	4a
1	4b
2	4b
3	4a
4	3c
5	4a
6	4a
7	4b
8	4b
9	4b
10	4b
11	4c
12	4c
13	4a
14	5b
15	4b
16	4b
17	4c
18	4b
19	4a
20	4c
21	4c
22	3c
23	4a

Vallée de la Mée - Potala

CIRCUITS

Orange AD+	●
Blue D	●
Red TD+	●
Off-circuit	✗

Previous page:
Falling is part of the
spice of bouldering.

Below:
Jacky Godoffe on Le
surplomb *in the*
Vallée de la Mée.

When you go to the Rocher du Potala, you will see the remains of ancient dwelling places, where every climber would have liked to live so as to be right in the heart of his playground. But the rocks themselves are a bit further on in an ochre bower which irresistibly prompts a desire to climb. A reasonable height, an unusual feel to the rock, mean technique and delicacy is what is required here, rather than strength. You may have to walk a little to find certain problems, but always in excited anticipation of what may be coming next. It was a route on an overhang which made this area famous, because for many years it was a real myth: a grade eight. Although the myth no longer exists, there is still a very hard problem which attracts climbers from the four corners of the world.

Vallée de la Mée - Potala
orange circuit

ORANGE CIRCUIT

route	boulder	grade	name	route	boulder	grade	name
1	34	3b	Le Klem	23	59	4a	La vire tournante
2	33	4a	Le rouleau californien	24	58	3b	Le Cervino
3	31	4a		24b	58	2c	Le Cervino *(lefthand finish)*
4	32	3c	L'équilibriste	25	55	3b	Les pattes de mouche
5	33	4a	Ventre bleu	25b	55	3a	
6	33	3b	La traversée des confettis	26	62	2c	
7	35	2c	L'écartelée	27	63	3c	
8	35	2c	La vire à bicyclette	28	64	3b	
9	35	3b	L'inessorable reptation	29	66	3a	La grande dalle du Coutant
10	36	3c	Le baquet de Pierre	29b	66	4a	La petite dalle du Coutant
11	37	4b	Le crochet	29t	65	2a	
11b	37	2c		30	66	2b	La traînée blanche
12	40	2a	Le pas de la mule	31	70	2b	
13	41	3c	Le feuillet décollé	32	70	4b	Le mauvais angle
14	44	4a	Le pousse pied	33	71	3b	L'allonge de l'escalier
15	45	4b	La traversée du poussin	34	71	3c	Le mauvais pas
16	48	3a	L'accroupie	35	72	3c	Le nouvel angle
16b	49	2c		36	74	4a	La fissure humide
17	52	3b	Les petits rognons	36b	74	4b	
18	52	4b		37	76	4a	La déviation
19	53	2c		38	78	4a	Les deux baignoires
20	54	3a	La patinoire	39	80	2c	La bleausarde
21	54	3a	La cheminée de l'obèse	40	81	3b	La traversée des tortues jumelles *Slab variation 4c*
22	56	3c					

Getting the feel of the rock.

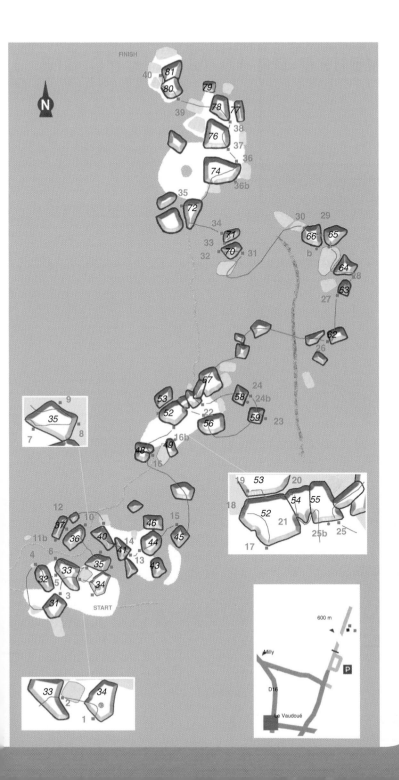

Vallée de la Mée - Potala
blue circuit

First moves in the sunshine.

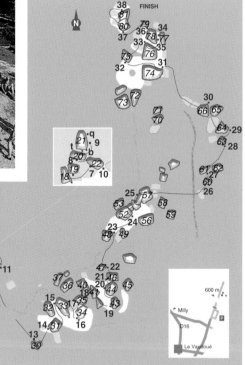

Tim starting the orange circuit.

BLUE CIRCUIT

route	boulder	grade
0	10	3a
1	13	4a
2	12	4b
3	14	3c
4	15	3c
5	16	3c
6	18	4b
7	22	5a
7b	19	5c
8	20	5b
9	21	4a
9b	21	4b
9t	21	4c
9q	21	3a
10	22	4a
11	23	4a
12	24	4c
13	30	4a
14	31	4a
15	33	5a
15b	33	5b
16	34	3c
16b	34	5b
17	35	2c
18	41	3c
19	43	4b
20	44	4b
21	46	3b
22	47	3c
23	48	4c
24	52	4b
25	57	3c
26	60	4a
27	61	2c
28	63	4c
29	64	4b
30	66	4a
31	74	4a
32	75	4a
33	76	4a
34	77	4a
35	78	4c
36	79	3b
37	80	3b
38	81	4c

Vallée de la Mée - Potala
red circuit

On the final rotational moves of the red circuit.

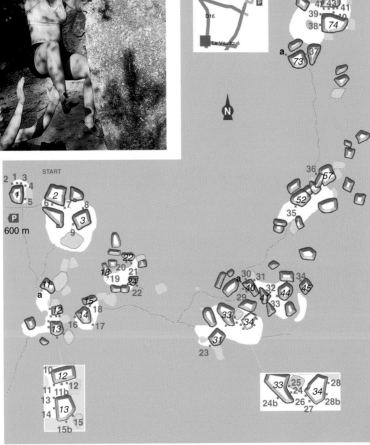

RED CIRCUIT

route	boulder	grade	name	route	boulder	grade	name
1	1	5a		26	34	5a	
2	1	5a		27	34	5a	
3	1	5b		28	34	5c	
4	1	5c		28b	34	6b+	
5	1	5b		29	40	5c	
6	2	6a		29b	40	6a	
7	2	5b		30	40	6b	
8	3	6a		31	40	5c	
9	3	5b		32	41	5c	
10	12	5c		33	44	5a	
11	12	5b	Les trois lancers	34	45	5b	Le toit du châtaignier
11b	12	6a		35	52	5c	
12	12	5c		36	57	5a	
13	13	5a		37	73	5c	
14	13	5b		38	74	5c/6b	Selon méthode
15	13	6b		39	74	5a	
15b	13	5a		40	74	5b	
16	14	5c		41	76	5c	
17	14	5c		42	76	5a	
18	15	5b		42b	76	5c	Les rasoirs
19	18	6b	La voie lactée	43	76	5b	La fissure au marbre
20	22	6a		44	78	5a	Corner
21	22	5c	La clé de pied	44 b	78	5b	
22	24	5b	La contorsion	45	78	5c	Les petits pieds
23	31	5b		46	78	5b	
24	33	6a		46 b	78	6b	
24b	33	6a		47	80	5b	
25	33	5b	Le mur jaune	48	81	6a	L'angle des tortues jumelles

Vallée de la Mée - Potala
off-circuit

OFF-CIRCUIT

boulder	route	grade	name
81	a1	8a+	Le surplomb
81	a2	7c	La traversée
11	a	6c+	Eclipse *G > D (L > R) traverse*
40	a	7b+	Etrange étrave
73	a	7a+	Prophétie *D > G (R > L) traverse*

Rocher fin

CIRCUITS

Yellow PD	●
Orange AD	●
Blue D	❑
Red TD+	●

The climbing is very delicate, with precarious balancing moves and subtle footwork required; which is why it attracts technical climbers. But whatever your standard, your fingers and feet will have a hard time, the friction never fails to surprise and the crimps are aggressive to say the least. For beginners there is a short and varied yellow circuit (but polished in places). Although this is one of the areas furthest from a car-park, at the weekend it attracts those who like to combine sport with picnicking. Here there are not only the rocks to climb on, but there is a yellow ochre sand and a special quality of light. During the week, it is a desert island in an ocean of sand. And finally, its hillside location means it dries quickly after rain.

Previous page:
Nadia Hrina on the marbled rock of Rocher fin.

Below:
Le cube, a very delicate 6a.

Rocher fin

yellow circuit

red circuit

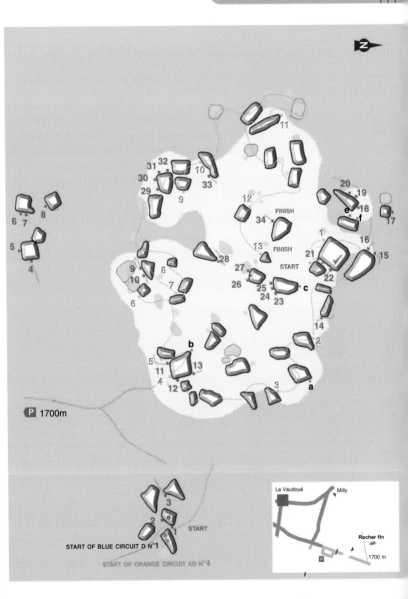

FINISH

11

31 32
30
29
10
33
9

12
34   FINISH

13   FINISH

START

20
19
18
17
16
21   15
22

28

27
26   25
24   23

14

2

b

5
11   13
4
12   3   a

6 7   8

5
4

9
10
8
7

6

P 1700m

3
2   START
1

START OF BLUE CIRCUIT D N°1

START OF ORANGE CIRCUIT AD N°4

Le Vaudoué   Milly

Rocher fin

P   1700 m

On the arête of Le Cube.

YELLOW CIRCUIT

route	grade	name
D	2a	Départ
1	3b	Le cube
2	3b	La déversante
3	2c	Le pas à droite
4	2c	La sinueuse
5	3b	La niche
6	2b	Le chemin de ronde
7	2c	Les bossettes
8	3a	L'éperon
9	2c	Le promenoir
10	2c	La voie du trou
11	2b	L'adhérence
12	2b	La dalle marbrée
13	2c	Le menhir

RED CIRCUIT AND OFF-CIRCUIT

route	grade	name	route	grade	name
1	5b	L'angle ingrat	21	6a	La traversée à Taupé
2	6a	Ascendance	22	6a	Coup de pompe
3	5b	Choux blancs	23	4c	Dinomania
4	4c	Pastiche	24	5b	Gras double
5	5a	C.Q.F.D.	25	5a	Chien fou
6	5c	Colin-maillard	26	6a	Coup de griffe
7	5c	Grande manœuvre	27	6a	Doigt dans l'œil
8	4b	Contre vérité	28	5b	Envie et nécessité
9	5b	Nombril de Vénus	29	5b	Bras de fer
10	5c	Syracuse	30	6a	Soleil brûlé
11	5c	Sale gueule	31	5a	Système F
12	4c	Le tas de sable	32	5b	Regain
13	5c	L'art de vivre	33	5c	La Micholeg
14	5a	Tronche à noueux	34	5c	Coup de rein
15	5b	L'apostolat	a	7a	L'envol du Martinet
16	5c	Torticolis	b	7b	Mémoire d'outre tombe
17	6a	Théorème	c	7a	Intégrale *(traverse)*
18	6b	Plein pot	d	7a+	Forty-ssimo
19	5c	La belle d'Ivry	e	7b	Les Croates
20	6a	Grosse caisse	f	7b	Les Serbes

J. A Martin

CIRCUITS

White children's circuit ❑
Yellow PD- ❑
Orange AD+ ❑
Sky blue D ❑
Blue D+ ●
Red TD+ ❑

A vast jumble which is reminiscent of the Gorges d'Apremont because it is so difficult to find your way around. The circuits which run across the slopes of these small hills (pignons) are relatively mixed. But they are very user-friendly and this combined with the technical aspect of the climbing attracts many weekend climbers.

J. A Martin

blue circuit |||

off-circuit |||

Jo Montchaussé on L'étrave.

This very mixed circuit is an example of the interest in route marking, generally represented by little coloured arrows. This circuit was first marked towards the end of the sixties, then repainted about thirty years later and completed to created the present route. How history evolves.

OFF-CIRCUIT

route	grade	name
a	7b+	L'étrave
b	6c	Bibi Fricotin
c	6c	Le printemps du Martin
d	7a+	Coup de cymbale

OFF-SITE

route	grade	name
A	7b+	Jardin secret *G>D (L>R) traverse*

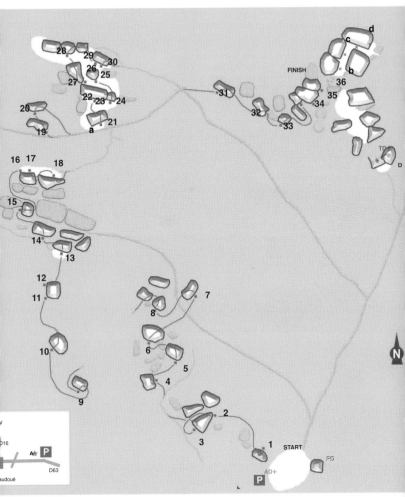

BLUE CIRCUIT

route	grade	name	route	grade	name	route	grade	name
1	4b	Le starter	13	5a	La trapèze	25	4b	Le coup de pied
2	5a	Le pommeau	14	4b	L'opposition	26	4c	L'échappatoire
3	4a	La déchirure	15	3c	Le carré de chocolat	27	4b	L'arête dorsale
4	4a	Le mur en faïence	16	3c	Un coin de paradis	28	4c	Fissure contractuelle
5	5b	Le tour de main	17	5a	Truc et astuce	29	4c	L'ardu
6	5b	La voie du forçat	18	4c	La brasse crawlée	30	4b	Eclats de verre
7	4c	L'entrechat	19	4c	Attention fragile	31	4c	Le coup de cymbale
8	4c	L'incertitude	20	5a	La force de caractère	32	4b	La voie inquiète
9	4c	La brosse à ongles	21	4a	La fissure de l'étrave	33	4a	La poussée d'Archimède
10	4b	La jaunisse	22	5a	Dérapage contrôlé	34	4c	Le casse pied
11	4a	La dalle cirée	23	4b	La grande nouvelle	35	5b	Le jeu de paume
12	3c	Le croche-pied	24	4a	La conduite forcée	36	4c	Carrefour

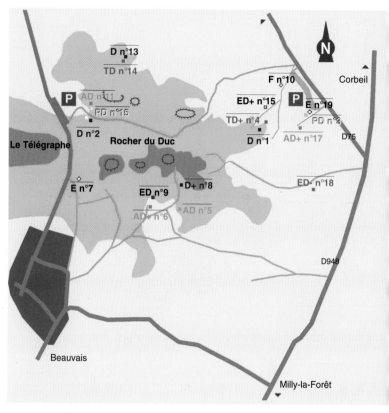

Beauvais Rocher du Duc.

Beauvais - Rocher du Duc

CIRCUITS

ROCHER DU DUC EAST

White children's (n°19) ❖
Easy/family white (n°10) ❑
Yellow PD (n°3) ❑
Orange AD+ (n°17) ❑
Blue D (n°1) ●
Red TD+ (n°4) ●
Red ED- (n°18) ❑
Black & White ED+ (n°7) ●

ROCHER DU DUC CENTRE

Saffron AD (n°5) ❑
Orange AD+ (n°6) ❑
Blue D+ (n°8) ❑
Black ED (n°9) ❑

ROCHER DU DUC WEST

White children's (n°7) ❑
White F (n°16) ❑
Yellow PD (n°12) ●
Orange AD (n°11) ❑
Blue D- (n°2) ❑
Blue D (n°13) ❑
Red TD (n°14) ❑

Although a little away from the heart of Fontainebleau, Beauvais, in the Grands Avaux forest is nevertheless a very popular area.

Firstly because of the large number of reasonably graded and very interesting circuits, particularly the white one for children (no.19); probably the best in the whole forest.

Secondly, the boulders are not very high, which makes it easier to work on problems. Finally, the hardest circuits concentrate particularly on traversing. Another speciality: sloping holds of all shapes and sizes.

Climbers seem to be coming here in ever greater numbers if the East car-park, which has tripled in size recently, is anything to go by.

In springtime the ground is carpeted with violets which are a delight to see. The air is dry and pleasant up on the hill but under the chestnut trees, which are magnificent in autumn, dampness clings to the rocks after rain.

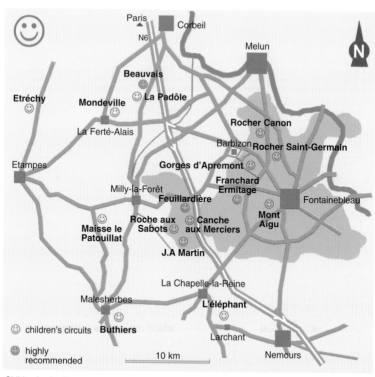

☺ children's circuits

☻ highly recommended

10 km

Children's circuits.

CLIMBING ... CHILD'S PLAY

If you agree with the fundamental reasoning that a child can climb before he can walk, then surely climbing is child's play.

The preconceived idea that climbing and danger go hand in hand has long been given the lie. Over the last two decades, climbing has grown into an organised activity in the towns and its popularity amongst young children and adolescents continues to grow. The values of personal freedom, freedom of choice, self-regulation of risk and a return to nature are particularly fashionable today.

Children are not only good at climbing but are wanting to do so in ever greater numbers. Fontainebleau is no exception to the rule, which is why the white circuits for children, not to be confused with the white top grade circuits, have been created.

The idea of these circuits, a cause championed by the FSGT which got on its high horse over the issue, was based on the premise of encouraging more children to climb in a safe environment. Safety of course is relative and must be looked at in conjunction with the other aspects of climbing, principally those of self-evaluation of risk and greater safety in using a spotter.

So there are about twenty marked children's circuits in the forest, which are easy enough for even the first time climber to use. Every spring these circuits attract classes for beginners, school outings and school holiday groups.

Rock boots are not essential, but it is important to stress that the sandstone is easily damaged by the rubbing of sandy shoes and you do not get the same feel for the rock as you do in rock boots.

Perhaps more than anywhere else in the forest, the white trails have been methodically thought out, often by experienced educationalists. Basically, the main stumbling block is the distance between the holds which nature has dispersed in a somewhat random matter. To progress to a higher grade, yellow, even blue or red depending on the colour coded gradings, could prove to be a problem, mainly because when the circuits were created, it never occurred to anyone that children might hurt themselves bouldering. So they will have to wait a while, and grow a little, to make the most of the joys of climbing at Fontainebleau.

On the "plus" side when considering morphology and age, is the fact that slab climbing is easier for those of a small, slight build, giving them the opportunity to broaden their repertoire of techniques which will be useful to them when they grow up.

La Feuillardière.

Beauvais-Rocher du Duc east
white children's circuit

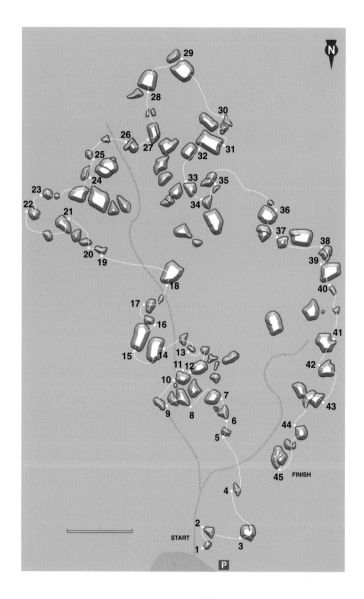

This is a children's climbing area in every sense of the word because this is the part of the forest to which it is most popular to bring school children for their first taste of climbing.

For that reason this trail is both technical and rewarding, with much longer problems than are to be found on other children's circuits.

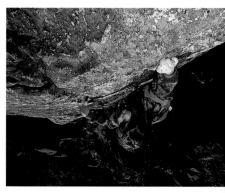

WHITE CHILDREN'S CIRCUIT

route	difficulty	name
1	☺	Le petit riquiqui
2	☺☺	La surprise cachée
3	☺☺	Le gros mif
4	☺	La montagne blanche
5	☺	Le phoque
6	☺	La tête du lion
7	☺☺	La grotte de l'ogre
8	☺	La queue de la langouste
9	☺	Le petit fado
10	☺☺☺	Le petit difficile
11	☺	Le rocher des bébés
12	☺☺	Le chat perché
13	☺☺	Le bébé clown
14	☺☺☺	Le gugus
15	☺	La maman clown
16	☺	L'oiseau de Beauvais
17	☺	La pierre de cristal
18	☺	La queue du long cou
19	☺☺	Le diamant
20	☺☺	La boule de neige
21	☺☺	La galipette supérieure
22	☺☺	L'éléphant
23	☺☺	La pieuvre

route	difficulty	name
24	☺	L'hippopotame
25	☺☺☺	Le gros dur
26	☺☺	Le petit cochon
27	☺☺☺	Le dinosaure
28	☺	Le toboggan de New York
29	☺	La baleine bleue
30	☺☺☺	Les gros muscles
31	☺☺	Le livre de la jungle
32	☺	La tortue ninja
33	☺☺	Le dragon
34	☺	La cascade
35	☺	La bouche ouverte de la grenouille
36	☺☺☺	Le gros pépère
37	☺☺	La chouette
38	☺☺☺	Le poisson d'avril
39	☺	Le chévrefeuille
40	☺☺	L'escalier
41	☺☺	Le pélican
42	☺	Le zéro prise
43	☺	Le sanglier
44	☺☺	La rampette
45	☺☺☺	Les deux amphores

Beauvais-Rocher du Duc east
blue circuit

BLUE CIRCUIT

route	boulder	grade	name
1	45	3a	La chaufferette
1b	45	4a	
2	42	3c	Ventre dur
3	42	4b	Le pt'it coin
4	37	3c	La motte de beurre
5	34	3c	La prise en compte
6	33	3a	Le bœuf sous le toit
7	29	3a	L'hypothénuse
8	38	4b	La fissure close
9	40	3a	Les pieds dans la semoule
10	32	3a	L'incertitude
11	31	3c	L'appuie-tête
12	31	4b	L'éclopé
13	38	3c	Le poussif nocif
14	22	4b	Pour Olympe
15	22	5a	Agoraphobie
16	19	4b	Les gros bras
17	19	4b	Le pendule des Avaux
18	17	3c	La toile de cinoche
19	16	4a	Objectif grâce
20	15	4a	La pierre de l'édifice
21	15	3c	L'évidence
22	13	4a	L'écailleux
23	10	4c	Comme un singe en rut
24	10	3c	Les dégâts limités
25	11	3b	La dalle de la Carrière
26	12	3c	Le quartier de citron
27	24	4c	Errare humanum est
28	8	4b	Perseverare diabolicum
29	6	4b	Le pin bonsai
30	5	4a	La traversée des cieux
31	2	4a	Le plat garni
32	1	4a	New deal
33	3	4c	Du rouge pour les bleus
34	4	4a	Le long fleuve tranquille
35	25	4a	La bidouille
36	26	4a	Le bloc de poche
37	27	2c	Le trait d'union
38	28	4b	Le complexifié
39	40	3c	La dulf' du vieux cimetière
40	41	4b	Des bogues plein les pognes
41	49	4a	Lacoïonnade
42	50	3b	La frousse bleue
43	52	4a	Le grattounet
44	53	4a	Tête de colombe
45	55	3c	Bouleau chagrin
46	56	4b	Aller simple
47	57	4a	Pas d'affolement pour miss Vibram
48	58	4b	Au gré du grès
49	59	4a	Le bon choix
50	47	4a	Voici le temps du monde fini

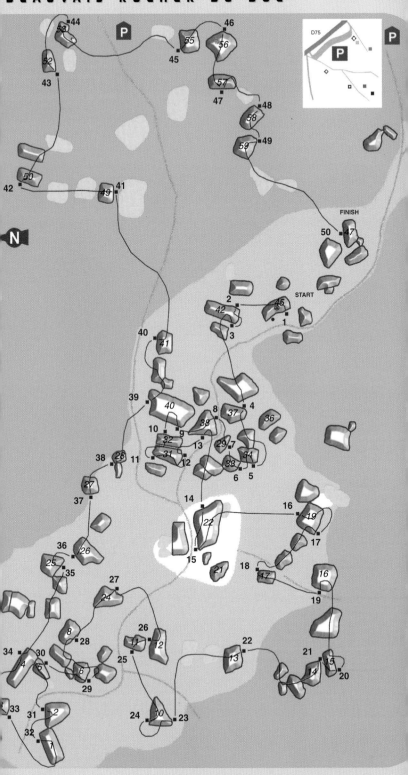

Beauvais-Rocher du Duc east

red circuit

black and white circuit

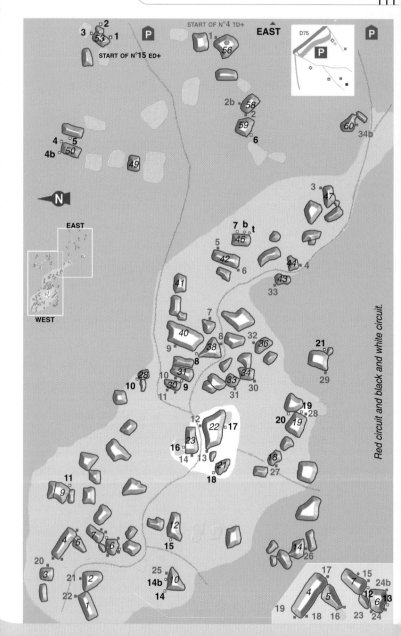

Clarity of light in the forest.

RED CIRCUIT

route	boulder	grade	name	route	boulder	grade	name
1	56	5b	La traversée du désir	22	1	5b	La kaléidoscope
2	58	5c	Le coq six	23	6	6a	La traversée du bonsai
2b	58	5c	Le sot poudrage	24	6	5c	Syndrome albatros
3	47	5b	Un bien beau superlatif	24b	6	6a	Manu : tension
4	44	5c	Soleil cherche futur	25	10	5a	La rogaton
5	42	5b	L'amoch'doigt	26	14	6a	D.o.s 6
6	42	5a	L'has been	27	18	5b	Le folklo
7	39	6a	Blatte runner	28	19	5c	Le biodégradable
8	38	5b	Foot bloc	29	35	5b	L'appel du bistrot
9	40	5a	La rimaye	30	34	6a	L'ouvre-boîte
10	31	5b	L'oubli	31	33	5c	Néanderthal roc
11	30	5c	Le confit de canard	32	36	5b	La dure mère
12	22	5b	Caresses amères	33	43	5c	Roc autopsie
13	22	5c	Art pariétal	34	61	5b	La traversée des filles
14	23	5c	Le bœuf carotte	34b	60	5c	La traversée des garçons
15	7	5b	En bref	35	66	6a	Le coup de boule
16	5	5c	L'étrave	36	67	5c	Mauvais sang
17	4	5c	L'étambot	37	68	5b	Sans l'arrêt
18	4	5b	Les chaires mobiles	38	65	5b	Le trou des garçons
19	4	5b	Trompe la mort	39	65	5b	Le trésor public
20	3	5a	J'ai fantaisie	39b	63	6a	La tripack
21	2	5b	Le distingo	40	65	5b	Tu ne voleras point

Beauvais-Rocher du Duc east

red circuit

black and white circuit |||

The characteristic feature of the black and white circuit is undoubtedly the predominance of traverse problems. The small size of the boulders has forced the climbers to literally scale down their climbing so it takes a more horizontal direction, although there are also some longer routes such as the superb *Etrave à sucre*. If you find the grade too difficult, try the red circuit which is just as enjoyable, but a little less demanding.

Steely climbing under a steel blue sky.

BLACK AND WHITE CIRCUIT

route	boulder	grade	name
1	53	7a	L'éloge de la différence
2	53	6c	le mouton noir
3	53	6a	Sang d'encre
4	50	6c	Coup de blues
4b	50	7b	L'étrave à sucre
5	51	6c+	Le grain de beauté
6	59	6a	Bagdad café
7	46	7a+	Mathilde
7b	46	7b	Je broie du noir
7t	46	7b	Le sectaire
8	38	7a+	Le nègre en chemise
9	31	7a	La mouche
10	28	7a	Le black out
11	9	6b	Les abysses
12	7	6b	Le petit ramoneur
13	6	6c	Les ongles en deuil
14	10	6c	Le cliché N&B
14b	10	7b+	La gueule du loup
15	12	6c	La magie noire du derviche
16	23	6b	M&M's
17	22	7a	L'anthracite
18	21	6b	Le brou de noir (statique)
19	19	6b	L'onyx
20	20	6b	La limonite
21	35	6b	La dame noire
22	62	6c	Le cambouis du diéseliste
23	64	6a	L'Amoco
24	71	7a	L'œuvre au noir
24b	72	7c	Le dahlia noir
24t	73	7a	La ballade du champion
25	74	6b	La veuve du fossoyeur
26	70	6a	Le mâle blanchi
27	65	6a	Le café crème
28	65	6b	Le capuccino
29	66	6c	Le crawl en mer noire
30	67	6b	L'ébène
30b	67	6c	La perle de jais
30t	67	7a	Danse macabre

Red circuit and black and white circuit.

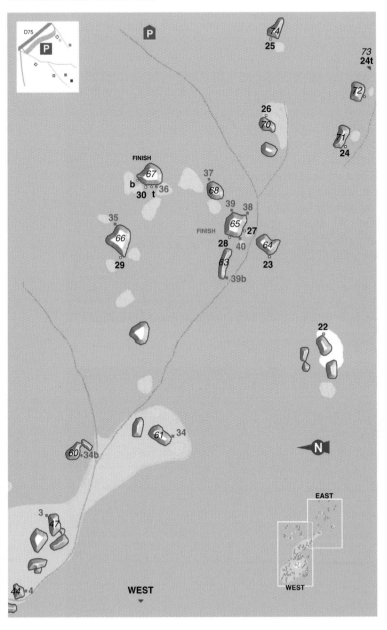

Beauvais-Rocher du Duc west
yellow circuit

Gently does it on the Canon at area 95.2.

route	grade
1	1c
2	2a
3	2b
4	2c
5	2c
6	2c
7	1c
8	2a
9	2b
10	2a
11	2a
12	2c
13	2c
14	2b
15	2a
16	2a
17	2c
18	2b
19	2a
20	2b
21	2a
22	2b
23	2b
2 variations 1c	
24	2b
25	2c
26	2a
27	2a
28	2a
29	2b
30	2b
variation 2c	
31	2c
32	2b
33	2a
34	2a
35	2b
36	2c
37	1c
38	2b
variation 2c	
39	2c
40	2a

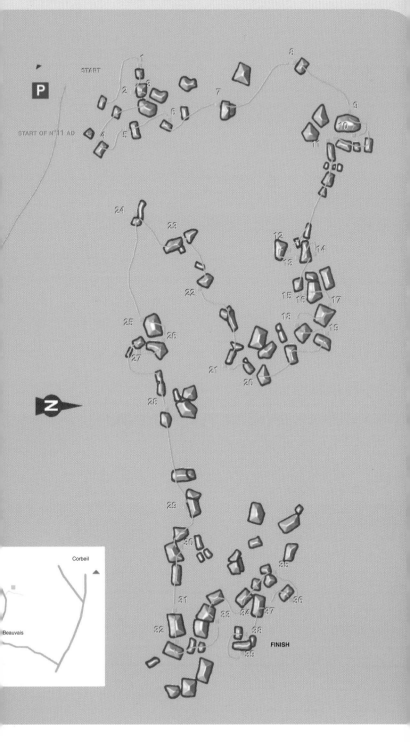

LA PADOLE

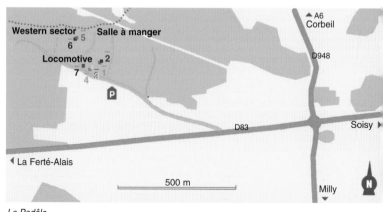

La Padôle.

Hymn to nature on Le mur à Jacques.

La Padôle

CIRCUITS

Yellow PD n°3 ❏
Orange AD n°4 ❏
Blue D n°6 ❏
Blue D+ n°2 ❏
Red TD n°5 ❏
Red TD+ n°1 ❏
Black ED+ n°7 ❏

Selected problems:

Locomotive and Salle à manger sectors

Who would imagine finding rocks such as these in the middle of the countryside and in such a lovely setting. So luxuriant is the vegetation, that in springtime it would be easy to imagine yourself in the tropics, rather than at Fontainebleau. To the rocks, whose height and feel leave a feeling of surprise and delight.

The commitment needed here is bordering on exposure on many of the routes of all grades. The grain of the sandstone here is the finest and the roughest in the forest and leaves you with the impression that your fingers are sticking to the rock. This area is quiet and generally little used, in fact around some of the boulders it appears that nature is taking over again. You have to come here to climb now and again to sample the delights of an area where the demands of the climbing blends perfectly with the atmosphere of the place.

La Padôle

selected problems |||

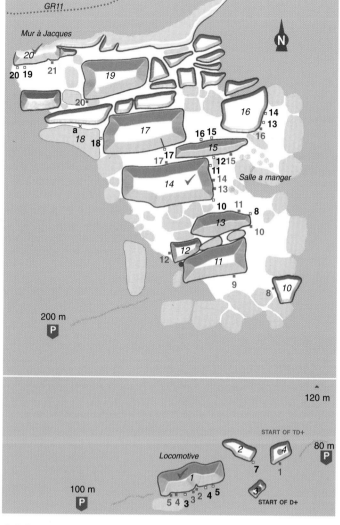

Salle à manger and Locomotive sectors.

LA PADOLE

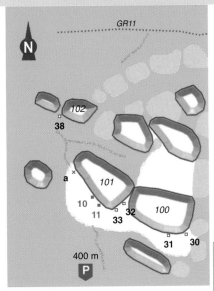

Western sector.

Tropical cameo at La Padôle.

SELECTED PROBLEMS

boulder	route	circuit	grade	name
1	2	●	5a	Le cheminot
1	3	●	4c	Les bavures jaunes
1	4	●	5c	
1	5	●	5b	Fissure de Tender
1	3	●	6b	TGV
1	5	●	7b	Carte orange
1	4	●	7a	La vie du rail
2	7	●	6b	Odeur de vestaire
10	8	●	5c	
11	9	●	5c	
12	12	●	4c	La nord ouest du sandwich
13	8	●	6a	Anti takat
13	10	●	6a	La gitane
13	11	●	4c	Mur de son
14	10	●	6b	Les aventuriers
14	13	●	5b	Salle à manger
14	14	●	5b	L'écho muet
14	11	●	6c	La dernière croisade
14	17	●	5c	Service compris
15	12	●	7a+	
15	15	●	6b	Sabbah
15	15	●	6c	L'ami bernard
15	16	●	6c	Bagdad café
16	16	●	5b	Enfin heureux
16	13	●	6b	La cache
17	18	●	7a+/7b	Tyama arachi *7b start at the bottom*
17	17	●	6a	Tien Anmen
18	a	✗	6b/7a	Tani otochi *7a start at the bottom*
19	20	●	5c	L'expo
20	21	●	5b	Le mur à Jacques
20	19	●	6a	Tombé du ciel
20	20	●	6b	Alertez les bébés
100	31	●	6b	Kalimantan
101	a	✗	7c+	Fin de journée *Traverse finishing on black 32*
101	11	●	4c	Paroles
101	33	●	6b+	Kango
101	32	●	7a	Délice choc
102	38	●	6b	Le petit écolier

The magic of nature, these aeroliths are a mystery.

La Dame Jouanne

CIRCUITS

Yellow PD	❑
Mauve AD+	● (grey)
Orange AD	❑
Blue D-	❑
Red TD-	❑
White ED	○
Black ED+	●

Jumps

One of the favourite games that our glorious forefathers liked to play was that of jumping from one boulder to another. The SAMU did not exist then. Amongst the most impressive are several at the Dame Jouanne area of the forest and the most incredible of all is that which consists of jumping from the plateau on to the Dame Jouanne boulder.
Fashions change … today jumping is out, climbers prefer to protect their backs.

Twelve metres!!! That is the height of the tallest boulder at Fontainebleau. Curiously enough, when the first tourists came here at the beginning of the last century, they made derisory comments about the small size of this rocky peak when compared to those of the Alps. If they could see how popular these rocks are now, no doubt they would be very surprised. This area is principally known for its famous mauve circuit which gives a thousand metres of up and down climbing. Many well known Parisian alpinists prepared for their alpine season here, on this very long and generally exposed circuit.

The fashion today is less for the linking of problems than for boulder to boulder climbing, and there are a large number of circuits threading their way amongst this huge jumble of boulders. Knowing where you are is sometimes difficult but the views are so wonderful that it is worth coming here for this alone.

Cocteau's grave at Milly.

La Dame Jouanne

mauve circuit

MAUVE CIRCUIT

route	grade	name
1	2b	Le réta du pof
2	3b	Le mur à Jules
3	3c	La traversée du fada
4	4b	La mine aux demis
5	3a	La cheminée du gruyère du requin
6	3b	Le génevrier
7	2b	Le rocher bouffé aux mites
8	3b	La traversée du temple
9	3c	La traversée du rocher rond
10	3a	L'accès au Simplon
11	3b	Le rateau de chèvre
12	3c	La fissure à Tom
13	3a	La traversée verte
14	3c	L'angle des J3
15	2b	La takouba
16	4a	Le réta vicelard
17	3a	La traversée du jardin
18	3b	La fissure à pipi
19	2b	La boite aux lettres
20	4a	La tubulaire
21	3b	La voie cassée
22	3c	Les assiettes
23	3b	La paroi aux trois grottes
24	3b	La pesée
25	4a	Le dièdre baveux
26	4b	La patinoire
27	3b	Le coude désossé
28	3c	Le n°1 de la dalle aux pigeons
29	3c	La muraille de Chine
30	3c	La muraille de Chine (suite)
31	4a	Les grattons du french cancan
32	3b	La voie des lacs
33	3b	La voie qui mérite un numéro
34	3b	Les trous de gauche de la Caroline
35	3b	La forêt vierge
36	2b	Les grattons des petits enfants
37	3c	Les maquereaux au vin blanc
38	4b	L'envolée du tank

route	grade	name
39	2c	La fissure des dames
40	3a	Le mur de la gitane
41	3a	Les oreilles de cocu
42	2b	Le rocher du Gaulois
43	3b	Le mur des préliminaires
44	4a	La fissure Souverain
45	4a	L'angle sud-ouest de la calanquaise
46	3a	La balançoire
47	3c	La goulotte de la rampe
48	3c	Les tripes à Géo
49	3a	La face sud de l'hippopotame
50	2b	
51	3b	La tour de Pise
52	3c	L'arête de Larchant
53	3c	La voie du cheval
54	2b	Le rocher de la dalle aux Mathieux
55	3a	Le rocher du tremblement de terre
56	3a	L'empruntée
57	3c	La fissure sud de l'ours
58	3a	L'arête nord-ouest de l'ours
59	4a	Le face-à-main
60	3c	La dalle Brégeault
61	3c	Le rateau de bouc
62	3c	La fausse glissière
63	3b	Le parapluie
64	3b	Le cache Baba
65	3c	Le Baba coulant
66	3b	La dalle du radio circus
67	3b	La traversée du Rigoulot
68	3b	La dalle de feu
69	3b	Le rocher du jeune marié
70	3a	Le pas de Barbe-bleue
71	3c	La traversée du petzouille
72	3c	Le pas de la chaise électrique
73	4b	La traversée à Mimiche
74	3c	La face nord du petit minet
75	3b	L'arête de la petite noire
76	3c	La traversée du tourniquet

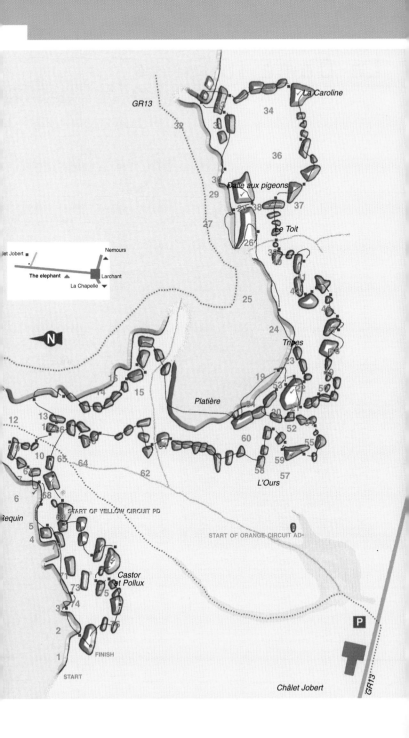

GR13

La Caroline

34

36

Dalle aux pigeons

29

30

38

37

Le Toit

27

26

25

24

Tripes

23

19

Platière

20

52

60

55

59

58

57

L'Ours

62

15

14

18

16

13

12

11

10

65

64

68

START OF YELLOW CIRCUIT PD

START OF ORANGE CIRCUIT AD

Requin

5

4

6

69

Castor
et Pollux

73

74

3

76

2

1

FINISH

START

P

Châlet Jobert

GR13

The elephant

Jet Jobert

Nemours

Larchant

La Chapelle

N

La Dame Jouanne

black circuit

white circuit

WHITE CIRCUIT

route	grade	name
1	6b	Le pied là
2	6a	Le grand noir
3	6b	Le toit du koala
4	6c	Culbutor
5	5b	La dalle verte
6	6b	Le trou normand
7	6a	Le trou de secours
8	6b	Extractor
9	5c	La rampe
10	5c	La gouttière
11	6a	L'ours blanc
12	6b	Le tendu
13	6c	Le trou de l'Anord
14	6b	Spélman
15	6c	Le dernier empereur
16	5c	Sans l'angle
17	5b	L'angle mort
18	6a	Le Pontet bas
19	6b	L'expo supo
20	6b	Le bras carré
21	6c	Prédator
22	6a	Le pied-main
23	7a+	L'angle parfait
24	5c	Les p'tits plats
25	6a	La tranchante
26	6c	Anse Lazio
27	6a	Les grottes de Kocamador
28	6a	L'écaille cassée
29	6b	Le surbac plomb
30	6a	Tetehamor
31	6b	La crampe à Rachid

A dance on rock at sunset.

BLACK CIRCUIT AND OFF-CIRCUIT

route	grade	name		route	grade	name
a	6b+	Vertibloc		k	7b	Dévertige
b	6b+	Moselle		m	8a+	Hibernatus
c	7a+	Baladium		n	7a+	Strechin
d	7b+	Scolopendre		o	6c	Arrêt sur image
e	7a+	Monumendalle		p	7a+	La grenouillère
f	7b+	Etoile		s	7b+	L'angle plus que parfait
g	7b+	Nuage		t	7a+	Chair et cuir
h	7b+	Le plafond		u	8b	Unforgiven
i	7a+	Murmur				
j	7a+	Anti G				

Black circuit ED+ : marked throughout with a capital letter

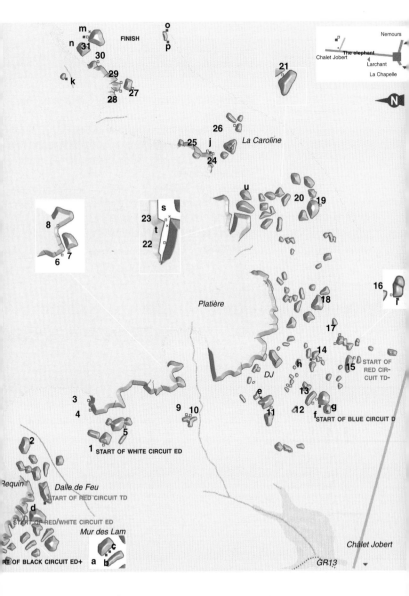

m
x
n 31
FINISH
30
29
k
28 27

o
p

21

26
25 j
La Caroline
24

u
20 19

23 s
t
22

8
7
6

16
f

Platière

18

17

14
h
15 START OF RED CIR-CUIT TD-

3
4
DJ
e
13
9 10
11 12 g
f START OF BLUE CIRCUIT D

1 START OF WHITE CIRCUIT ED

2

Requin
Dalle de Feu
START OF RED CIRCUIT TD
d
START OF RED/WHITE CIRCUIT ED
Mur des Lam
c
RT OF BLACK CIRCUIT ED+ a b

Châlet Jobert
GR13

Nemours
The elephant
Chalet Jobert
Larchant
La Chapelle

N

Maunoury

This area is very quiet because of its proximity to its neighbour, Dame Jeanne.

So you will find peace and quiet on all these circuits, the problems on which are generously supplied with holds. The routes are less bold than at Dame Jeanne, although they are still of a good length.

A footnote: it was here that Bernard Giraudeau started climbing together with two of the greatest alpinists of the last century, Lucien Bérardini and Robert Paragot, who are the area's most fervent supporters and who were the originators of many of the problems.

Maunoury

blue circuit

BLUE CIRCUIT

route	grade	name	route	grade	name
1	3c	Le bilboquet	16	4a	La traversée du nid
2	3b		17	4b	La traversée de la grande Monique
3	4c	La vire à bicyclette	18	3c	Le château fort
4	3b	Le miroir aux alouettes	19	2b	La pâtissière
5	4c	Le super toboggan	20	3b	La descente de la loco
6	3c	L'arête ronde	21	4a	La dalle du clodo
7	4b	Le surplomb du boxeur	22	3c	La petite fresque
8	3a	Les fesses	23	4b	La traversée du camembert
9	4a	Le surplomb du cuveton	24	3c	Le petit !
10	4a	La gifle	25	3c	La fissure du bec
11	4b	Le surplomb du prélude	26	4b	Le surplomb des tétons
12	3c	L'arête du triangle	27	3a	La cheminée du rouge-gorge
13	4b	La boîte	28	4a	La face est du motard
14	3a	La dalle des paras	29	4a	La traversée de Rigoulot
15	4a	Le rocher de Sacha	30	4b	La petit z

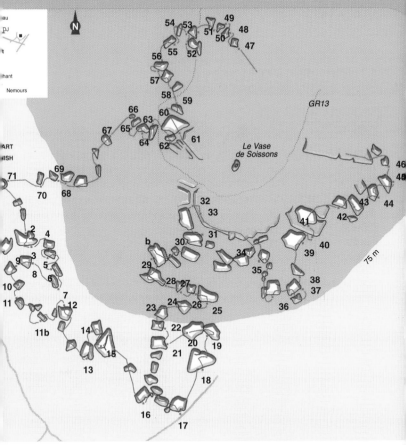

route	grade	name		route	grade	name
31	3c	Le surplomb du porte-manteau		52	3c	Le spoutnik 2
32	4b	La traversée du vieux marin		53	3c	Le trou du souffleur
33	4a	Le pas de géant		54	3b	Le jeton
34	4b	Le dévers		55	4b	Le mètre pliant
35	3c	La traversée du calbar		56	3b	Le piano à queue
36	3b	Le réta du trésor		57	5b	Les orgues
37	3c	Le contour du pilastre		58	3c	La brique réfractaire
38	3b	La petite plaque de marbre		59	3b	La glissière à Toto
39	3c	La paire de bretelles		60	3b	L'aérolithe
40	4b	La fissure des signes rupestres		61	3a	Le coupe-gorge
41	2c	L'embrasse-moi		62	3a	Le surplomb de la dégonflée
42	4a	Le mur blanc		63	3a	La poignée de métro
43	3b	Les planqués		64	3c	Le surplomb de Fakstind
44	4b	Le pot de moutarde		65	3c	L'étrave
45	3b	La tour de l'Orient		66	4a	L'échelle de coupée
46	4a	La tour Denecourt		67	3b	La traversée des pattes de tortue
47	3b	La sauce verte		68	4a	Le bec de gaz
48	3c	La sauce blanche		69	3b	L'arête du poivrot
49	3b	Le menhir		70	3a	Le marchepied de l'autobus
50	3b	Le collier du dogue		71	3c	La voie de la fin
51	4b	Les spoutniks				

The elephant

Who would expect to find what is without doubt the most famous boulder in the forest, after its near neighbour Dame Jouanne, in the middle of the countryside. Under the rocks there is the wonderfully fine sand to walk on, which is one of the forests most valuable attributes. Paradoxically, the climbing is quite bold. Firstly, the boulders are quite high and secondly and more importantly, the ground underneath some of the routes is littered surprisingly with roots and small

boulders. This is not the case for the famous Elephant boulder, which is covered on every side with routes of all grades. The holds are usually very good, which is why the boulders are particularly popular in springtime and even in summer when the heat makes climbing on crimps and edges impossible. Nature has given strange shapes to some of the rocks which take on a fantastic appearance in the of the setting sun. Many circuits were created at the Elephant area. Many of the painted markers are gradually disappearing and moss is taking over on some of the boulders. Here boulder to boulder climbing has become popular, which is why we have listed some problems in the form of a topo list and not in circuits. The only thing which all the problems have in common, is their length. Note that a rock to stand on or two crash mats on top of each other are necessary for the dyno start on Partenaire Particulier.

The elephant

selected problems

SELECTED PROBLEMS

boulder	route	circuit	grade	name
1	1	●	3c	*Traverse under the roof, blue finish, 6a*
1	1	●	6a	
1	1b	●	4a	
1	1	●	4b	
1	2	●	5c	L'y
2	3	●	6a	La chute du moral
3	4	●	5c	
3	3	●	4a	
4	a	✗	7c	Coup de lune
4	5	●	5c	
5	a	✗	7b+	Vache folle
5	b	✗	7c+	Egarement
5	6	●	5c	
5	7	●	5c	
5	7b	●	5b	
6	a	✗	7a	La figure de proue
6	b	✗	6c	Le piler Droyer
6	8	●	5c	Le mur de la mort *Very exposed*
7	a	✗	5b	*D>G (R>L) traverse*
8	a	✗	7a	
10	17	●	4c	L'aigle déployé
10	12	●	6b	La directe de l'aigle *Bold*
11	15	●	4c	
11	10	●	6b	Le lancer
12	18	●	5a	
12	11	●	5c	L'appui
12	13	●	6a	
12	14	●	6c	
13	23	●	4c	Départ du bloc
13	31	●	6b	Le toît du loup
13	a	✗	7a	Traversée des dieux *D>G (R>L) traverse*
13	32	●	6c+	Voie du flirt
13	33	●	4b	
13	24	●	5c	
14	a	✗	7b	Haut de gamme
14	33	●	6c+	Le pilier légendaire
15	a	✗	8a+	Partenaire particulier
21	a	✗	7b+	Monsieur plus *G>D (L>R) traverse*

boulder	route	circuit	grade	name
21	23	●	6a	
21	24	●	6a	
21	26	●	5b	
22	22	●	6c	
22	26	●	4c	
23	24	●	3b	
23	22	●	3c	
23	19	●	6b	Fissure du trio
23	18	●	5b	Le trou du trio
23	29	●	5a	
24	17	●	6b	Les quatre cents buts
24	30	●	5b	
24	16	●	5b	Le médaillon
25	a	✗	7a	Le lépreux *G>D (L>R) traverse*
25	b	✗	7a	
25	20	●	6a	
26	26	●	6c+	Le bouton
26	42	●	4c	
26	25	●	5b	
27	a	✗	7b+	Etat d'urgence *Roped*
27	b	✗	6c	Protection rapprochée *Sandy*
28	27	●	5c	
28	46	●	5a	
29	25	●	3c	
30	35	●	5b	
32	36	●	7a	Le cœur
33	a	✗	7c	Envie d'ailes
33	b	✗	7b+	Envie d'air *Traverse*
33	37	●	5b	
34	38	●	6b	
35	39	●	6c	
36	40	●	5c	Dalle à Poly
36	40b	●	4c	Dalle à Poly
36	a	✗	6b	Dalle à Poly
A	a	✗	7a	Le bout du monde *D>G (R>L) traverse*
A	b	✗	7b	Le bout du monde *G>D (L>R) traverse*
A	a, b	✗	7c	Le bout du monde *Two traverses linked*

AROUND LARCHANT

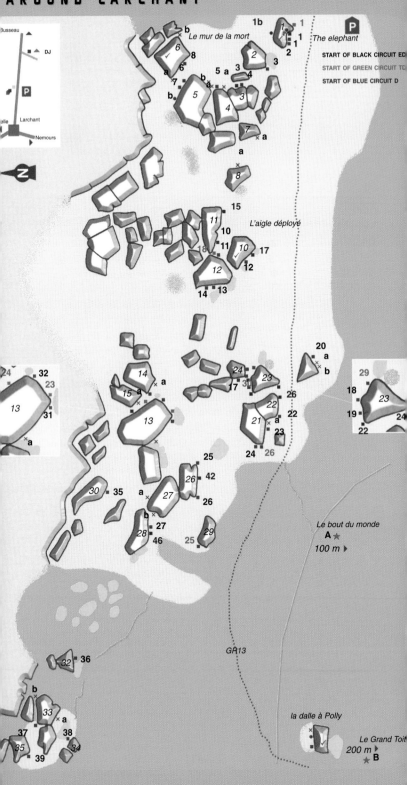

Le mur de la mort

The elephant

START OF BLACK CIRCUIT ED

START OF GREEN CIRCUIT TD

START OF BLUE CIRCUIT D

L'aigle déployé

Le bout du monde
A ★
100 m ▶

GR13

la dalle à Polly

Le Grand Toit
200 m ▶
★ B

Busseau

DJ

P

Larchant

Nemours

Petit bois

CIRCUITS

Yellow PD+/AD-	❏
Blue D	●
Red TD+	❏
Black ED+	●

Close to the centre of Nemours, Petit Bois is well named. It is, in fact, a small wooded area, situated beside a residential zone and very close to the town hall. Before the advent of the circuits which today are the pride of their creator, not many climbers made the foray to this southern limit of the Fontainebleau forest. However over the last three years it has become much more popular. The wide range of problems which you will encounter on the four circuits has probably got something to do with this. But even discounting the charm of the place it is possible to climb here even in high summer. Not far away, the Rocher Gréau has some fine challenges, mostly very hard with a commitment bordering on boldness. A little further away still, the Fosse aux Loups provides a different type of bouldering, not unlike British gritstone.

Bernard Théret on a hidden traverse.

WORDS FROM THE LOCAL EXPERT

Climbing areas don't appear out of the ground as if by magic. How the Petit Bois area became a new place to climb, although it had always existed, is a revealing example.

A meeting with Bernard Théret, creator of some two hundred and fifty routes at Petit Bois, makes us aware of some of the essential qualities necessary for a person prepared to take on such a task: passion and a willingness to work for love and not money. And underlying everything, curiosity: "While out on my trials bike behind my house, I discovered the Petit Bois. Attracted by the lines, I contacted the town hall to find out who owned it." It was communal land. Then, it was a lot of painstaking work: "Three years of brushing, clearing and all kinds of exploration followed. Three years during which every route became an integral part of a circuit in my mind before they materialised on the ground in the form of small painted arrows. I wanted to give other climbers something of what was left; and the two hundred and fifty bouldering problems are a present."

A physical effort as well: " I used I don't know how many wire brushes to clean all the holds. It was striving for purity that kept me going; every square centimetre of moss might hide some treasure ..."

Finally, the moment came to tell others about it: "When, in '97, I told the community about the first blue circuit, I felt a sense of achievement but also an immense regret. It was finished. I must now look elsewhere. It's true, that the ultimate reward is that of giving pleasure to the climbers who come to Petit Bois today and above all, the fact that they keep coming back."

What's next?

"The story will continue elsewhere, in another part of the forest which I am going to scour, in the hope that I will find something else in the same vein. Don't ask me why, I simply know how I am going to do it, but not yet exactly where."

And thus it has been since climbers first set their hands on Fontainebleau sandstone.

No, a climbing area definitely does not appear out of the ground as if by magic.

Petit bois

blue circuit

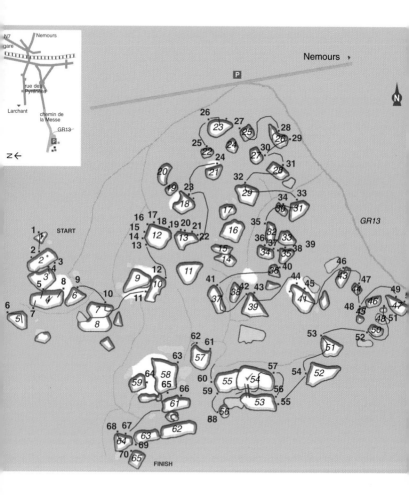

La Baleine (the Whale), one of the most striking boulders in the forest.

BLUE CIRCUIT

route	boulder	grade	name	route	boulder	grade	name
1	1	4b	Carapace	35	32	4b	Muraille
2	2	4a	Nid d'abeilles	36	34	4a	Le rouge est miss
2b	2	4b	Nid d'oiseaux	37	34	4b	Du rail
3	2	4b	Rêve d'Eiger	38	35	4b	Chercheur d'or
4	3	4a	La vague	39	35	4a	Sur le fil
5	4	4a	Face nord	40	36	4a	Que dalle
6	5	4a	Sans les mains	41	37	4a	Le buffet
7	4	4a	Toute confiance	42	39	4b	P'chy cause
8	4	4b	Silence	43	39	4b	Le roncier
9	6	4b	Haut les pieds	44	41	4b	Le rempart
10	7	4b	Hésitation	44b	41	4a	Ramping
11	10	5a	Rondeurs ennemies	45	41	4a	Don jon
12	10	4b	Emotions	46	43	4a	Contre bras
13	12	4a	Petites formes	47	44	4a	Le plan incliné
14	12	4a	Plat du jour	48	45	4b	Pain de sucre
15	12	4a	Rando bleu	49	47	4b	Le gruyère
16	12	4a	Etroiture	50	47	4b	Sans comté
17	12	4b	Dans les nuages	51	48	4a	Angle roc
18	12	4b	Angle gauche	52	50	4a	Dans l'ombre
19	13	4b	La bonne taille	53	51	4c	Squat
20	13	4a	Pour les mains	54	52	4b	Convexasse
21	13	4b	Blocage	55	53	4c	L'aboréta
21b	13	4a	Des blocages	56	53	4b	Fuillangle
22	13	4a	Dérapage	57	54	4c	Bruit de couloir
23	18	4b	Ténéré	58	56	4b	L'excentré
23b	18	4b	Super Ténéré	59	55	4a	Le muret
24	21	4b	Le réveil matin	60	55	4c	L'élinante
25	22	4b	En trave	61	57	4b	La dérive
26	23	4b	L'hélicol	62	57	4a	Compression
26b	23	4a	Le super frelon	63	58	4b	Le merisier
27	25	4a	L'acrobate	64	59	4a	Gratangle
28	26	4b	Bil Boquet	65	58	4a	Près des anges
29	26	4b	Boule Boquet	66	61	4b	Extorsion
30	27	4b	Action plus	67	64	4b	Déroutage
31	28	4b	Belle à faire	68	64	4a	Le penchant
32	29	4a	Le guépier	69	63	4a	Le fond de grès
33	31	4a	L'allonge	70	65	4a	L'arrêt qu'on pense
34	30	4a	Achille t'as long				

Petit bois

black circuit |||

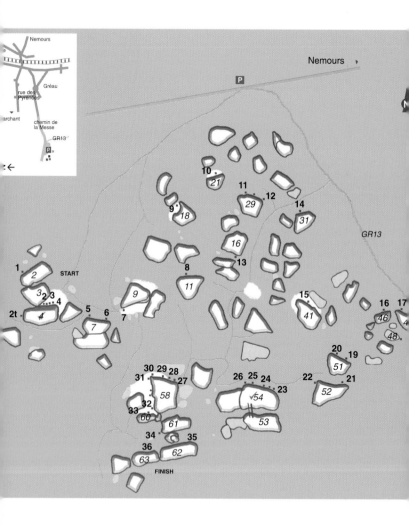

On the characteristic sandstone of Fosse aux Loups, one of the incomparable areas.

BLACK CIRCUIT

route	boulder	grade	name
1	2	5b	Préchauffe
2	4	6c	La balade de Jim
2b	4	7a+	T comme Tarzan *Exposé*
2t	4	6c	L'œuf
3	4	7a+	Passage à l'acte *Exposé*
4	4	6c	Big Jim *Engagé*
5	7	6b+	Le dolmen
6	7	6b+	Rataplazip
7	9	7a	La baleine
8	11	6b	Le triangle d'or
9	18	6a	Remise à l'heure
10	21	6a	Big Ben
11	29	6b	Le casse-tibia
11b	29	7c	Morte plaine
12	29	6a+	Les petits vérins
13	16	6b	Parapente
14	31	6b	Le GR bloc
15	41	6b+	Les douves
16	46	6a	Big bloc
17	47	6c	Bidoigts pour monocéphal
17b	47	7b	Convulsions
18	48	6a	L'escalier

route	boulder	grade	name
19	51	6b+	L'ange mobile
20	51	6b+	Le doigt carré
21	52	7a	Rebord retord
22	52	7a	La prise clef
23	54	6a+	L'Emoréta
24	54	6b	Ligne de force
24b	54	7a+	Pro-pulse
25	54	6b	Sur prises
26	54	6b	Le plat pays
27	58	6c	Vacances à Bombay
27b	58	6c	Conduite rapide
28	58	6a+	Elongation
29	58	6c	Machine à jambon
30	58	6b+	L'angle rotulien
31	58	6b+	La cruxi friction
31b	58	7c	Le mur du son
32	58	6b	Le beau quartier
32b	58	7a	L'arc Angel
33	60	6b	La vengeance des triceps
34	61	6a	Des pieds, des mains
35	62	6c	Vive les vacances
35b	62	7b	Travaux forcés
36	63	6b	Le chat de gouttière

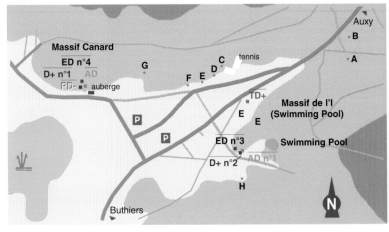

Buthiers.

Christophe Laumône, great pioneer of lost boulders.

Buthiers, Malesherbes

CIRCUITS

CANARD SECTOR

Yellow PD-	❏
Orange AD	❏
Blue D+	❏
Black ED	❏

SWIMMING POOL SECTOR

White children's circuit (2 circuits)	❏
Orange AD-	❏
Blue D+	●
Red TD+	❏
White ED	●
Off-circuit	✗
Off-site	★

Malesherbes is the southernmost climbing area. Its success is doubtless due in large part to the building of a leisure centre in the heart of the bouldering area, so saving it from privatisation in the seventies. There was climbing here before, but the fact that climbing is now available to thousands of youngsters has led to every avenue being explored.

We must not forget that it is thanks to the passion of two climbers, instructors at the centre, that the first traverses were created here in this open air laboratory. You will also find here relics from the time when aid climbing was in vogue in the fifties; and numerous pitons are still to be found in some boulders.

Today, climbing at Buthiers is still very varied, with both traverses and boulder problems which are true markers of their grade, and some of them are even collectors items. Exposure is ever-present.

Partage (Sharing), a name which is very meaningful on this amazing boulder.

Buthiers, Malesherbes
blue circuit

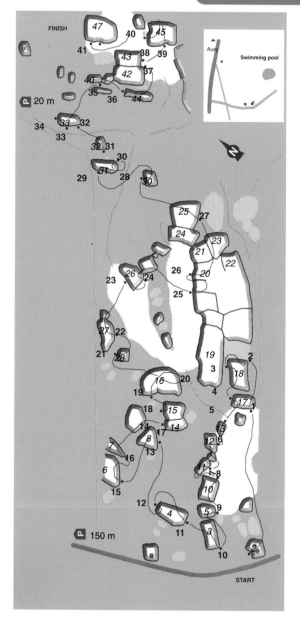

BLUE CIRCUIT

route	boulder	grade	name	route	boulder	grade	name
0	2	4b	Départ	22	27	4b	L'enjambée
1	17	4a	La jambe en l'air	23	26	4c	Le général direct
2	18	4b	La rampe de l'escalier vert	24	26	3c	Les grattons du général
3	18	4b	La vire à Bibi	25	20	4c	La fissure du sherpa
4	17	4c	La lime à ongle	26	20	4b	Le dé rance
5	13	4c	L'as tactique	27	25	4b	La bien planquée
6	12	4c	Le petit Cervin	28	30	3c	La vite fait
7	11	4b	L'onglier	29	31	4c	La Descheneaux
8	10	4c	La dalle de marbre	30	31	4b	L'envers de la Descheneaux
9	5	4c	Le jeté tentant	31	32	3a	L'histoire de
10	3	4a	L'angle du grincheux	32	38	4c	Le surplomb des poings
11	4	4c	L'andouille de vire	33	38	3b	Les poings à gauche
12	4	4c	Le quadriceps gauche	34	38	4b	La fissure des poings
13	8	4a	Les doigts sous le pied	35	40	4b	Le plaisir des dames
14	8	4b	La dalle du pin	36	44	3a	Le plaisir à personne
15	6	4c	Le jazz	37	42	4a	Le minaret
16	7	3c	La java	38	43	3c	Les trous du gruyère
17	14	4a	Le quadriceps droit	39	45	5a	La fissure de l'I
18	15	4a	Les pieds à plat	40	45	5a	La fissure verte
19	16	4a	Les doigts coincés	41	47	4c	La mine à Rey
20	16	4a	Les mains à plat	42	47	4c	La fissure Brutus
21	28	3c	Les baquets				

Buthiers, Malesherbes

black circuit

This circuit was created by Alain Michaud, who was the precursor of the very hard routes at the end of the seventies. He did several exceptional new routes here which are still technical and physical references for the highest grades in climbing today.

BLACK CIRCUIT

route	boulder	grade	name	route	boulder	grade	name
1	1	6a	L'envers des fesses	20	43	6c	La voie Mercier
2	3	5b	Le pare brise	21	47	5c	La super angle Brutus
3	10	6a	Surplomb de marbre	22	47	6a	La Brutus
4	10	6b	Le grand angle	23	50	6b	La traversée du culot
4b	10	5c	La jojo	24	51	5c	La dynamostatique
5	12	5c	La directe du petit Cervin	25	55	6a	L'étrave
6	19	5c	Le marchepied	26	53	5c	L'angle de la fresque
7	16	6a	Les supers grattons	27	53	6c	La super fresque
8	16	6a	Les grattons	28	54	6b	L'ultra son
9	21	6a	Les pédales	29	56	5c	La coupe rose
10	24	6b	L'orléanaise directe	30	57	6c	Le surplomb taillé du pique nique
11	22	5c	La piscine	31	58	5c	La dalle Poulenard
12	31	5c	La Descheneaux	32	58	5c	Le surplomb de l'Usi
13	31	5c	L'envers de la Descheneaux	33	60	5b	La sup direct des Minets
14	34	6a	La voie lactée	34	60	5b	Le directissime des Minets
15	36	6b	L'excuse	35	60	6a	Le charleston
16	37	6c	Le Cource doigt	36	60	6b	Le swing medium
17	42	5c	Le perlinpimpin	37	62	6b	Rêve de singe
18	44	5c	La Yano	38	63	5c	L'allumeuse
19	45	6b	La duchesse	39	64	5c	La réfractaire directe

Catherine Miquel on the extreme Halloween.

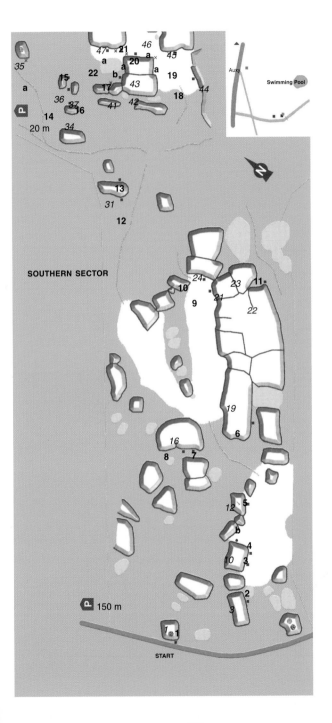

SOUTHERN SECTOR

START

Solitude on the boulders of Boigneville.

Buthiers, Malesherbes
off-circuit and off-site

OFF-SITE

route	grade	name
A	7c	Magic Bus
B1	7a	Attention chef d'œuvre
B2	8a	Partage
C	7c	Flagrand désir
D	8a	Coccinelle *G>D (L>R) traverse*
E	7a	Les monos
F	7b+	La mygale *G>D (L>R) traverse*
G	7c+	Halloween
H	8b	Atomic playboy *G>D (L>R) traverse*

OFF-CIRCUIT

boulder	route	grade	name
35	a	7b	Traversée D>G
43	a	7b	Master edge
43	b	8a	Misanthropie
45	a	7c	Furyo
47	a	7b+	L'âge de pierre *Roped*
52	a	7a+	Lady big claques
60	a	7c	Strappal

Total exposure

Risk taking is an inherent part of bouldering. As soon as you leave the ground, it takes on various guises from insignificant to, in most cases, "you must not fall". At Puiselet, where two circuits and many unmarked routes were created in the beginning of the eighties, this dimension often borders on maximum risk. It is enough to say that the area is no longer popular and that nature has once again taken over covering the boulders with lichen. It is possible that this trend, linked principally to the fashions of the day, is not irreversible. Which is why you should not come here without your brush and a strong head. Even with the development of crash mats, there is a serious feeling about the place.

Some areas where boldness more usually equates to exposure :

Le rocher Gréau ; La Padôle ; Les Gros Sablons ; La Dame Jeanne ; La Roche aux Oiseaux.

64
38
63
65
39
62
37
61
ARRIVÉE
36
a
60
33
35 34

**NORTHERN
SECTOR**

31   32
58
30
57

56
29

P 20 m

27 28
26   55
53 54
25

52
a
50
24
23

47   45
b
22 20 a
a 19
21 43 a 18

Practical Information

Note: When making a telephone call to France from abroad, dial 00 33 and then the French number without the first 0 (zero) in the Paris area code 01.

HOW TO GET HERE ?

• By car
It is normally the quickest way. The maps in this guide will help you to find the different areas without difficulty.

If you are coming from Paris, remember that the rush hours are between 7am and 9am in the morning and late afternoon to early evening.

There are car-parks beside the climbing areas but avoid leaving anything in your car, unfortunately there are thieves about.

• By train
It is possible, but you will have to do some walking. All the train timetables are available on the Internet (www.sncf.fr), on the telephone (01 53 90 20 20) or on Minitel (3615 SNCFIDF).

Many trains from Paris-Gare de Lyon stop (in less than an hour) at the stations from which it is easiest to reach the climbing areas.

From Bois-le-Roi station
You can walk to Rocher Canon (2.5km), Rocher Saint-Germain (4.5km) or Cuvier (5km) ...

From Fontainebleau station
You can get to the Rochers du Calvaire (2km uphill), Mont Aigu (5km) ...

To be original (many Japanese tourists do it): you can hire a bike at the station (01 64 22 36 14), a mountain bike costs 120 francs a day for a mountain bike, negotiate for longer periods. Arm yourself with a good IGN map (TOP25 n° 2417) and lots of spirit and take

the small forest roads and tracks to Rochers d'Apremont or Cuvier. Allow about an hour. You can also hire a mountain bike in the centre of Fontainebleau, at La Petite Reine, 32 rue des Sablons (01 60 74 57 57).

From Malesherbes station
You can get to Buthiers, only 2km down the road.

WHERE TO SLEEP ?

There are not many campsites in the area. One of the most useful is the one at La Musardière near the Trois Pignons (see Milly-la-Forêt) as is the one at Samoreau (see Fontainebleau).

Hotels on the other hand are very numerous. We list a few of the fairly inexpensive ones. The price given is a rough guide.

You could also rent somewhere (gîte) or stay in a bed and breakfast (about 250 french francs for two people). We list the ones nearest to the climbing areas but you can buy the guide to gîtes and bed and breakfasts from the Maison des Gîtes de France, 59 rue Saint Lazare, 75439 Paris Cedex 09 (01 49 70 75 75). You can rent a gîte in the Seine et Marne region directly through the Internet site: www.tourisme77.net.

Advance booking is advised as the region is very popular with tourists.

The main forest has several serviced 'bivouac' areas (there is running water but no sanitation) which are run by the Office National des Forêts: they are free but you can only stay a maximum of two nights. You are advised to contact the nearest Maison Forestière to enquire about availability, the one at Cuvier in particular is packed on certain weekends.

• Fontainebleau
(Tourist office: 01 60 74 99 99). Hôtel Richelieu (4 rue Richelieu, 01 64 22 26 46), double room from 320 french francs.

Hôtel Ibis (18 rue Ferrare, 01 64 23 45 25), double room from 385 french francs.

The nearest campsite is in the village of Samoreau (follow signs for Montereau/Provins): municipal campsite open from 15 March to 30 October (11 rue de l'Eglise, 01 64 23 98 91).

Two bivouac sites are available. The first is situated near the Hippodrome de la Solle: take the N6 out of Fontainebleau towards Melun, after about 3km turn left towards the Hippodrome and after 500m you will see the bivouac site on your left. There is another one near Bourron-Marlotte: take the N7 and follow signs for this village, at the Croix de Saint-Hérem turn left towards Thomery then take the first road on the right to the Maison Forestière de la Grande Vallée (01 64 45 96 46).

• Bois-le-Roi
Hôtel Le Pavillon Royal (40 avenue de Général-Gallieni, 01 64 10 41 00), rooms from 295 french francs (swimming pool).

There is a serviced bivouac site on the edge of Bois-le-Roi near the D138, in the direction of Samoreau, route des Larmières.

• Barbizon and surrounding area
(Tourist Office 01 60 66 41 87). Hôtel L'Auberge des Alouettes (4 rue Antoine Barye, 77630 Barbizon, 01 60 66 41 98): rooms from 270 french francs.

Hôtel Campanile (346 rue Capit, 77190 Dammarie Les Lys, 01 64 37 51 51): rooms from 295 french francs.

Bed and Breakfast: M. et Mme Bourdin (23 rue de la Mairie, 77930 Cély en Bière (01 64 38 05 96).

Gîte: Saint-Fargeau Ponthierry (01 60 39 60 39), 2 people.

There is a bivouac site near Cuvier (500 metres): it is just beside the Maison Forestière at Bas Bréau, on the N7. There is room for 20 people, but no sanitation (running water supplied). You are advised to telephone (01 64 37 29 96) to check availability. Crossing the N7 near the village of Barbizon (centre 1 km) is dangerous, be careful.

• Milly-la-Forêt and surrounding area (Tourist Office 01 64 98 83 17). Hotel Au colombier (26 avenue de Ganay, 01 64 98 80 74), rooms from 145 french francs.

Gites
— Noisy-sur-Ecole (28 rue d'Aubers, 77123, 01 64 24 54 67): the Gîte des Trois Pignons has 4 bedrooms, kitchen and sitting room for 75 french francs per person.
— Moigny-sur-Ecole (01 64 97 23 81), sleeps 7.
— Le Vaudoué (01 60 39 60 39) sleeps 3.

Bed and Breakfasts
— M. Desforges (route de Gironville, Ferme de la Grande Rouge, 91490 Milly-la-Forêt, 01 64 98 94 21)
— M. Lenoir (9, rue du Souvenir, 91490 Moigny-sur-Ecole, 01 64 98 47 84)
— M. Roulon (10, sentier de la Grille, 91490 Moigny-sur-Ecole, 01 64 98 49 97).
— Mme Brouard (23, rue d'Auvers, 77123 Noisy-sur-Ecole, 01 64 24 79 12).
— Anne et Patrick Pochon (9, rue des Saules, Marianval, 77760 Boissy-aux-Cailles, 01 64 24 57 69.

The campsite at Musardière (Route des Grandes Vallées, 91490 Milly-la-Forêt, 01 64 98 91 91) is 1.5 km from the car-park at the Croix Saint-Jérome (access from here to

area 95.2). It costs 30 french francs per person, 17 francs per car and 15 francs per tent. It is advisable to book for Easter and the month of May.

•Larchant and surrounding area (Nemours)
Chalet Jobert (Route de Larchant at Busseau, 91 64 28 16 23): a few hundred metres from the famous Dame Jeanne climbing area, this hotel-restaurant has been frequented by climbers for several decades! There are a few simple rooms for 130 french francs (often booked by regulars) and they are used to feeding climbers. In summer, you can sit outside under the trees, in winter climbers gather around the fire, surrounded by photographs of the alpinists and rock climbers who used to come here.

There are several hotels at Nemours (Tourist Office 01 64 28 03 95), some of them are very good value and are near the exit from the A6 motorway: Formula 1 (ZA d'Ecuelles, place des Moines, 01 64 29 17 64), Mister Bed (route des Moines, 01 64 78 06 32).

There are various gîtes to let in the villages around Nemours and in Larchant itself. They are all managed by the Gîtes de France central reservations service (01 60 39 60 39).

• Malesherbes and surrounding area
Hôtel L'Ecu de France (10, place du Martroy, 02 38 34 87 25) : rooms from 140 to 350 french francs.

Bed and Breakfasts
— Anne et Patrick Pochon (9, rue des Saules, Marianval, 77760 Boissy-aux-Cailles, 01 64 24 57 69).
— Laurent et Nadine Stelmack (Mainbervilliers, 77760 Boissy aux Cailles, 01 64 24 56 77).

Gîtes
There are several gîtes in this very rural area, contact the central reservations service (01 60 39 60 39).

RESTAURANTS, SHOPPING

The area is very popular with tourists, there are many restaurants, for all budgets and all tastes.

You will generally find a grocer and a baker in the villages; chemists in all the towns (and some villages, Barbizon, Chailly-en-Bière, Le Vaudoué …) . The shops are open on a Sunday in Barbizon.

There is a big commercial centre 5 km from Cuvier (centre commercial Carrefour, Villiers-en-Bière, RN7, from Chailly-en-Bière towards Paris): Décathlon shop (rock boots, chalk …), restaurants, the shops are closed on a Sunday.

The mobile workshop SOS Escalade is in the Roche aux Sabots car-park at the weekend (Noisy-sur-Ecole – cemetery): repairs rock boots, sells topos, hardware, crash mats (01 48 53 38 77), http://www.sosescalade.fr

The crash mats "TRIPLE PAD" designed by Jo Montchaussée are available in Barbizon: 32, rue Gabriel-Séailles, 01 60 66 47 78, http://members.aol.com/innovbbz

In Paris there are two specialist climbing shops: Au Vieux Campeur (48, rue des Ecoles, 75005 Paris, 01 43 29 12 32) and Passe Montagne (95-102, avenue Denfert-Rochereau, 75014 Paris, 01 43 22 24 24).

RAINY DAYS, REST DAYS

You could perhaps still climb … on an artificial structure (all situated near Paris):

— Mur Mur, 55, rue Cartier-Bresson, 93500 Pantin (01 48 46 11 00).
— Antrebloc, 5, rue Henri-Barbusse, 94800 Villejuif (01 47 26 52 44).
— Centre Européen d'Escalade, 3, rue des Alouettes, zone Sénia, 94320 Thiais (01 46 86 38 44).

And for those very hot days and simply rest days, there are two leisure centres in the area (often packed in summer):

– Base de loisirs de Bois-le-Roi (on the banks of the Seine, access direction Fontaine-le-Port, 01 64 81 33 00) : beach, windsurfing, climbing wall …
– Base de loisirs de Buthiers, in the heart of the climbing area (01 64 24 12 87) : very good swimming pool in the middle of the boulders, climbing wall …

You will also find cinemas and swimming pools (good for a shower after a night's bivouac) at Fontainebleau, Milly-la-Forêt, Nemours…

There are lots of walking and mountain biking trails in the forest (see the guides in the bibliography).

But if you have hopes of something a little more cultural and you are wondering who the Bartizon artists are, go and visit the museum in the Auberge Ganne. There is a good slide show which outlines the story behind the artists (92, rue Grande, 01 60 66 22 27).

Les châteaux of Fontainebleau (01 60 71 50 70) and of Vaux-le-Vicomte, near Melun (01 64 14 41 90) are a must (1000 candles are lit in the château of Vaux-le-Vicomte every Saturday evening from May to mid-October). The village of Moret-sur-Loing is worth a visit (he inspired the impressionist painter, Sisley).

1 km from Milly-la-Forêt (rue Pasteur, then signposted, 01 64 98 83 17), the Swiss sculptor Jean Tinguely put 20 years and 300 tons of steel into creating Cyclops: the head is of some considerable size (22 metres, climbing it would not be a good idea!) and there is a labyrinthe inside.

TELEPHONE NUMBERS AND USEFUL ADRESSES

In the event of an accident :
– Sapeurs pompiers (fire service): 18 (be very precise as to the location of the incident: area, which car-park, nearest road or crossroads …)
– Police-Gendarmerie : 17.
– SAMU (medical emergency) : 15.

– Office national des forêts (ONF) : 217 bis, rue Grande, 77300 Fontainebleau, 01 60 74 93 50.
– Comité de défense des sites et rochers d'escalade (CO-SI-ROC) : Bâtiment 510, Centre universitaire, 91405 Orsay Cedex, http://www.lps.u-psud.fr/cosiroc
– Fédération française de la montagne et de l'escalade (FFME) : 8-10, quai de la Marne, 75019 Paris, 01 40 18 75 50, http://www.ffme.fr
– Club alpin français (Ile de France) : 24, avenue de Laumière, 75019 Paris, 01 42 02 24 18, http://members.aol.com/cafactiv/escalade/bleau.html
– Météo (Seine et Marne) : 08 36 68 02 77.
– Météo (Essonne) : 08 36 68 02 91.
– Association des amis de la forêt de Fontainebleau (AAFF), 26, rue de la Cloche, BP 14, 77301 Fontainebleau Cedex, 01 64 23 46 45.
– Fédération sportive et gymnique du travail (FSGT), 14-16, rue Scandicci, 93508 Pantin Cedex, 01 49 42 23 19.
– Groupe universitaire de montagne et de ski (GUMS), 53, rue du Moulin-Vert, 75014 Paris, 01 45 43 48 37.

BIBLIOGRAPHY

• Climbing guides
Escalade à Fontainebleau, tome 1 : « Les Trois Pignons », CO-SI-ROC, 1998. Trois autres tomes à paraître.

• Walking and mountain biking guides
Guide des sentiers de promenade, édité par l'AAFF.
La forêt de Fontainebleau, 33 itinéraires de découvertes, ONF, éditions Ouest France.
Guide VTT Evasion Forêt de Fontainebleau, IGN.

• General reading
Bleau, la forêt de Fontainebleau et ses rochers, Sylvain Jouty, éditions ACLA, 1982, épuisé, réédition prévue.

• On the Web
Cotations, Bleau de 7 à 8 :
http://www.multimania.com/bleauelu.
Photos : http://www.multimania.com/jomontch.

PHOTO CREDITS

Jacky Godoffe : pages 9,10, 11, 12, 13, 17 lower, 18, 20, 21, 23, 25, 27, 30, 33, 44, 54, 56, 59, 61, 65, 67, 70, 71, 73, 74-75, 77, 78, 79, 81, 83, 85, 87, 90, 91, 93, 95, 97, 99, 103 lower, 105, 115, 119, 121, 122, 123, 127, 129, 133, 134, 135, 137, 138, 141, 149, 160, 163, 166, 169 right, 171, 173, 175, 176, 179, 181, 182, 185, 186, 187, 188, 189, 190, 191, 193, 194, 201 right, 203, 205, 207, 209, 210, 211, 213, 215, 217, 219 right, 222-223, 226, 229, 231, 232, 233, 235, 236. Jo Montchaussé : pages 17 top, 34, 39, 41, 43, 47, 49, 51, 88, 89, 114, 117, 143, 153, 169 left, 183, 198, 201 left, 219 left. Françoise Montchaussé : pages 103 top, 151. Aurore Godoffe : pages 106, 107.

GENERAL LISTS

B	bleu / blue
Bc	bleu ciel / sky blue
Bf	bleu foncé / dark blue
Bal	bleu baltique / baltic blue
Ou	bleu outremer / ultramarine blue
Bl	blanc / white
N	noir / black
N/Bl	noir et blanc / black and white
R	rouge / red
R/Bl	rouge et blanc / red and white
J	jaune / yellow
O	orange
S	saumon / salmon
Fr	fraise écrasée / crushed strawberry
OC	off-circuit
OS	off-site

This is a directory of the areas where the boulders have been numbered.
The lists are classified by boulder number. With the map of a given area and the appropriate list, the reader can find any desired reference.

Bas Cuvier

page 19

boulder	route	circuit	grade	name	boulder	route	circuit	grade	name	boulder	route	circuit	grade	name
1	1	R	5c	L'envers du un	23	5	OC	5c	La genouillère	40	4b	Bl	7b	L'angle incarné
1	1	Bl	6c	La Lili	23	5	B	4a	Pilier	40	5	Bl	7a	La boucherie
1	2	R	5c	La goulotte sans la goulotte	23	6	B	4c	Le coq	40	9	B	4c	Le tuyau Morin
1	2	B	4c		23	7	B	4c	Le coq droite	40	10	B	4c	La solitaire
1	3	B	5a	Le surplomb N.O.	23	13	O	2a	La fissure sud du coq	40	13	B	5a	Le surplomb du réveil matin
1	7	O	3b	La voie de l'arbre	23	14	O	2a	La traversée de la crête du coq	40	28	O	3a	La rigole ouest de la solitude
1	a	OC	7b	Croix de fer	24	10	R	5b	La bijou	40	a	OC	7c	Infidèle
2	3	R	5c	Le trou du tondu	24	15	B	4a	L'inexistante	40	b	OC	7c	Hypothèse
2	8	O	2b	La dalle du tondu	25	3	Bl	6a	Le dernier jeu	40	c	OC	7c+	Antithèse
3	9	O	3b	L'envers du J	25	3b	Bl	6b	La Ravensbruck	40	d	OC	7a	Araignée
6	10	O	3b	L'oreille cassée	25	24	O	4a	Le tire bras	40	e	OC	7a	Le picon bière
7	2	Bl	6a	L'emporte pièce	26	8	B	4a	La poule	40	f	OC	8b	Mouvement perpétuel *Girdle traverse D>G (R>L)*
7	2b	Bl	7c	L'aérodynamite	26	25	O	3a	Le mur aux fênes	41	6	Bl	6c	La défroquée
7	4	R	6a	Le trou du Simon	26	a	OC	7c	Photo sensible *D>G (R>L) traverse*	41	9	R	6c+	La daubé
7	11	O	2b	La dalle de l'élan	27	6	R	5c	La gugusse	41	14	B	4c	Fissure Morin
8	a	OC	7a	Platinium	27	7	R	5c	Les frites	41	a	OC	7a	Cortomaltèse
9	a	OC	7a	La tonsure	27	8	R	5b	La vire Authenac	44	6b	Bl	7a	L'abattoir
10	1	B	5a	La sans les mains	31	27	O	3a	Le petit surplomb	44	6t	Bl	7b+	Le carnage
10	6	O	2b	La sans les mains	33	a1	OC	8b	Encore *Obsession + Biceps dur*	44	6q	Bl	7c	L'abbé Résina
10	a	OC	7b	Fluide magéntique	33	a2	OC	7c+	Obsession *G>D (L>R) traverse*	44	a	OC	6c+	Coton tige
15	17	O	2c	La deux temps	33	b	OC	7b	Pince mi	44	b	OC	7c/7c+	Balance *Depends on the technique used*
16	17	B	4c	Le K	33	c	OC	7b+	Vers Nulle part	44	c	OC	7a	Hélicoptère
16	17b	B	5b	Le faux K	33	d	OC	7b+	Vers Claire *7c sitting start*	44	d	OC	7c+	Apothéose
16	a	OC	7c	Plats toniques	33	e	OC	7b	Biceps mou	45	11	B	4c	Les grattons Morin
17	16	O	3a	La tenaille	33	f	OC	7c+	Biceps dur *D>G (R>L) traverse*	45	12	B	4c	La dalle du réveil matin
18	15	O	2c	La proue	33	g	OC	7a	Holey Moley	45	30	O	2c	La fissure des enfants
20	4	B	5c	Fissure Authenac	34	a	OC	7c	La Gaulle *Sitting start*	45	a	OC	7a	
20	a	OC	7a+	Le mur du feu *Stand on stone to start*	40	4	Bl	6c	La charcuterie	48	29	O	2b	La delta
20	b	OC	6c+							51	31	O	2a	La grenouille
21	26	O	2a	Le « trois »										
22	12	O	2b	La petite côtelette										

I

boulder	route	circuit	grade	name
54	a	OC	6c	Béatrice
54	b	OC	6b	Sanguine
54	c	OC	7c+	Raideur digeste
60	20	O	2a	La fissure est de la gamelle
61	21	O	2c	La traversée du bock
62	11	R	5c	Le ligament gauche
62	16	B	5a	Faux ligament
63	3b	B	4c	La demi dalle
65	22	O	2c	La petit angle
67	23	O	2c	Le muret
70	19	O	2b	La dalle du pape
71	7	Bl	6b	La résistante
71	8	Bl	6c	La forge
71	25	B	5a	Le dernier des six
71	36	R	6a	Le soufflet
71	a	OC	7a	La bouiffe
73	9	Bl	6b	La folle
73	9b	Bl	6b	L'enclume
73	9t	Bl	7a	La rhume folle
73	23	B	5b	Le coup
73	a	OC	7a+	Fruits de la passion
74	24	B	5a	La nouvelle
74	35	R	5b	Les esgourdes
74	37	R	5c	Le coup de rouge
74	a	OC	8a	Digitale
75	18	O	2a	La voie bidon
76	10	Bl	7a	La vie d'ange
76	10b	Bl	6b	La dix tractions
76	18	B	5b	Le fantôme
76	39	R	5c	La clavicule
76	41	R	5c	L'ectoplasme
76	a	OC	7b	Kilo de beurre G>D (L>R) traverse
76	b	OC	7c	L'angle
77	11	Bl	6c+	La clé
77	22	B	5b	La fissure
77	38	R	5c	La bicolore
77	a	OC	7a	la clé de droite
77	b	OC	7a+	Casse tête
80	5	O	2c	Le onzième trou
80	a	OC	7b	Technogratt'
81	4	O	3a	Le second rétab
82	3	O	3a	L'envers des trois
82	a	OC	7c	L'aconqueàdoigt
83	2	O	2c	La fissure de l'auto
84	42	R	6a	La fauchée
84	a	OC	7b	Dalle siamoise Righthand variation
85	21	B	4c	Le vide ordure
85	40	R	5b	L'orientale
85	a	OC	7b+	Banlieue nord G>D (L>R) traverse
86	1	O	2b	Le petit rétab
87	11b	Bl	6c	La tour de Pise
87	19	B	4c	La dalle de la rouge
87	20	B	5b	La Borniol
87	a	OC	7b	Tour de pise directe
90	15	Bl	6b	La stalingrad
90	16	Bl	6c	La chalumeuse
90	17	Bl	7b+	La super Prestat
90	27	B	5b	Le quartier d'orange
90	32	R	5c	La dalle du baquet
90	44	B	5a	La nationale
90	48	B	4c	La Paillon directe
90	50	O	3c	La Prestat Finish
90	a	OC	7c	L'ange gardien
90	b	OC	6c	L'angle
91	30	R	6a	La Couppel
91	31	R	6a	Les grattons du bàquet
91	47	B	5b	Le baquet normal
92	28	R	5c	Le Nasser
92	29	R	5b	Le réveil matin
92	45	B	4c	La fissure de la lionne
92	46	B	5a	Les grattons du réveil-matin
92	49	O	2c	L'envers du réveil matin
93	33	R	5c	La dalle au chocolat
94	34	R	5c	La côtelette
95	23	R	5b	La bizuth
95	26	R	5c	L'huitre
95	a	OC	7c+	L'idiot
96	13	Bl	7a	La joker
96	14	Bl	6c	Le 4ème angle
96	22	R	6a	La Marie Rose Bleau's first 6a
96	24	R	5c	La troisième arête
96	40	B	5b	
96	42	B	5b	La face nord
96	43	B	4c	Le bidule
96	a	OC	7b	Cornemuse
96	b	OC	7c	Le joueur
97	25	R	5c	L'angle rond
97	41	R	5b	L'Innominata
100	0	O	2a	La fissure de la place du Cuvier Start
100	12	Bl	6c	La chicorée
100	21	R	6a	La nescafé
100	a	OC	6b+	La Marco
101	18	R	5c	La parallèle
101	19	R	5c	La Leininger
101	20	R	6a	La Suzanne
101	38	B	5c	Le jus d'orange
101	39	B	5a	La Porthos
101	a	OC	8a	Golden feet
101	b	OC	7c+	Lune de fiel
102	14	R	6b	Les bretelles
102	15	R	5b	L'Authenac
102	16	R	5b	La V1
102	17	R	5c	La traversée Authenac
102	34	O	4a	La jarretelle
102	37	B	5c	L'angle Authenac
102	a	OC	7a	La Cinzano
103	26	B	4b	L'angle olive
103	27	B	4c	La dalle olive
103	33	O	3a	La traversée de la dalle des flics
103	a	OC	7b	Alter mégot
104	29	B	4c	La dalle d'ardoise
104	35	O	2b	Le zéro sup
105	30	B	4c	Le 7 sup
105	36	O	2c	Le boulot
107	12	R	5b	La dalle au trou
107	13	R	5c	La voie de la vire
107	28	B	5a	Le baquet
107	32	O	3b	La dalle aux trous
107	a	OC	8a+	Coup de feel No longer possible, the crucial hold has broken
110	48	O	2c	L'envers de pascal
112	47	O	3c	Le petit mur
114	46	O	3b	La déviation
115	45	O	2c	La verte
121	44	O	2b	Les lichens
122	35	B	5a	Le surplomb du doigt
122	36	B	4c	Le dièdre du doigt
122	43	O	3c	La traversée du doigt
123	40	O	1c	Le coin du 5
123	42	O	2c	Les pinces
124	41	O	2b	Les lunettes
126	32	B	5b	La dalle au pernod
126	39	O	3c	La dalle du 106
127	33	B	5b	La dévisante
127	34	B	5c	Les tripes
127	38	O	3a	Les tripes
128	31	B	3b	La dalle au demi
128	37	O	2b	La dalle aux demis

Apremont Bisons

page 58

boulder	route	circuit	grade	name
1	1	O	3c	
2	1	R	4b	3b variation
2	2	O	3c	
3	3	R	4b	
3	3	O	3a	3b variation
4	2	R	5a	Dyno
4	2b	R	5b+	
4	4	O	4a	3c variation
4	5	O	2c	
5	4	R	4c	
5	6	O	3b	
6	7	O	3c	
6	7b	O	3a	
6	7t	O	4b	
7	8	O	2b	
7	9	O	3b	
8	5	R	4c	6a variation
8	10	O	4c	
8	10b	O	3c	
8	11	O	3c	
9	6	R	5a	
9	7	R	4a	
9	8	R	4a	
9	12	O	3b	
9	13	O	3a	
10	9	R	5a	
10	9b	R	5a	
10	10	R	4c	
10	14	O	2c	
10	14b	O	3c	
11	11	R	5b	
12	15	O	4c	
13	16	O	3a	
14	17	O	3a	
15	26	O	3a	
15	26b	O	3c	

boulder	route	circuit	grade	name
16	12	R	4c	
16	13	R	5a	G>D (L>R) traverse variation 6a
16	24	O	4b+	
16	24b	O	2c	
16	25	O	3a	
17	14	R	4c	
17	23	O	2c	
18	18	O	3c	
19	15	R	5c	
19	22	O	3b	
19	22b	O	3c	
20	21	O	3a	
21	19	O	4a	
22	20	O	4a	
23	17	R	4a	
24	18	R	5a	
24	18b	R	5c	
24	19	R	4b	
25	28	R	4c	
26	20	R	4a	
27	21	R	4b	5a variation
28	22	R	4b	
29	23	R	4a	
30	25	R	4c	
31	24	R	4a	
32	26	R	4c	
33	27	R	5b	
34	16	R	5c	
35	32	O	4b	4c variation
36	31	O	3c	
37	27	O	3c	
38	28	O	4c	
39	29	O	3a	
39	30	O	3c	
40	37b	R	4c	
40	48	O	3a	
41	33	O	4a	
41	37	R	3c	
42	36	R	4b	
43	36	O	3a	
44	35	O	3b	
45	34	O	4a	
46	29	R	4c	
47	37	O	3b	4a variation
48	43	O	2b	
49	32	R	4b	
49	42	O	4a	3c variation
49	44	O	3b	
50	31	R	4b	
51	30	R	6a	
51	33	R	4b	
51	40	O	3b	4b variation
51	41	O	2c	
52	38	O	3c	4a variation
52	39	O	2c	
53	45	O	3c	
54	34	R	3c	
54	46	O	4a	
55	35	R	5b	
55	47	O	3b	
56	38	R	5b	
56	38b	R	5b	
57	39	R	4a	4c variation
58	40	R	5b	
58	41	R	5a	
58	41b	R	5a	
59	42	R	5b	
60	43	R	5a	

Les Gorges d'Apremont

page 35

boulder	route	circuit	grade	name
				ZONE A
1	1	R/Bl	5c	Start
1	2	R/Bl	6a	
1	57	S	4c	
2	3	R/Bl	6a	
2	4	R/Bl	5c	
2	56	S	5a	
2	a	OC	7a+	
3	5	R/Bl	5c	
3	54	S	4a	
3	55	S	5b	
4	6	R/Bl	5b	
5	53	S	4a	
6	7	R/Bl	5b	
6	8	R/Bl	5c	
7	9	R/Bl	5c	
8	10	R/Bl	5c	
9	11	R/Bl	5c	
9	12	R/Bl	5b	
9	52	S	4a	
10	13	R/Bl	5c	
10	13b	R/Bl	5c	
11	15	R/Bl	5c	
12	14	R/Bl	5b	
13	17	R/Bl	5b	
13	51	S	4c	
13	a	OC	7a	Super Stalingrad
13	b	OC	7a	Tendance de droite
14	a	OC	7c+	Jolie Môme
15	18	R/Bl	5c	
15	19	R/Bl	5b	
16	16	R/Bl	5c	
19	a	OC	7a	Hiéroglyphe
20	a	OC	7c+	Jolie Môme
21	20	R/Bl	5b	
22	50	S	4a	
24	21	R/Bl	5c	
25	22	R/Bl	5c	
26	23	R/Bl	5b	
27	24	R/Bl	5c	
28	25	R/Bl	5c	
28	26	R/Bl	5b	
29	27	R/Bl	5b	
31	a	OC	7a	
32	28	R/Bl	5c	
33	29	R/Bl	5b	
33	30	R/Bl	5c	
34	31	R/Bl	5a	
34	32	R/Bl	5c	
35	33	R/Bl	5a	
37	34	R/Bl	5c	
38	40	R/Bl	5c	Finish
40	39	R/Bl	5a	
40	35	R/Bl	5c	
40	36	R/Bl	5c	
41	38	R/Bl	5b	
42	37	R/Bl	4c	
				ZONE B
1	1	Ou	4a	
2	2	Ou	3b	
3	3	Ou	4b	
3	4	Ou	3b	
4	5	Ou	3c	
5	6	Ou	4b	
6	7	Ou	4a	
7	8	Ou	3c	
8	73	S	4b	
9	9	Ou	3c	
9	74	S	4c	Finish
10	10	Ou	3c	
11	11	Ou	3c	
12	13	Ou	4c	
12	72	S	5a	
13	12	Ou	4b	
13	71	S	5a	
14	40	J	3a	
15	14	Ou	4b	
16	9	Bc	5b	La pavane
16	15	Ou	3c	
17	10	Bc	4c	Le sabre
17	11	Bc	4c	Le goupillon
17	17	Ou	3c	
18	12	Bc	6c	Le mur des lamentations
18	18	Ou	3c	
18	19	Ou	4a	
18	42	J	2c	Finish
19	41	J	2c	
19	a	OC	7a	Clin d'œil
20	22	Ou	4b	
21	16	Ou	4c	
21	23	Ou	3c	
21	69	S	4c	
21	70	S	4c	
21	a	OC	7c+	Koala Exposed
22	20	Ou	4a	
22	67	S	5a	
22	68	S	4c	
22	a	OC	6c	
22	b	OC	6c	
22	c	OC	6c	D>G (R>L) traverse 7a
22	d	OC	6b	
23	21	Ou	4c	
24	24	Ou	3c	
25	8	Bc	6a	L'empire des sens
25	25	Ou	4b	

boulder	route	circuit	grade	name	boulder	route	circuit	grade	name	boulder	route	circuit	grade	name
25	64	S	4c		12	10	J	2b		64	8	R	5b	Le triste portique
26	7	Bc	6a	Le gibbon	12	13	J	2b		64	15	S	5a	
26	26	Ou	4c		13	11	J	2b		65	20	Bc	4c	La lanterne
27	63	S	4b		14	12	J	2b		65	21	Bc	5b	Le pont Mirabeau
28	62	S	4b		15	14	J	2c		66	19	Bc	5a	La vessie
29	6	Bc	7a	Le toit tranquille	16	15	J	3b		67	9	R	5b	Le toboggan
30	60	S	4b		17	16	J	2a		67	10	R	5b	Le vieil os
30	61	S	5b		18	17	J	2c		67	16	S	4a	
31	a	OC	7b	Faux contact	19	18	J	2a		68	11	R	6a	Les yeux
32	27	Ou	3c		19	19	J	3a		69	12	R	5c	Le château de sable
33	28	Ou	4a		20	20	J	3c		70	17	S	5b	
33	66	S	5c		21	21	J	3a		70	22	Bc	5b	La super simca
34	4	Bc	4b	L'effet yau de poele	22	22	J	3a		71	13	R	5b	La durandal
34	5	Bc	4a	La bagatelle	23	5	R	5a	La traversée de la fosse aux ours	71	18	S	4c	
34	29	Ou	3c							72	14	R	5c	La rampe
35	4b	Bc	5c		24	23	J	2b		74	5	N/B	6c	L'ébréchée
35	4t	Bc	5c		25	24	J	2c		74	15	R	5c	Le marchepied
36	3	Bc	5a	L'anti gros	26	25	J	2a		74	23	Bc	6a	Ignès
37	30	Ou	3c		27	7	S	5a		75	18	R	5b	Le bonheur des dames
38	31	Ou	4a		27	26	J	2c						
38	65	S	5b		28	27	J	2c		76	16	R	5b	La longue marche
40	59	S	4c		28	28	J	2b		78	6	N/B	6c	La ténébrante
41	58	S	4a		29	6	S	4c		79	17	R	5c	Le bouleau
42	49	S	4c		30	29	J	2a		79	19	S	5a	
43	33	Ou	4b		31	30	J	3a		80	29b	R	5c	Les chiures
44	2	Bc	5c	L'esprit du continent	31	31	J	2c		80	31	R	5c	La que faire
44	2b	Bc	6c	Le poulpiquet	32	32	J	2c		81	20	S	6a	
44	32	Ou	4b		33	14	Bc	5c	L'ostétoscope	81	24	O	3b	
44	34	Ou	4b		33	33	J	2c		81	30	R	5b	La valse
45	35	Ou	4c		34	5	S	3c		82	25	O	3c	
46	36	Ou	4c		34	34	J	2c		82	28b	R	6a	Les fausses inversées
47	1	Bc	5c		34	a	OC	6b	*Traverse*	82	28	O	3b	*Finish*
47	37	Ou	3c		35	35	J	2c		82	29	R	5c	L'ancien
47	37b	Ou	4b		36	4	S	4a		83	24	Bc	5c	La salamandre
47	48	S	5c		36	36	J	2c		83	25	Bc	5c	La vie lente
47	a	OC	7b	Une idée en l'air	37	3	S	4a		83	27	R	5a	Le pilier
49	0	Bc	5c	Le croque mitaine	39	2	S	4a		83	28	R	6a	La conque
49	a	OC	7b+	Le marginal	40	13	Bc	5a	Le rince dalle	83	a	OC	7a+	Dalle d'Alain
50	38	Ou	4c		40	37	J	2c		84	27	O	3c	
51	39	Ou	3c		41	38	J	2c		84	a	OC	7a+	Futur antérieur
52	40	Ou	3b		41	a	OC	6c+	Egoïste *Sitting start 7a+*	85	19	R	5b	La freudienne
53	41	Ou	4b		42	1	S	5c	*Start*	86	26	Bc	5c	La muse hermétique
54	42	Ou	4a		42	39	J	2a		87	26	R	5b	La claque
55	43	Ou	4b		43	1b	Ou	5b		87	26	O	4c	
55	44	Ou	4a	*Finish*	50	2	R	5b	La sans l'arête	88	21	S	5a	
56	47	S	5c		50	3	R	5a	Les trois petits tours	89	24	R	6b	Les verrues
57	45	S	4a		50	4	R	6a	Le piano à queue	89	a	OC	7b	Coup de cœur
58	46	S	3c		51	1	R	5c	*Start*	90	25	R	5a	Le réta gras
59	44	S	5a		52	3	N/B	6b	La croix et la bannière	90	28	Bc	5b	Icare
60	43	S	5c		52	6	R	5c	Le trompe l'oeil	90	28b	Bc	5c	
61	42	S	4a		53	9	S	5c		92	20	R	5a	Le coin pipi
62	41	S	4b		54	10	S	4c		92	27	Bc	5c	L'angle obtus
63	40	S	4a		55	8	S	5a		93	22	S	5b	
64	38	S	4c		56	11	S	5b		94	7	N/B	6c	L'oeuf
64	39	S	4a		58	12	S	4a		94	21	R	5a	L'angulaire
65	37	S	5a		58	a	OC	6b	D>G (R>L) traverse	94	23	S	5a	
66	36	S	4a		59	17	Bc	4c	L'across en l'air	95	22	R	5b	Le baiser vertical
67	35	S	4a		60	a	OC	6a	Surplomb	101	17	O	3c	
				ZONE C	61	2b	N/B	7a	Médaille en chocolat	103	38	R	5c	La râpe grasse
					61	13	S	4c		104	13	N/B	6c	La tarentule
3	1	J	2b	*Start*	62	1	N/B	7a	L'hyper plomb	104	18	O	4b	
4	2	J	2b		62	7	R	6a	Les crampes à Mémère	104	28b	S	5c	
5	3	J	2a							105	12	N/B	6c	L'arc d'Héraclès
6	4	J	2a		62	7b	R	6a		106	37	R	5c	Le médius
7	5	J	2b		62	18	Bc	5c	L'astrolabe	107	11	N/B	6c	Le fruit défendu
8	6	J	2a		63	2	N/B	7a	La dalle du dromadaire	108	15	Bc	5c	Les fesses à Simon
9	7	J	2b							108	27	S	5a	
10	8	J	3a		63	7t	R	5c		108	34	S	5c	La science friction
11	9	J	3c		63	14	S	4c		110	28	S	4c	
					64	4	N/B	6a	La dalle du toboggan	110	35	R	5c	Le pilier japonais

Franchard Isatis

boulder	route	circuit	grade	name
6	10	R	5b	
6	12	Bl	5b	
6	13	Bl	5b	
6	14	Bl	5c	
6	a	OC	7c	Gnossienne
6	b	OC	7b+	Le mur des lamentations
6	c	OC	7c	Gymnopédie
7	3	B	3c	
7	4	B	3c	
7	8	B	5b	
7	10	Bl	6a	Le statique
7	11	R	4b	
7	11	Bl	6b	
7	15	Bl	5b	
7	a	OC	7a	
7	b	OC	7a	
7	c	OC	7a	
8	7	B	3c	
9	8	B	5a	
9	12	R	5a	
9	13	R	5a	
9	14	R	5b	
9	15	R	5a	
9	16	R	5a	
9	18	Bl	6b	La zip zut
9	19	Bl	6b	L'envie des bêtes
9	a	OC	6c+	
11	9	B	5a	
11	17	R	5a	
11	18	R	4b	
11	a	OC	6c	
12	10	B	4a	
13	19	R	4c	
13	20	R	4b	
13	a	OC	7c+	Le vin aigre *Morpho*
14	11	B	3b	
14	17	Bl	5b	
14	21	B	4c	
15	16	Bl	6a+	Beurre marga
15	a	OC	6c	Les troubadours
20	20	B	3a	
21	21	B	4a	
21	a	OC	6b+	
22	17	B	3a	
22	26	R	4c	
23	19	B	3b	
23	20	Bl	6b	La planquée
23	21	Bl	6a	
23	22	Bl	5c	
24	18	B	3b	
24	22	B	4b	
24	23	Bl	5c	
24	24	Bl	6a	
24	25	Bl	5c	
24	27	R	4c	
24	28	R	5c	
24	29	R	5c	
26	24	B	4a	
27	23	B	3c	
30	26	B	5a	
30	a	OC	7a+	
31	16	B	3b	
31	25	R	4b	
31	27	B	6a	
32	15	B	3a	
33	14	B	4a	
33	23	R	4c	
33	24	R	5b	
33	28	Bl	6a	
33	29	Bl	5b	
34	13	B	5c	
35	12	B	4b	
35	22	R	5a	
37	25	B	3c	
37	26	B	3c	
38	27	B	2c	
39	28	B	4b	
39	28b	B	5a	
39	30	R	5b	
39	30	Bl	5b	
40	29	B	3a	
41	35	B	4c	
43	31	Bl	6b	
43	32	Bl	6a	
43	34	B	4c	
43	a	OC	6c	
43	b	OC	7c	Alta
43	c	OC	8b	Enigma
44	30	B	3b	
44	31	R	5b	
44	32	R	5a	
44	33	R	5b	
44	33	Bl	5a	
44	34	Bl	5c	
44	35	Bl	6a	
44	36	Bl	6b	
45	34	R	5c	
46	31	B	3b	
46	35	R	4c	
46	37	Bl	6a	
48	37	R	4b	
48	38	R	5b	
48	38	Bl	6a	
48	39	Bl	6a	
49	33	B	3c	
49	36	R	6a	
50	42	Bl	5b	
51	32	B	3b	
51	32 b	B	3c	
51	40	Bl	6b	
51	41	Bl	6a	
51	a	OC	7a	
52	36	B	4c	
53	39	B	3c	
54	38	B	3c	
55	37	B	4b	
56	40	B	3c	
58	41	B	4a	
59	42	B	4b	
59	a	OC	7a+	El poussif
61	a	OC	7a	El poussah
70	43	B	3b	
70	44	B	4a	
72	41	R	4c	
72	42	R	5b	
72	44	Bl	5b	
72	45	B	3b	
72	45b	B	3a	
72	46	B	4a	
73	43	R	4c	
73	44	R	4b	
73	47	B	3c	
73	a	OC	6b	
73	b	OC	?	*Project*
73	c	OC	7b	La Mernel
74	45	R	4c	
74	45	Bl	5b	
74	46	Bl	6c	Le Cervin
74	47	Bl	5b	La patinoire
74	48	B	3b	
75	46	R	5b	
75	47	R	5b	La bissouflante
75	48	Bl	6c	
75	49	B	4a	*Finish*
75	49	Bl	6a	
77	40	R	5b	
79	43	Bl	6a	
80	50	Bl	6b	
80	a	OC	7c	L'arrache cœur
100	48	R	4a	
101	49	R	5a	
102	50	R	5a	
102	a	OC	8a	Iceberg
103	53	R	4c	
103	54	R	5a	
104	51	R	5a	
104	52	R	4c	
104	55	R	4c	
105	56	R	4c	
106	57	R	4a	
107	58	R	4c	
107	59	R	5b	
107	60	R	5b	
108	62	R	5b	*Finish*
109	61	R	4c	

Franchard Sablons

page 73

boulder	route	circuit	grade	name
1	1	B	3b	L'accueil tranquille
1	1	R	5c	L'accroche doigt
1	2	B	4a	
2	2	R	5b	La réticence
2	3	B	4c	La verdâtre
2	3 b	B	3c	
3	3	R	5b	Le passe plat
3	4	B	4b	L'oiseau B
3	4 b	B	4a	
3	4	R	5b	La promptitude
3	a	OC	6c	Dos d'âne
3	b	OC	6c	Le fer à repasser
4	5	B	4b	Le 4x4
4	5	R	5c	La dérobade
4	6	R	5c	Morsure aux doigts
4	a	OC	7b+	Traînée de poudre G>D (L>R) traverse, finish up scoop
4	b	OC	7c+	Fragment d'hébétude D>G (R>L) traverse, 5 R finish

boulder	route	circuit	grade	name
5	6	B	4a	La voie du gynécologue
6	a	OC	6c+	Gros tambour *G>D (L>R) traverse*
7	7	B	4b	L'ascenseur
7	a	OC	7a+	Canyon *G>D (L>R) traverse*
8	8	B	4b	Le gros bidon
9	9	B	4b	Le bloc du forestier
11	10	B	4c	L'équilibriste
12	7	R	5c	Les racines
12	12	B	4b	La montagne russe
12	12b	B	4c	La Migouze
12	13	B	5a	Une voie d'orange.S.
13	8	R	5b	Saccage au burin
13	14	B	4b	Les fourmis vertes
14	9	R	5b	Le chien assis
14	16	B	4a	
14	a	OC	7a	Peine forte *7b+ G>D (L>R) traverse, sustained*
15	15	B	4a	L'enchaînement
18	17	B	4c	
18	a	OC	7a	Duralex
19	12	R	5a	Le nez
19	19		B3b/5c	Le trou morpho
19	a	OC	7b+	Modulor
20	11	R	5b	La traversée
20	18	B	4a	
21	10	R	5b	L'arête du poisson
21	11	B	3c	L'amanite vaginée
21	11 b	B	4c	
22	20	B	4b	Le bon point à Danièle
23	13	R	4c	L'accalmie
24	21	B	3a	La médaillon
25	14	R	4b	Mise en train
26	16	R	6a	La dalle à Clément
26	22	B	5a	La grat'à Marc
26	a	OC	7b	Jokavi *Jeté*
26	b	OC	7a	La vérité
27	23	B	4b	
28	a	OC	6b	Sale affaire
29	24	B	4c	
30	17	R	4b	Orgasme
31	18	R	4a	La dalle bleue
31	19	R	5c	Prise de tête
31	25	B	4a	La Gillette
31	25b	B	3a	La débonnaire
31	25t	B	3c	La Gillette bleue
31	a	OC	7a+	Talons aiguilles
32	26	B	4a	L'anonymat
34	27	B	4a	L'arraché
35	28	B	3c	
36	29	B	4b	
37	30	B	4c	
38	31	B	4b	La réserve du Président
39	32	B	3c	Le rouleau californien
40	20	R	6a	Dalle funéraire
41	33	B	4a	La soucoupe volante
42	34	B	4a	L'arête vive
44	35	B	4a	
45	37	R	3a	La Fonta stick
46	36	B	4b	
47	38	B	3c	
48	39	B	4a	
49	40	B	4b	La multiprise
50	15	R	5a	Coup de canon *Sustained 6a*
A	B		7a	Voltane *8a when traversed*

Franchard Cuisinière

page 78

boulder	route	circuit	grade	name
1	1	Bl	5c	Départ
2	2	Bl	4b	
3	a	OC	7c+	Coté coeur
4	1	R	4b	Départ
4	2	R	4c	
4	3	Bl	4c	
4	3b	Bl	5a	
7	6	Bl	6a	
8	7	Bl	4b	
8	a	OC	7a	
8	b	OC	6c	
8	c	OC	6a	
9	a	OC	7b	Alaxis
10	a	OC	8a	The beast *Traverse*
13	a	OC	6b	
13	b	OC	6c	
14	a	OC	7c	La jouissance du massétar
16	3	R	4c	
16	4	R	4c	
16	4	Bl	5b	Le hareng saur
16	5	Bl	5c	
16	a	OC	7c+	Les yeux pour pleurer
17	5	R	6a	
18	8	Bl	5b	
18	8b	Bl	6a	
18	9	Bl	5b	
18	10	Bl	6b	
18	10b	Bl	6c	
19	6	R	4b	
19	a	OC	6c	
19	a	OC	6a+	
21	7	R	4c	
21	8	R	5a	
21	a	OC	7b	Entorse *Morpho*
21	b	OC		*Project*
22	a	OC	7a+	Impasse du hasard
23	a	OC	7b+	Les petits poissons
23	b	OC	6a	
24	a	OC	6c	
30	30	R	4c	*Finish*
30	a	OC	8a	Karma
30	b	OC	7a	Bizarre bizarre *Eliminate*
31	26	R	5a/5c	
31	43 b	Bl	6b	
32	29	R	4c	
33	28	R	4c	
33	a	OC	6b+	
34	27	R	4a	
35	a	OC	6c	
37	a	OC	7a	Traversée
38	44	Bl	5c	
38	a	OC	8a+	Liaisons futiles *Traverse*
39	45	Bl	4c	
40	a	OC	7c	Eclipse *Traverse*
40	b	OC	7a+	Pensées cachées
40	c	OC	7c	Atomic power
41	46	Bl	6a	
41	47	Bl	6a	
41	a	OC	6b	
41	b	OC	6c	
42	48	Bl	6b	*Finish*
43	25	R	4c	
43	43	Bl	6b	
43	a	OC	7a	
50	9	R	5a	
50	9b	R	4c	
50	11	R	5c	
51	10	R	4b	
51	12	Bl	4c	
51	12b	Bl	4b	
52	11	R	4c/5c	
53	12	R	5a	
53	13	R	4a	
53	13	Bl	5a	
54	a	OC	7a+	Terre promise *(7c) sitting start*
55	14	R	6a	
55	15	R	4b/6b	
55	15	Bl	5c	
56	14	Bl	4c	
56	16	R	4c	
58	17	Bl	5a	
59	22	Bl	5a	
60	23	Bl	5a	
62	16	Bl	5b	
63	18	Bl	4b	
63	a	OC	6c	
64	19	R	4b	
65	17	Bl	5c	
65	18	R	4c	
65	19	Bl	5c	
66	20	Bl	5c	
66	a	OC	7b+	Corps accord
68	21	Bl	5b	
68	a	OC	7b	Haute tension
68	b	OC	7b	La déferlante *Exposed*
69	20	R	5a	
75	24	R	5b	
75	41	Bl	5c	
75	42	Bl	5c	
76	39	Bl	5b	
76	40	Bl	5b	
77	23	R	4b	
77	38	Bl	6b	
78	37	Bl	5b	
79	22	R	4c	
80	21	R	4c	
80	36	Bl	6b	
82	28	Bl	5b	
83	27	Bl	6a	
83	29	Bl	5c	
84	26	Bl	5a	
84	26b	Bl	5b	
85	24	Bl	5c	
86	25	Bl	5c	

Rocher canon

Bois-Rond

boulder	route	circuit	grade	name	boulder	route	circuit	grade	name	boulder	route	circuit	grade	name
13	8	O	3c		24	26	R	5b	Razorback	39	26	O	3a	
13	17	R	5c		25	a	OC	7a+	Bande passante *G>D (L>R) traverse*	40	23	O	4a	
13	18b	B	6c+	La Michaud						40	27	R	3b	
14	8	B	4b		26	a	OC	7b	Les plats *G>D (L>R) traverse*	40	32	R	6c	
14	18	R	6c		27	14	B	4c		41	23b	B	4c	
15	10	B	4c		27	16	B	4c		42	23	B	4b	
15	10	O	3a		27	19	O	3b		42	37	R	5c+	Le long fleuve tranquille
16	9	O	2c		27	24	R	5c		43	36	R	5b	
17	9	B	5a		27	25	R	6a		44	22	B	4c	
17	19	R	6a	Prise de becquet	27	24b	R	7a		44	22	O	2b	
17	20	R	6a	Ponction lombaire	28	20	O	3b		44	33	R	5c+	L'otan en emporte le vent
18	11	O	3b		30	31	O	3a		44	34	R	6c	Galla lactique
19	11	B	4b		31	3	R	6a		44	35	R	6c	Constellation des amoureux
19	12	O	3a		31	28	B	5b		45	24	B	5b	
19	13	O	3a		31	32	O	4a		45	28	O	3a	
19	15	O	3a		32	21	O	2c		45	38	R	6b+	Le vélo de max
19	21	R	5b		33	17	B	5a		45	39	R	5c	L'appui acide
20	12	B	4c		33	27	R	6a	Gilette pare dalle	45	a	OC	7a	Le Boudha peste *High G>D (L>R) traverse*
20	14	O	3a		33	28	R	5c		46	25	B	5b	
20	21b	R	7a	Le tourniquet du 93.7 *Girdle traverse of the boulder*	34	18	B	4a		47	29	O	3a	
21	16	O	3b		35	19	B	5a		48	40	R	5c	
21	17	O	3b		35	19b	B	4b		49	1	R	5b	*Start*
23	15	B	4b		35	29	R	6c	Aero beuark	49	2	R	6a	
23	22	R	6a	Le meilleur des mondes	36	30	R	6b	Super vista	49	26	B	4c	
23	9	R	6a+	La théorie des nuages	37	20	B	4b		49	27	B	4c	
23	a	OC	7a+	Spyder bloc	38	21	B	4c		49	30	O	3c	
24	13	B	4c		38	25	O	3b		49	41	R	5c	Fritz l'angle *Finish*
24	18	O	2c		38	31	R	5b						
					39	24	O	3a						

Canche aux Merciers

page 122

boulder	route	circuit	grade	name	boulder	route	circuit	grade	name	boulder	route	circuit	grade	name
1	3	B	4b		20	12	O	2c		36	29	R	6b	Les doigts d'homme
1	3	O	5c		21	9	R	5b	Le beau final	36	29b	R	6c	Kaki dehors
1	4	R	4c	La débonnaire	22	9b	R	5c	variante	37	41	B	4b	
2	0	O	2c	Départ	22	10	B	4c		38	25	R	5c	La conti
2	1	B	4c	Départ	22	10b	B	4a		38	26	R	6a	Uhuru
2	1	O	3b		22	13	O	3a		38	41	O	3c	*Finish*
2	3	R	5c	L'autoroute du Sud	23	17	B	5a		38	44	B	5b	*Finish*
2	3b	R	5c		24	11	B	5b		38	44b	B	4b	
3	2	B	5a		26	33	R	4c	Récupactive	38	a	OC	7a	Double face *(7b using lower holds)G>D (L>R) traverse*
3	2	O	3a		26	33b	R	5c	Gros os *Finish*	39	27	R	5c	L'air de rien
3	5	R	5c	Maurice Gratton	27	12	B	3b		39	40	O	3a	
3	6	R	6a	La goulotte à Dom	27	12b	B	3c		39	42	B	5a	
3	a	OC	7a+	Infusion du soir	28	15	B	4c		40	23	R	5b	Lune rousse
4	4	B	5a		29	14	O	3a		40	24	R	5c	Rêve de chevaux blancs
4	4b	B	4a		29	16	B	5a		40	28	R	5b	L'hésitation
4	4	O	3a		29	16b	B	4b		40	36	B	3c	
5	2	R	5c	Les nineties	30	15	O	3c		41	37	B	3b	
6	5	O	2c		31	10	R	6a	Bobol's come back	42	38	B	4b	
7	6	O	3b		31	16	O	3a		42	a	OC	7b	P'tit bras *D>G (R>L) trav*
8	1	R	5a	Ça dérape sec *Départ*	31	18	B	4a		43	39	B	4c	
10	5	B	4a		32	17	O	4a		43	39	b	B	4a
10	7	O	4b		32	19	B	5b		43	a	OC	6b	Les bons plats *D>G (R>L) traverse*
10	7	R	5b	Le croisé magique	33	14	B	4b		44	a	OC	7b	*D>G (L>R) traverse*
11	6	B	4a		33	14b	B	5b		44	b	OC	6c+	Le nez *Toit*
12	7	B	4c		33	32	R	6b	Glycolise	45	21	R	5a	Triste sire
13	8	B	5a		33	40	B	4a		45	22	R	5c	Grande classique
13	8	O	3a		33	a	OC	7a	Crise de l'énergie *Low level traverse*	45	35	B	5a	
13	8	R	5c	Par Toutatis	34	13	B	3c		45	39	O	3b	
14	9	O	3b		34	30	R	5c	La femme léopard	46	19	R	5a	Beau pavé
15	9	B	3c		34	31	R	5b	Hatari	46	20	R	6a	Okilélé
15	10	O	2c		35	a	OC	7a	*G>D (L>R) traverse*					
16	11	O	3a											

boulder	route	circuit	grade	name	boulder	route	circuit	grade	name	boulder	route	circuit	grade	name
46	34	B	4b		55	24	B	3c		70	27	O	1c	
46	34b	B	4b		56	21	O	2c		71	36	O	2c	
46	38	O	4a		56	23	B	4c		72	28	O	2a	
47	37	O	1a		56	23b	B	3c		73	29	O	3c	
48	33	B	4b		57	22	O	3c		74	30	O	3a	
50	20	B	4b		57	22b	O	2b		75	29	B	4b	
51	18	O	2b		57	a	OC	6c	*D>G (R>L) traverse*	75	30	B	3c	
51	19	O	3b		58	23	O	3a		75	31	O	2b	
51	21	B	3c		59	24	O	2c		76	32	O	4b	
52	11	R	6a	Pas pour Léon	60	15	R	6a	L'enfer des nains	77	16	R	6b	Chouchou chéri
52	12	R	6b+	Gueule cassée	60	15b	R	7a	Coup bas	77	31	B	5a	
52	13	R	6a	Jeu de jambes	60	25	O	2b		77	33	O	3b	
52	13b	R	5c	Le piston	61	26	O	3b		78	34	O	2a	
52	22	B	4b		61	26b	O	4a		79	17	R	5c	Vous avez dit gros bœuf
52	a	OC	7b+	Rage dedans	61	a	OC	7b	*D>G (R>L) traverse*	79	18	R	5c	Equilibriste
52	b1	OC	8a	Jacadi *Sitting start, on the left*	62	25	B	5a/4a		79	32	B	4b	
52	b2	OC	8a	saut de puce *Sitting start, on the right*	64	26	B	4b/6b		79	35	O	3b	
52	c	OC	7a	Fissure	65	27	B	5b		A		OS	7a+	Ni vieux ni bête *D>G (R>L) traverse*
53	20	O	3c		65	27b	B	4b		B		OS	7c	Soléa pour Valérie *G>D (R>L) traverse*
53	22b	B	4b		68	a	OC	7b	Séance friction *D>G (R>L) traverse*	C		OS	8a	La colonne Durruti *G>D (R>L) traverse*
54	14	R	5c	Sortie des artistes	69	28	B	4b						

95.2

page 138

boulder	route	circuit	grade	name	boulder	route	circuit	grade	name	boulder	route	circuit	grade	name
1	2	B	4b		22	13	B	4c		38	9	Bl	5b	
1	31	R	4b		22	23	R	4b		38	10	Bl	6a	
2	1	B	4b	Départ	23	14	B	3c		38	10b	Bl	6b	
2	28	R	5a		23	24	R	4b		38	15	R	4c	
2	29	R	5a		25	11	B	3c		38	19	B	4c	
3	4	B	3c		26	34	Bl	5c		38	21	B	3c	
4	36	Bl	5b		26	35	R	4c		39	17	B	4b	
4	37	Bl	5c	*6b direct variation*	27	36	R	4a		40	a	OC	7a+	Le p'tit toit
5	1	Bl	5b	Le kilo de beurre	28	26	B	3c		41	11	Bl	5b	
5	32	R	5a		28	27	B	4a		41	11b	Bl	6b+	
5	a	OC	7a+/7c+	L'ange naïf *Grade depends on technique used*	28	32	Bl	7a	La fosse aux ours	41	18	B	3c	
6	2	Bl	6b	La Poincenot *7a without the chipped hold*	28	32b	Bl	7a	Danse avec les loups	42	12	Bl	5c	
7	3	B	4c		28	32t	Bl	7a		42	13	R	4c	
7	3	Bl	5c		28	37	R	5a		43	13	Bl	5b	
7	3b	Bl	7a+	Le bloc à Bertrand	28	38	R	4c		43	14	R	4b	
7	3 t	Bl	7a+		29	25	B	4a		44	12	R	4b	
7	30	R	4b		29	33	Bl	5c		45	11	R	5b	
8	5	B	4c		29	39	R	4b		46	10	R	4c	
9	6	B	4c		30	28	B	4c		48	8	R	3c	
9	27	R	5b		31	24	R	4b		48	14	Bl	5a	
10	9	B	4b		32	23	B	4b		49	7	R	4b	
11	7	B	3b		32	42	R	5a		50	9	R	4c	
12	20	R	4c		33	22	B	3b		50	15	Bl	5a	
12	a	OC	7b+	Le médaillon	33	29	Bl	5c		50	16	Bl	5b	
13	4	Bl	6a		33	29b	Bl	7a	Miss KGB	51	6	R	4c	
13	5	Bl	6b		33	30	Bl	6a		51	17	Bl	5c	
13	6	Bl	5a		33	30b	Bl	7a+	Mister proper	51	18	Bl	6b	
13	21	R	4c		33	31	Bl	5c		52	19	Bl	6a	
14	35	Bl	5b		33	31b	Bl	7a	Tarte aux poils	53	5	R	4c	
15	10	B	4b		33	40	R	4c		54	4	R	4b	
15	34	R	5a		34	41	R	4c		54	20	Bl	5b	
16	8	B	5a		35	15	B	4b		55	3	R	4c	
16	12	B	4b		36	7	Bl	6a		55	21	Bl	5b	
16	33	R	4c		36	16	B	5b		56	1	R	4a	*Start*
17	26	R	4b		36	17	R	5c		56	2	R	4b	
19	22	R	5b		37	16	R	5a		56	22	Bl	5b	
20	18	R	4a		37	20	B	4b		56	23	Bl	5b	
21	19	R	5b		38	8	Bl	5b		60	29	B	4b	
										61	30	B	3c	

X

boulder	route	circuit	grade	name
62	31	B	3c	
62	43	R	5b	
63	28	Bl	4c	
63	28b	Bl	7a	
63	45	R	5b	
64	27	B	5b	
64	32	B	4b	
64	44	R	5b	
64	46	R	4c	
65	26	Bl	5b	
65	33	B	4b	
65	35	B	5a	
66	36	B	3c	
67	24	Bl	5c	
67	24b	Bl	6b	
67	25	Bl	6a	
67	34	B	4c	L'ectoplasme
67	47	R	5c	Finish
67	a	OC	7c+	Futurs barbares
68	37	B	3b	
68	a	OC	7b+	Absinthe
69	a	OC	7a	Pierre précieuse (Yaniro)
69	b	OC	7a+	Arête de gauche
A		OC	7a	Oxygène/Oxygène actif 7b D>G (R>L) there and back traverse
B		OC	7b	Yogi
C		OC	7b	Prouesse
D		OC	7a+	Extraction terrestre
E		OC	7a	Surplomb du bivouac

La Roche aux Sabots

page 155

boulder	route	circuit	grade	name
1	1	B	4b	
1	2	B	4b	
1	3	B	4b	
1	20	J	2c	
2	4	B	4b	
2	5	B	4a	
2	13	R	5b	Red one
2	21	J	2c	
2	a	R/Bl	7a+	C'est assis, mais c'est tassé
2	b	R/Bl	7c	Le poil de la bête D>G (R>L) low level traverse
3	6	B	4c	
3	7	B	4a	
3	8	B	3b	
3	9	B	4b	
3	14	R	6b	L'angle de la pierre ôtée
3	15	R	6a+	Coup de patte
3	a	R/Bl	6b	
3	b	R/Bl	7a	Lime à ongles
3	c	R/Bl	7b	La bas-bas cool G>D (L>R) low level traverse
3	d	R/Bl	7a	Prima G>D (L>R) traverse,14 R finish
3	e	R/Bl	6b	
4	21b	J	3a	
4	a	R/Bl	6b	D>G (R>L) traverse
5	10	B	3c	
5	11	B	3b	
5	22	J	2c	
5	a	R/Bl	6b	Silence, on tourne G>D (L>R) traverse
5	b	R/Bl	7b	Lucifer
6	10	R	5c	Danger majeur
6	11	R	5c	L'arrache-moyeu
6	12	R	5c	L'angle à Gilles
6	19	J	2c	
6	19	B	4b	
7	18	J	1c	
7	20	B	4a	
7	a	R/Bl	6c	Anglomaniaque Start on n°20 B
7	b	R/Bl	7a	Jeux de toit 7b variation
8	12	B	5a	
8	17	R	5a	Vol au vent
8	18	B	4b	
8	24	J	3a	
8	a	R/Bl	8a	Déviation
8	b	R/Bl	6b	Le bond de l'hippopotame
8	c	R/Bl	6c	Le flipeur
9	23	J	2c	
10	13	B	3b	
10	14	B	4a	
10	15	B	4a	
10	16	B	4c	
10	16	R	5b	Le mode d'emploi
10	25	J	3b	
11	17	B	5b	
11	21	B	4a	
11	26	J	3a	
12	16	J	2b	
13	17	J	2b	
14	22	B	4a	
14	23	B	5a	
14	27	J	2b	
14	a	R/Bl	6b	Chapeau chinois
15	14	B	2c	
16	9	R	5b	Little Crack
16	15	J	3b	
16	29	B	5a	
17	18	R	6a+	Le mur à Robert
17	19	R	6a+	les joyeuses de Noël
17	24	R	4c	
17	a	R/Bl	7a	Angle
17	b	R/Bl	6b	L'inversée satanique 6c+ direct variation
17	c	R/Bl	6b+	Angle
18	25	B	3c	
19	26	B	4c	
19	28	J	2b	
20	20	R	5b	Passage à l'acte
20	21	R	5b	Mine de rien
20	27	B	4c	
20	28	B	3c	
20	29	J	2a	
20	a	R/Bl	7a	Amanite dalloïde
20	b	R/Bl	6c	Bazooka jo
21	22	R	6a+	Le tiroir/Rien de bon
21	23	R	6a	Bon à rien
21	24	R	6a	Les grattons belliqueux
21	25	R	6b+	L'angle à Jean-Luc
21	30	B	5a	
21	30b	B	5a	
21	a	R/Bl	6b+	Angle Ghersen
21	b	R/Bl	7a+	Sphincters toniques All on the hands
21	c	R/Bl	7c	Pets O2 max Combination of routes on the main wall
21	d	R/Bl	7a+	A l'impossible
21	e	R/Bl	7b	Ongle jo
22	13	J	2c	
23	26	R	5a	Le goût du jour
23	27	R	5c	Crosse en l'air
23	28	R	6a+	Service compris
23	29	R	6b	Le mur à Michaud
23	30	J	3b	
23	30	B	5b	La barquette de beurre
23	31	B	3b	
23	31	b B	4b	
23	a	R/Bl	7a	Jet set
23	b	R/Bl	7b	Jack's finger
23	c	R/Bl	7a	Les yeux
23	d	R/Bl	7b	7c D>G (R>L) traverse, 28 R finish
23	e	R/Bl	7b+	Le parallèlogramme
24	11	J	2a	
24	12	J	3a	
25	10	J	1c	
26	8	R	5b	Beauf en daube
26	9	J	3b	
26	9b	J	3b	
26	44	B	4a	
26	45	B	4c	
26	46	B	4b	
27	35	B	3c	
28	31	J	2b	
28	31b	J	3a	
28	31	R	5b	Servir frais
28	32	B	4b	
28	32	R	5c	Le pain total
28	33	B	4b	
28	33	b B	4b	
28	33	R	5c	Le théorème de Pascal
28	34	B	4a	
28	a	R/Bl	6c+	Rumsteak en folie
29	8	J	2c	
30	6	R	5c	Le porte à faux
30	7	J	3b	
30	7	R	4c	Le mur Badaboum
30	a	R/Bl	7a	Achille Talon
30	b	R/Bl	7b+	100% pulpe
30	c	R/Bl	7a	Jus d'orange
31	6	J	2c	
31	43	B	4a	
32	5	J	3a	
32	41	B	3c	
32	42	B	4a	
33	4	J	1c	
33	5	R	5b	Le passage à tabac
33	40	B	4c	
33	a	R/Bl	7c	Sale gosse 8a sitting start
33	b	R/Bl	7a	Gravillon Overhanging corner
33	c	R/Bl	7a	Graviton

boulder	route	circuit	grade	name	boulder	route	circuit	grade	name	boulder	route	circuit	grade	name
33	d	R/Bl	7b+	Vieille canaille *G>D (L>R) traverse*	35	a	R/Bl	7a+	Partie de jambes en l'air *D>G (R>L) traverse*	37	34	R	6a	L'auriculaire - Toit aux frelons
34	36	B	4b		36	3	J	2b		37	a	R/Bl	7a	Le tourniquet *Girdle traverse of the boulder*
34	37	B	4a		37	1	J	2c						
34	38	B	3c		37	1	R	6a	Le saute-montagnes	38	2	J	3a	
34	a	R/Bl	6c+	Surplomb des frelons *D>G (R>L) traverse*	37	2	R	6a	Le coup de genoux	38	4	R	5b	La dalle de cristal
35	39	B	3c		37	3	R	6a	Le surplomb à coulisse	A		OS	7c	Miss world *G>D (L>R) traverse*
										B		OS	7c	Le dernier angle

91.1

page 166

boulder	route	circuit	grade	name	boulder	route	circuit	grade	name	boulder	route	circuit	grade	name
1	31	R	4b		21	23t	R	6a		36	a	OC	7a	Les pieds nickelés
1	31b	R	5a		21	37	J	3a		37	29	J	3c	
1	47	J	4b	*Finish*	22	18	J	5a		38	9	R	5a	
2	30	R	5b		22	33	J	2c		38	9b	R	5c	
3	32	R	5a		23	17	R	4c		38	26	J	3c	
3	42	J	3b		23	32	J	3a		40	6	R	4b	
3	43	J	3b		23	a	OC	7a	Le Sur Plomb	40	6b	R	5c	
3	a	OC	6c	*G<>D (L<>R) traverse*	24	16	R	5b		40	7	R	5b	
4	34	R	5c	*Finish*	24	25	R	4c		40	17	J	2c	
4	45	J	3c		24	25b	R	5a		42	5	R	4b	
4	46	J	4b		25	13	R	4c		42	16	J	2c	
5	33	R	4c		25	14	R	6a	La Goulotte	43	4	R	4a	
5	33b	R	6b		25	14b	R	5a		43	15	J	4a	
6	44	J	3b		25	31	J	3b		44	14	J	3a	
6	20	J	3b		26	30	J	3c		45	13	J	3c	
6	21	J	3b		30	22	J	3b		46	3	R	3c	
7	19	J	3a		31	24	J	3c		47	1	R	4c	*Start*
8	18	J	4c		32	8	R	4c		47	2	R	5b	
10	29	R	5b		32	8b	R	6a	Le Flipper	47	2b	R	6b	
11	27	R	4c		32	25	J	4b		47	11	J	4a	
12	40	J	3b		33	23	J	4a		48	12	J	4a	
13	39	J	3a		34	10	R	4b		50	10	J	3b	
14	28	R	4b		34	10b	R	5c		51	8	J	3b	
14	38	J	3c		35	11	R	4b		51	9	J	3c	
14	41	J	3b		35	11b	R	4b		52	7	J	3c	
15	24	R	4c		35	16b	R	5c		53	6	J	3a	
16	35	J	3b		35	26	R	4c		53	6b	J	3c	
17	36	J	2b		35	26b	R	6a	*G<>D (L<>R) traverse*	53	6t	J	4a	
18	21	R	4a		35	27	J	4a		54	5	J	3c	
19	22	R	4c		36	12	R	5c		55	4	J	4a	
19	34	J	3a		36	12b	R	6a	L'arc de cercle	56	3	J	3c	
21	19	R	5a		36	12t	R	6a	Le Grand dièdre	57	2	J	3c	
21	20	R	4b		36	15	R	5b		58	1	J	3a	*Start*
21	23	R	5b		36	15b	R	5a		58	1b	J	3c	
21	23b	R	5c		36	28	J	3a						

Rocher Guichot

page 171

boulder	route	circuit	grade	name	boulder	route	circuit	grade	name	boulder	route	circuit	grade	name
1	1	B	4a	*Start*	5	2	B	4c		7	4	O	2b	
1	1	O	2c	*Start*	5	2	O	2b		8	5	O	2a	
2	4	B	4a		5	3	R	6b		9	7	O	3a	
3	5	R	6b		5	3	B	4b		9	18	B	5b	
3	5	B	4c		5	4	B	6b		9	19	R	6a	
3	6	B	5a		5	20	B	5a	*Finish*	9	19	B	4c	
3	26	O	3a		5	21	R	6a	*Finish*	9	20	R	6b	
4	27	O	2b		5	28	O	3b	*Finish*	10	6	O	3a	
5	1	R	5b	*Start*	5	a	OC	8a	*D>G (R>L) traverse*	11	9	O	3a	
5	2	R	6a		6	3	O	2b		11	10	O	2b	

Vallée de la Mée

boulder	route	circuit	grade	name	boulder	route	circuit	grade	name	boulder	route	circuit	grade	name
76	43	R	5b	La fissure au marbre	78	46	R	5b		81	40	O	3b	La traversée des tortues jumelles *4c variation on slab*
77	34	B	4a		78	46b	R	6b						
78	35	B	4c		79	36	B	3b		81	48	R	6a	L'angle des tortues jumelles *Finish*
78	38	O	4a	Les deux baignoires	80	37	B	3b						
78	44	R	5a	Corner	80	39	O	2c	La bleausarde	81	a1	OC	8a+	Le surplomb
78	44b	R	5b		80	47	R	5b		81	a2	OC	7c	La traversée
78	45	R	5c	Les petits pieds	81	38	B	4c	*Finish*					

Beauvais Est

boulder	route	circuit	grade	name	boulder	route	circuit	grade	name	boulder	route	circuit	grade	name
1	22	R	5b	La kaléidoscope	23	16	N/Bl	6b	M&M's	52	43	B	4a	Le grattounet
1	32	B	4a	New deal	24	27	B	4c	Errare humanum est	53	1	N/Bl	7a	L'éloge de la différence
2	21	R	5b	Le distingo	25	35	B	4a	La bidouille	53	2	N/Bl	6c	le mouton noir
2	31	B	4a	Le plat garni	26	36	B	4a	Le bloc de poche	53	3	N/Bl	6a	Sang d'encre
3	20	R	5a	j'ai fantaisie	27	37	B	2c	Le trait d'union	53	44	B	4a	Tête de colombe
3	33	B	4c	Du R pour les bleus	28	10	N/Bl	7a	Le black out	55	45	B	3c	Bouleau chagrin
4	17	R	5c	L'étambot	28	38	B	4b	Le complexifié	56	1	R	5b	La traversée du désir
4	18	R	5b	Les chaires mobiles	29	7	B	3a	L'hypothénuse	56	46	B	4b	Aller simple
4	19	R	5b	Trompe la mort	30	11	R	5b	Le confit de canard	57	47	B	4a	Pas d'affolement pour miss Vibram
4	34	B	4a	Le long fleuve tranquille	31	9	N/Bl	7a	La mouche	58	2	R	5c	Le coq six
5	16	R	5c	L'étrave	31	10	R	5b	L'oubli	58	2b	R	5c	Le sot poudrage
5	30	B	4a	La traversée des cieux	31	11	B	3c	L'appuie-tête	58	48	B	4b	Au gré du grès
6	13	N/Bl	6c	Les ongles en deuil	31	12	B	4b	L'éclopé	59	6	N/Bl	6a	Bagdad café
6	23	R	6a	La traversée du bonsaï	32	10	B	3a	L'incertitude	59	49	B	4a	Le bon choix
6	24	B	5c	Syndrome albatros	33	6	B	3a	Le boeuf sous le toit	60	34b	R	5c	La traversée des garçons
6	24b	R	6a	Manu : tension	33	31	R	5c	Néanderthal roc	61	34	R	5b	La traversée des filles
6	29	B	4b	Le pin bonsaï	34	5	B	3c	La prise en compte	62	22	N/Bl	6c	Le cambouis du diéseliste
7	12	N/Bl	6b	Le petit ramoneur	34	30	R	6a	L'ouvre-boîte	63	39b	R	6a	La tripack
7	15	R	5b	En bref	35	21	N/Bl	6b	La dame noire	64	23	N/Bl	6a	L'Amoco
8	28	B	4b	Perseverare diabolicum	35	29	R	5b	L'appel du bistrot	65	27	N/Bl	6a	Le café crème
9	11	N/Bl	6b	Les abysses	36	32	R	5b	La dure mère	65	28	N/Bl	6b	Le capuccino
10	14	N/Bl	6c	Le cliché noir&blanc	37	4	B	3c	La motte de beurre	65	38	R	5b	Le trou des garçons
10	14b	N/Bl	7b+	La gueule du loup	38	8	B	4b	La fissure close	65	39	R	5b	Le trésor public
10	23	B	4c	Comme un singe en rut	38	8	R	5b	Foot bloc	65	40	R	5b	Tu ne voleras point
10	24	B	3c	Les dégâts limités	38	8	N/Bl	7a+	Le nègre en chemise	66	29	N/Bl	6c	Le crawl en mer noire
10	25	R	5a	La rogaton	38	13	B	3c	Le poussif nocif	66	35	R	6a	Le coup de boule
11	25	B	3b	La dalle de la Carrière	39	7	R	6a	Blatte runner	67	30	N/Bl	6b	L'ébène
12	15	N/Bl	6c	La magie noire du derviche	40	9	B	3a	Les pieds dans la semoule	67	30b	R	6c	La perle de jais
12	26	B	3c	Le quartier de citron	40	9	R	5a	La rimaye	67	30t	N/Bl	7a	Danse macabre
13	22	B	4a	L'écailleux	40	39	B	3c	La dulf' du vieux cimetière	67	36	R	5c	Mauvais sang
14	26	R	6a	D.o.s 6	41	40	B	4b	Des bogues plein les pognes	68	37	R	5b	Sans l'arrêt
15	20	B	4a	La pierre de l'édifice	42	2	B	3c	Ventre dur	70	26	N/Bl	6a	Le mâle blanchi
15	21	B	3c	L'évidence	42	3	B	4b	Le pt'it coin	71	24	N/Bl	7a	L'oeuvre au noir
16	19	B	4a	Objectif grâce	42	5	R	5b	L'amoch'doigt	72	24b	N/Bl	7c	Le dalhia noir
17	18	B	3c	La toile de cinoche	42	6	R	5a	L'has been	73	24t	N/Bl	7a	La ballade du champion
18	27	R	5b	Le folklo	43	33	R	5c	Roc autopsie	74	25	N/Bl	6b	La veuve du fossoyeur
19	16	B	4b	Les gros bras	44	4	R	5c	Soleil cherche futur					
19	17	B	4b	Le pendule des Avaux	45	1	B	3a	La chaufferette					
19	19	N/Bl	6b	L'onyx	45	1b	B	4a						
19	28	R	5c	Le biodégradable	46	7	N/Bl	7a+	Mathilde					
20	20	N/Bl	6b	La limonite	46	7b	N/Bl	7b	Je broie du noir					
21	18	N/Bl	6b	Le brou de noir *(static)*	46	7t	N/Bl	7b	Le sectaire					
22	12	R	5b	Caresses amères	47	3	R	5b	Un bien beau superlatif					
22	13	R	5c	Art pariétal	47	50	B	4a	Voici le temps du monde fini					
22	14	B	4b	Pour Olympe	49	41	B	4a	Lacoïonnade					
22	15	B	5a	Agoraphobie	50	4	N/Bl	6c	Coup de blues					
22	17	N/Bl	7a	L'anthracite	50	4b	N/Bl	7b	L'étrave à sucre					
23	14	R	5c	Le boeuf carotte	50	42	B	3b	La frousse bleue					
					51	5	N/Bl	6c+	Le grain de beauté					

boulder	route	circuit	grade	name
1	1	N	6a	L'envers des fesses *Start*
2	0	B	4b	Départ
3	2	N	5b	Le pare brise
3	10	B	4a	L'angle du grincheux
4	11	B	4c	L'andouille de vire
4	12	B	4c	Le quadriceps gauche
5	9	B	4c	Le jeté tentant
6	15	B	4c	Le jazz
7	16	B	3c	La java
8	13	B	4a	Les doigts sous le pied
8	14	B	4b	La dalle du pin
10	3	N	6a	Surplomb de marbre
10	4	N	6b	Le grand angle
10	4b	N	5c	La jojo
10	8	B	4c	La dalle de marbre
11	7	B	4b	L'onglier
12	5	N	5c	La directe du petit Cervin
12	6	B	4c	Le petit Cervin
13	5	B	4c	L'as tactique
14	17	B	4a	Le quadriceps droit
15	18	B	4a	Les pieds à plat
16	7	N	6a	Les supers grattons
16	8	B	6a	Les grattons
16	19	B	4b	Les doigts coincés
16	20	B	4a	Les mains à plat
17	1	B	4a	La jambe en l'air
17	4	B	4c	La lime à ongle
18	2	B	4b	La rampe de l'escalier vert
18	3	B	4b	La vire à Bibi
19	6	N	5c	Le marchepied
20	25	B	4c	La fissure du sherpa
20	26	B	4b	Le dé rance
21	9	N	6a	Les pédales
22	11	N	5c	La piscine
24	10	N	6b	L'orléanaise directe
25	27	B	4b	La bien planquée
26	23	B	4c	Le général direct
26	24	B	3c	Les grattons du général
27	22	B	4b	L'enjambée
28	21	B	3c	Les baquets
30	28	B	3c	La vite fait
31	12	N	5c	La Descheneaux
31	13	N	5c	L'envers de la Descheneaux
31	29	B	4c	La Descheneaux
31	30	B	4b	L'envers de la Descheneaux
32	31	B	3a	L'histoire de
34	14	N	6a	La voie lactée
35	a	OC	7b	D>G (R>L) traverse
36	15	N	6b	L'excuse
37	16	N	6c	Le Cource doigt
38	32	B	4c	Le surplomb des poings
38	33	B	3b	Les poings à gauche
38	34	B	4b	La fissure des poings
40	35	B	4b	Le plaisir des dames
42	17	N	5c	Le perlinpimpin
42	37	B	4a	Le minaret
43	20	N	6c	La voie Mercier
43	38	B	3c	Les trous du gruyère
43	a	OC	7b	Master edge
43	b	OC	8a	Misanthropie
44	18	N	5c	La Yano
44	36	B	3a	Le plaisir à personne
45	19	N	6b	La duchesse
45	39	B	5a	La fissure de l'I
45	40	B	5a	La fissure verte
45	a	OC	7c	Furyo
47	21	N	5c	La super angle Brutus
47	22	N	6a	La Brutus
47	41	B	4c	La mine à Rey
47	42	B	4c	La fissure Brutus *Finish*
47	a	OC	7b+	L'âge de pierre *Roped*
50	23	N	6b	La traversée du culot
51	24	N	5c	La dynamostatique
52	a	OC	7a+	Lady big claques
53	26	N	5c	L'angle de la fresque
53	27	N	6c	La super fresque
54	28	N	6b	L'ultra son
55	25	N	6a	L'étrave
56	29	N	5c	La coupe rose
57	30	N	6c	Le surplomb taillé du pique nique
58	31	N	5c	La dalle Poulenard
58	32	N	5c	Le surplomb de l'Usi
60	33	N	5b	La sup direct des Minets
60	34	N	5b	Le directissime des Minets
60	35	N	6a	Le charleston
60	36	N	6b	Le swing medium
60	a	OC	7c	Strappal
62	37	N	6b	Rêve de singe
63	38	N	5c	L'allumeuse
64	39	N	5c	La réfractaire directe *Finish*

Dépôt légal avril 2001
Imprimé en France